Flann O'Brien & Modernism

Flann O'Brien & Modernism

Edited by
Julian Murphet, Rónán McDonald
and Sascha Morrell

BLOOMSBURY
NEW YORK · LONDON · NEW DELHI · SYDNEY

Bloomsbury Academic
An imprint of Bloomsbury Publishing Inc

1385 Broadway	50 Bedford Square
New York	London
NY 10018	WC1B 3DP
USA	UK

www.bloomsbury.com

Bloomsbury is a registered trade mark of Bloomsbury Publishing Plc

First published 2014

© Julian Murphet, Rónán McDonald and Sascha Morrell, 2014

All rights reserved. No part of this publication may be reproduced or transmitted in any form or by any means, electronic or mechanical, including photocopying, recording, or any information storage or retrieval system, without prior permission in writing from the publishers.

No responsibility for loss caused to any individual or organization acting on or refraining from action as a result of the material in this publication can be accepted by Bloomsbury or the author.

Library of Congress Cataloging-in-Publication Data
Flann O'Brien & Modernism/edited by Julian Murphet, Rónán McDonald, and Sascha Morrell.
pages cm
Includes index.
ISBN 978-1-62356-487-2 (hardback) – ISBN 978-1-62356-850-4 (paperback)
1. O'Brien, Flann, 1911–1966–Criticism and interpretation. 2. Modernism (Literature) I. Murphet, Julian, editor of compilation. II. McDonald, Rónán, 1970- editor of compilation. III. Morrell, Sascha, editor of compilation.
PR6029.N56Z675 2014
823'.912–dc23
2014004173

ISBN: HB: 978-1-6235-6487-2
PB: 978-1-6235-6850-4
ePub: 978-1-6235-6442-1
ePDF: 978-1-6235-6875-7

Typeset by Deanta Global Publishing Services, Chennai, India

Contents

Acknowledgements	vii
Contributors	viii
Introduction *Rónán McDonald and Julian Murphet*	1
1 Making Evil, with Flann O'Brien *Sean Pryor*	11
2 Mythomaniac Modernism: Lying and Bullshit in Flann O'Brien *John Attridge*	27
3 'The Outward Accidents of Illusion': O'Brien and the Theatrical *Stefan Solomon*	41
4 The Ghost of 'Poor Jimmy Joyce': A Portrait of the Artist as a Reluctant Modernist *Stephen Abblitt*	55
5 'Do You Know What I'm Going to Tell You?': Flann O'Brien, Risibility and the Anxiety of Influence *David Kelly*	67
6 *An Béal Bocht*, Translation and the Proper Name *Maebh Long*	77
7 Ploughmen without Land: Flann O'Brien and Patrick Kavanagh *Joseph Brooker*	93
8 Flann O'Brien's *Ulysses*: Marginalia and the Modernist Mind *Dirk Van Hulle*	107
9 'Truth is an Odd Number': Flann O'Brien and Infinite Imperfection *Baylee Brits*	121
10 'An Astonishing Parade of Nullity': Nihilism in *The Third Policeman* *Rónán McDonald*	135
11 Flann O'Brien and Modern Character *Julian Murphet*	149
12 'No Unauthorized Boozing': Flann O'Brien and the Thirsty Muse *Sam Dickson*	163

13 Soft Drink, Hard Drink and Literary (Re)production in Flann O'Brien and Frank Moorhouse *Sascha Morrell*	175
14 Flann O'Brien's Aestho-Autogamy *Mark Steven*	195
15 Modernist Wheelmen *Mark Byron*	213
Index	233

Acknowledgements

The editors would like to acknowledge the institutional support of the Centre for Modernism Studies in Australia and the Global Irish Studies Centre, both at the University of New South Wales, in the preparation of this volume. The School of the Arts and Media, also at the University of New South Wales, helped host the Flann O'Brien centenary conference in November 2011 from which this collection draws a number of revised and extended contributions. We would also like to thank the Consulate General of Ireland, Sydney, for their support and Angela McLoughlin, administrative officer of the Global Irish Studies Centre, who helped run the conference. The good-humoured support of Emeritus Professors John Kelly and Don Anderson on the day was particularly appreciated, as was the participation of Dr Frances Devlin Glass. At Bloomsbury, two anonymous press readers helped considerably in the tightening and strengthening of the collection as a whole. Laura Murray was resourceful, extremely helpful and a pleasure to work with. And Haaris Naqvi continues to cement his reputation as one of the best Literary Studies commissioning editors in the business. The editors would like to dedicate this volume to his first child, Leo, born while it was being drawn together.

Contributors

Stephen Abblitt recently received his PhD for a critical-creative thesis addressing some intellectual homologies between James Joyce and Jacques Derrida. He currently works in the Radical Learning Project at La Trobe University, where he is also an honorary visiting research fellow in the School of Humanities at La Trobe University, member of the Centre for Creative Arts, and joint managing editor of the interdisciplinary peer-reviewed open-access journal *Writing from Below*.

John Attridge is a lecturer in English in the School of the Arts and Media at the University of New South Wales. His essays on modern literature have appeared in journals such as *Modernism/modernity*, *ELH* and *The Times Literary Supplement*, and he is co-editor, with Rod Rosenquist, of *Incredible Modernism: Literature, Trust and Deception* (Ashgate, 2013). He is completing a book manuscript entitled '*The Invisible Vocation*': *Modernism, Impressionism and Professional Society,* dealing mainly with Ford, Conrad and James.

Baylee Brits holds a Research Masters in Cultural Analysis from the Amsterdam School for Cultural Analysis and is currently writing her doctorate at the University of New South Wales. Her current research project revolves around the mathematics of contingency in twentieth-century prose fiction.

Joseph Brooker is director of the Centre for Contemporary Literature at Birkbeck, University of London. His books include *Joyce's Critics: Transitions in Reading and Culture* (2004), *Flann O'Brien* (2005) and *Literature of the 1980s: After the Watershed* (2010). He has acted as editor for special issues of *New Formations, Journal of Law & Society* and *Textual Practice*.

Mark Byron is a senior lecturer in Modern British and American Literature in the Department of English at the University of Sydney. His current work is in developing digital scholarly editions of complex Modernist texts and their manuscripts, including the *Watt* module of the Samuel Beckett Digital Manuscript Project. His work also deals with critical and theoretical reflection upon scholarly editing techniques. He has published on nineteenth-century- and Modernist literature, and is the author of *Ezra Pound's Eriugena* (London: Continuum, 2014).

Sam Dickson Sam Dickson is completing his PhD at the University of Sydney. His research fields include twentieth-century literature and film theory.

David Kelly is senior lecturer in English at the University of Sydney. He is editor of *Sydney Studies in English*, and has published on contemporary film and literature.

Maebh Long is a lecturer in literature in the University of the South Pacific, Fiji. She is the author of the monograph *Assembling Flann O'Brien* (London: Bloomsbury, 2014). In addition to incursions into Irish Studies, her areas of engagement and publication are theory and philosophy, currently ironic and fragmentary forms in Derrida, Blanchot and Schlegel.

Rónán McDonald holds the Australian Ireland Fund Chair in Modern Irish Studies at the University of New South Wales. He is director of the Global Irish Studies Centre and president of the Irish Studies Association of Australia and New Zealand. His research interests lie in literary studies, especially Irish modernism, and ideas of 'value' in the humanities. He is the author of many articles and essays in these fields and his books include *Tragedy and Irish Literature* (2002), *The Cambridge Introduction to Samuel Beckett* (2007) and *The Death of the Critic* (2008).

Sascha Morrell is lecturer in English at the University of New England, Australia. Her research and publications examine dialectics of labour dependency and racial identity in a range of nineteenth- and early twentieth-century American and British fictions, and she has a particular research interest in symbolic appropriations of Haitian history and culture in the United States.

Julian Murphet is professor in Modern Film and Literature in the School of the Arts and Media, University of New South Wales, and Director of the Centre for Modernism Studies in Australia. He edits the journal *Affirmations: of the modern*.

Sean Pryor is a lecturer in English in the School of the Arts and Media at the University of New South Wales. He works on twentieth-century poetry, with a particular focus on modernism. His book, *W. B. Yeats, Ezra Pound, and the Poetry of Paradise* was published by Ashgate in 2011.

Stefan Solomon is a visiting research fellow in the Department of English at the University of Sydney. He completed his PhD in Film and Literature at the

University of New South Wales in 2012, and teaches both literary and film studies. He is currently interested in the changing nature of the novel in the face of new media, and is co-editor of a collection, *William Faulkner in the Media Ecology*, due for publication in 2014.

Mark Steven is a graduate student in the School of the Arts and Media at the University of New South Wales. His thesis maps the relationships between Modernist poetry, socialist revolution and the soviet state. He publishes on literature and cinema, and is co-editor of *Styles of Extinction: Cormac McCarthy's The Road*.

Dirk Van Hulle is professor of English Literature at the University of Antwerp (Centre for Manuscript Genetics). With Mark Nixon, he is co-director of the Beckett Digital Manuscript Project (BDMP) and editor-in-chief of the *Journal of Beckett Studies*. He is the author of *Textual Awareness* (2004), *Manuscript Genetics: Joyce's Know-How, Beckett's Nohow* (2008) and *The Making of Samuel Beckett's 'Stirrings Still' and 'what is the word'* (2011), co-author of *Samuel Beckett's Library* (Cambridge University Press, 2013) with Mark Nixon, editor of Beckett's *Company, Ill Seen Ill Said, Worstward Ho, Stirrings Still* (Faber and Faber, 2009), and with Shane Weller he has recently completed a genetic edition of *L'Innommable/The Unnamable* (2013), the second module of the BDMP (www.beckettarchive.org). He is currently preparing a monograph on *Modern Manuscripts* (Bloomsbury, 2014, forthcoming) and the second edition of the *Cambridge Companion to Samuel Beckett* (Cambridge University Press).

Introduction

Rónán McDonald and Julian Murphet

Flann O'Brien has always been hard to categorize. Born Brian Ó Nualláin (1911–66) to an Irish-speaking family in Co Tyrone, one of the six counties that would, in 1922, form part of partitioned Northern Ireland, he became a celebrated inventor of identities. Brother Barnabas, Count O'Blather, Matt Duffy, John James Doe, Myles na gCopaleen, Myles na Gopaleen and, the name under which he wrote his novels, Flann O'Brien, are just some of his pseudonymous creations. Working in the Irish Civil Service, there was good reason to self-conceal, especially given the satirical qualities of his journalistic pen which, when he fell afoul of his employers, would lead him into forced retirement in 1953. But there is also an insurgent quality to his multiple identities, a refusal to be pinned down or singularly named akin to the rebellious characters in his most famous novel, *At Swim-Two-Birds* (1939) who demand 'private life, self-determination and a decent standard of living' (21). In a late article, he argues that using a variety of pseudonyms and conscious self-creation 'ensures that the fundamental individual will not be credited with a certain way of thinking, fixed attitudes, irreversible techniques of expression. No author should write under his own name nor under one permanent pen-name; a male writer should include in his impostures a female pen-name, and possibly vice versa.'[1] There is then a perpetually elusive, determinedly multiple quality to self-identification that evokes Oscar Wilde's theories that the self is something invented rather than discovered or W. B. Yeats's doctrine of the 'mask'. This is a modernist notion of subjectivity that thwarts singular or positivistic ideas of a coherent, self-contained individual, which also has precursors in an Irish tradition of self-concealment or self-invention. Subjective experience evokes both difficulty and opportunity for O'Brien. If the observer cannot be fixed, then nor can the observed. If O'Brien's fiction deploys experimental and non-realist modes, including multiple narrative perspectives, a self-conscious investment in artifice, surreal elements, burlesque, and comic anomaly, it registers the recalcitrance and resistance of a world that defies pat representation. This indicates O'Brien's indebtedness

---

[1] Anthony Cronin, *No Laughing Matter: The Life and Times of Flann O'Brien* (London: Grafton, 1989), 225.

to European modernist currents, perhaps above all his fellow Irishman James Joyce, and also registers the specific social and cultural context in which he is writing: the Irish 'Free State', which, having recently gained a circumscribed independence, has adopted a strong social conservative and confessional ideology, marked by philistinism and censorship. The romantic nationalism that had fuelled the independence movement, still given lip-service by officialdom in O'Brien's time, had given way to disappointment and post-colonial torpor. This context of disappointment, combined with an uneven social development in a still primarily rural Ireland, underlies the peculiar combination of the mundane and the fantastic in O'Brien's work, a splicing of boredom with apocalypse that belongs both to an international context of epiphanic modernism and a peculiarly Irish tradition of literary anomaly.[2]

Indeed there is another, less nationally specific, way to construe this dogged flight from the inherited straitjacket of a named, self-consistent subjectivity. And that is to place it among other, comparable cases in the international pantheon of modernism – artists as reluctant to stand steadfast by the ethics of a proper name as they were to abide by standard definitions of the work of art, and whose biographical evasion of individual stability is carried over into the shedding of aesthetic skins that defined their praxis. The most extreme such case is that of the Portuguese poet Fernando Pessoa, who, not satisfied with the kinds of stylistic fracturing and formal tablet-breaking already made possible by a generation of avant-gardists, had recourse to no fewer than four alternative literary personae to prosecute the polyphonic effects his revolution was to have made.[3] Or, an inverted version of the same problematic, consider Picasso's serial self-reinventions and tactical disappointments of gathering market expectations, as if the fate of having to dwell uncomfortably within the confines of a brand name was only to be paid off through this constant act of self-refashioning in a chain of 'periods'. Pirandello's 'six characters in search of an author', Joyce's infamous 'new style per chapter', Schoenberg's conversion to, and away from, the serialism he had invented to escape the traps of tonality: there are any number of roughly contemporaneous instances of what Brian O'Nolan/Flann O'Brien spontaneously performed – the almost schizophrenic dismantlement of any unitary core of artistic responsibility into partial and more provisional identities, and a flight into aesthetic possibilities not tethered to any Goethean substance. The wide nocturnal

---

[2] Seamus Deane, *Strange Country: Modernity and Nationhood in Irish Writing since 1790* (Oxford: Clarendon Press, 1997), 145–97.
[3] For an excellent treatment of this, see John Frow, '"A Non-Existent Coterie": Pessoa's Names', *Affirmations: Of the modern* 1, 1 (Summer 2013): 196–213.

skies of Modernism are hung with brilliant constellations formed from the *noms-des-plumes* of artists who preferred not to stand by the responsibilities of their social stations and family names.

If O'Brien resists the strictures of biographical naming, then all the more so, one might think, does his work bristle against generic designation, categories, librarians' labels. One can undertake comparisons, detect shared energies, suggest influences, but why try to confine Flann O'Brien into a single word or a concept like 'modernism'? The answers to this question, which forms the justification of this collection, lie in the current position and scholarly understanding of modernism, especially the rise of the 'new modernist studies', which precisely resist singular ideas of modernism. There have been major shifts in our frames of understanding of modernism in recent years, a radical expansion of categories, genres and periods. Like other areas of literary studies modernism has grown more capacious, turning its attention to previously neglected forms – letters, diaries, notebooks – and to the material, institutional and intellectual histories that underpin cultural production. The questions of when modernism begins and ends and where, geographically, it takes place have been provocatively contested and richly complicated. This is not simply a question of perforating the conventional dates for artistic modernism, '1890–1930', or expanding its concerns from metropolitan Europe to a more global reach.[4] Some commentators insist that 'modernism' should not be attached to a period at all, but is rather indicative of an awareness of the inexpressibility of the world that we can find as early as the fiction of Cervantes or the engravings of Dürer.[5] If 'high modernism' once signified an art that afforded the route to transcend the nightmare of history, our contemporary sense of the term often emphasizes a pained awareness in the face of contradiction, contingency and abritrariness of a world shorn of the sacral.

This expansion in the sense of the term 'modernism' has overshadowed cognate terms like 'postmodernism' which now often seems a contrapuntal extension of 'modernism' rather than a rejection or inversion of it.[6] Whereas 20 years ago O'Brien seemed the quintessential postmodern writer, now his relationship to modernism is in pressing need of reassessment. This is a need that the current collection seeks to address. We are seeking a more adequate conceptualization of a literary oeuvre staked out in the immediate

---

[4] Laura Doyle and Laura Winkiel, *Geomodernisms: Race, Modernism, Modernity* (Bloomington, IN: Indiana University Press, 2005).
[5] Gabriel Josipovici, *What Ever Happened to Modernism?* (New Haven and London: Yale University Press, 2010).
[6] Julian Murphet, 'Introduction: On the Market and Uneven Development', *Affirmations: of the Modern* 1, 1 (Summer 2013): 1–20.

aftermath of the first, heroic generation of self-conscious 'moderns', but not yet abandoned to the free market of signs and styles associated with the postmodern break of 1968 or thereabouts. Tyrus Miller's astute development of the concept of 'late modernism' may well have more to say in this context;[7] but for now, the pressing task is to reorient the study of O'Brien away from a waning, if not yet obsolescent critical paradigm, and towards the extraordinary reinvention of modernism taking place today, a paradigm to which it could well be argued he always and already belonged as a reluctant second-generation black sheep.

Another reason for the timeliness of this intervention is the wider transformation of the relationship of Ireland to modernism. For the major critics of the mid-twentieth century, like Richard Ellmann or Hugh Kenner, the Irish modernists were modern insofar as they transcended their national background. Joyce and Beckett took their lead from international, cosmopolitan and generally metropolitan artistic currents, and were presented as deracinated Parisian bohemians, with universal as opposed to local concerns.[8] The opposition between the international modernists and the *völkish*, insular Irish revivalists, against whom they set their teeth and aimed their scorn, often calcified into a reductive duality between Joyce the pioneering modernist and Yeats the belated romanticist. It was a powerfully Manichean way of understanding Irish literary history that tended to marginalize a figure like O'Brien from the institutions of literary studies: experimental and open to European currents, scornful of the myths and pieties of the Irish Revival, but at the same time domiciled in Dublin, and profoundly attuned to the local and provincial dimensions of Irish life.

But our understanding of modernism's relationship to Ireland has been transformed in the last 20 years, not least by the impact of cultural studies and new historicism. No longer is there an implicit oxymoron in 'Irish modernism'. The circulation of primitivism, spiritualism, evolutionism and feminism in early twentieth-century Irish literary culture reveals it as part of a broader European interchange of ideas. Conversely, but consistently, our view of modernism has become much more alert to the local, national and peripheral energies that fed into it, despite the strongly metropolitan and

---

[7] See Tyrus Miller, *Late Modernism: Politics, Fiction, and the Arts Between the World Wars* (Berkeley and Los Angeles: University of California Press, 1999).

[8] Richard Ellmann, *James Joyce* (New York: Oxford University Press, 1959); Hugh Kenner, *The Pound Era* (London: Faber and Faber, 1971); Ezra Pound, *Literary Essays*, ed. T. S. Eliot (London: Faber and Faber, 1954); James Joyce, *Occasional, Critical and Political Writing*, ed. Kevin Barry (Oxford: Oxford University Press, 2008); and Samuel Beckett, *Disjecta: Miscellaneous Writings and a Dramatic Fragment*, ed. Ruby Cohn (London: John Calder, 1983).

universalist values of those modernist artists who flocked to the major capitals of Europe, and their early liberal humanist advocates within the academy. The image of deracinated modernist writers, who have transcended 'merely' historical or transient concerns, has been radically challenged. In the Irish case, the rise of a theoretically supple historical approach has demonstrated, first of Joyce and then Beckett, their inseparability from an Irish cultural, social and postcolonial context.[9] In short, over the last 20 years critical attention has shifted from the apparent collision between the Irish culture and international modernism to their previously obscured collusions.

These shifts provide a compelling case to understand Flann O'Brien's work within the context of the new modernist studies. Yet this is no simple re-categorization. If much of the art and literature that has been classed as modernist (including Flann O'Brien's novels) strains against resolved narratives and pat definitions, then the word 'modernism' itself is shot through with contradictory associations. In other words the instability of meaning in the word modernism is appropriate to the historical and cultural complexities and tensions that it denotes: it semantically enacts that which it signifies. Symbolism, vorticism, imagism, futurism, surrealism, cubism, Dadaism – as an artistic category the word modernism has long done duty for various artistic movements, not to mention the very different senses attached to the term by sociologists and cultural critics.[10] Even before the expansion of new modernist studies, modernism was stretched across many fields. The terms modern, modernism and modernity will not sit still, they refuse to deliver up their significations in the manner demanded by positivist linguistics. Perry Anderson notoriously called modernism the 'emptiest of all cultural categories'.[11] It could also be labelled the 'fullest', its elasticity worn thin from overuse. Yet those bulging significations are culturally informative. The evaluative charge of the word has oscillated along with its definitions. As Susan Stanford Friedman has pointed out, on an American campus during the 1960s, 'modernism' signified rebellion, excitement, rupture, 'make it new'; by the 1990s, modernism was elitism, the Establishment, 'High Culture',

---

[9] Indicative scholarly works include Emer Nolan, *James Joyce and Nationalism* (London: Routledge, 1994); Andrew Gibson, *Joyce's Revenge: History, Politics and Aesthetics in Ulysses* (Oxford: Oxford University Press, 2004); Sean Kennedy, ed., *Beckett and Ireland* (Cambridge: Cambridge University Press, 2010); and Emilie Morin, *Samuel Beckett and the Problem of Irishness* (Basingstoke: Palgrave Macmillan, 2009).

[10] This is one reason why one of the best products of the first wave of 'new modernist studies' made the decisive move of pluralizing its master concept. See Peter Nicholls, *Modernisms: A Literary Guide* (Berkeley and Los Angeles: University of California Press, 1995).

[11] Perry Anderson, 'Modernity and Revolution', in *Marxism and the Interpretation of Culture*, ed. Cary Nelson and Lawrence Grossberg (London: Macmillan, 1988), 332.

the authoritarian target of emancipatory postmodernism.[12] With the rise of the new modernist studies, the pendulum has swung back – 'modernism' has acquired once more the whiff of dissidence and disobedience, the glamorously unruly and rebellious, a connotation signalled by the title of a recent collection – *Bad Modernisms*.[13] Modernism has oscillated from the shock of the new, to tweedy campus orthodoxy and back again:

> the oppositional meanings of *modern/modernity/modernism* point to the contradictory dialogic running through the historical and expressive formations of the phenomena to which the terms allude. Order and disruption are symbiotically necessary to each other for each to have its distinctive meaning. The center comes into beings as it dissipates. Modernity's grand narratives institute their own radical dismantling. The lifeblood of modernity's chaos is order. The impulse to order is the product of chaos. Modernism requires tradition to "make it new." Tradition comes into being only as it is rebelled against. Definitional excursions into the meanings of *modern*, *modernity*, and *modernism* begin and end in reading the specificities of these contradictions.[14]

Definitional excursions need to be alert to the specificities of the contradictions, and this includes the contrary values between modernism and postmodernism. This ambidexterity, what could be dubbed the 'auto-antonymic' qualities of modernism as a term, is one reason why it is appropriate to place O'Brien in this discursive frame. A generation ago, criticism of Flann O'Brien focused on his 'postmodern' qualities, his ludic, parodic subversions of inherited forms, his refusal of metanarratives.[15] In the last 15 years, resonating with wider developments in Irish and modernist studies, scholars have grown more alert to the post-colonial aspect of O'Brien's work, its extravagant fabulism an inverse expression of a sclerotic, insular Ireland where he lived, with its bureaucracy, piety and post-colonial enervation.

The tug-of-war between the Irish O'Brien and the international experimental writer suggests a delimiting opposition that we would do well to refuse. Many of the essays in this collection look at O'Brien's work in the

---

[12] Susan Stanford Friedman, 'Definitional Excursions: The Meanings of Modern/Modernity/Modernism', *Modernism/Modernity* 8, 3 (September 2001): 493–513.
[13] Douglas Mao and Rebecca L. Walkowitz, eds, *Bad Modernisms* (Durham, NC: Duke University Press, 2006).
[14] Friedman, 'Definitional Excursions', 510.
[15] In book length studies, Keith Hopper, *The Portrait of the Artists as a Young Postmodernist* (Cork: Cork University Press, 1995) is representative of this critical response.

context of international currents while others attend to the Irish dimension. The collection is, among other things, a contribution to thinking beyond and through the binaries that have sometimes bedevilled thinking about O'Brien: Irish and European, local and international, Dublin 'character' and reclusive mandarin, journalist and novelist. These oppositions are themselves repeatedly parodied and dismantled in his work. The local and the universal in O'Brien continually juxtapose in his oeuvre rendering each other perpetually strange and uncanny. To treat one at the expense of the other is to adopt a restricted context or airy abstraction that is both incomplete and inadequate.

A corollary of the historically more plausible grouping of O'Brien with the modernists he both venerated and griped against – be they Irish or otherwise – is that modernism itself is by that act internally modified, in the manner of Eliot's 'tradition': 'for order to persist after the supervention of novelty, the *whole* existing order must be, if ever so slightly altered; and so the relations, proportions, values of each work of art toward the whole are readjusted'.[16] So it is that this volume offers a modernism 'ever so slightly altered' to accommodate a view of it much the more 'touched' by the industry of 'Messrs. Watkins, Jameson and Pim'; with a yet greater avocation for the philosophical challenges of nihilism; more heavily indebted to a Catholic conception of sin, yet (perhaps for that reason) giddy in its fascination with lying; more deeply animated by the 'anxiety of influence' than ever – between media and forms as much as within them; aspiring to a properly fractal and dissolute account of literary character; onanistic in sexual orientation; and of course bristling as never before with the erotic possibilities of bicycles. If the general conception of modernism has been radically adjusted and historicized in recent years, more given over to the rhythms and banalities of the quotidian, as well as to the austerity and gravity of the Event, then the consolidation of O'Brien as one of its more generative participants can only enrich that paradoxical portrait. For with O'Brien, modernism enters into a truly baffling circular chase after its own tail – a 'back to the future' game of hide-and-seek with modernism's least examined cultural source, in the wit and philosophical banter of eighteenth-century satire. More than any other modernist apart from Wyndham Lewis, O'Brien locates a delirious, and often anti-humanist energy in a satire that shows the facile verities of Humanism to be empty and sentimental; and yet, unlike his fellow 'late modernist', O'Brien manages to retrieve from that acid bath of corrosive wit a self-reflexive vision of artistic enterprise that is as beguiling and enabling as it is scabrous and

---

[16] T. S. Eliot, 'Tradition and the Individual Talent', in *Selected Prose*, ed. John Hayward (Harmonsworth: Penguin, with Faber & Faber, 1953), 23–4.

withering. For O'Brien, the anti-modern impulses that everywhere shape the fictional universes of his texts are part of an abiding modernist contempt for any easy or sanguine accommodation with a wider world actively dissolving the connective tissues of a truly social existence.

Within this broad thematic rubric, the essays in this collection variously explore form, style, voice, characterization, irony and parody in O'Brien's major works, in relation to ideas of 'the modern', encompassing scientific, religious, sexual, linguistic, literary, socio-economic and technological contexts. There has been an explosion of international academic interest in Flann O'Brien, as attested by the numerous conferences and symposia held around the world during his centenary in 2011. By bringing together different voices and perspectives on O'Brien, the book proposes a considered intervention in the given state of O'Brien scholarship at this time of critical and scholarly burgeoning. The book will allow students and academics to situate O'Brien's major work in relation to wider critical questions about modernist literature and art. It seeks to bring new perspectives and fresh interpretations to this increasingly recognized 'second generation' modernist. Rather than construe him as a postmodernist *avant la lettre*, these essays locate O'Brien's work as the product of a late modernist sensibility and cultural context. Similarly, while there should be no doubt of his Irishness, and his profound debts to Irish language, history and culture, this collection seeks to understand O'Brien's nationally sensitive achievement as the work of an internationalist whose formal preoccupations reflect global modernist trends away from particularist modes of identity.

The distinct themes and formal concerns tracked in these essays include *la vie moderne* (as an international structure of daily life); characterization in branching narrative forms; the ethics and paradoxes of naming; parody and homage; lies and deception; theatricality; sexuality; technology and transport and the inevitable matter of drink and intoxication. Taken together, these specific topics construct a mosaic image of O'Brien as an exemplary modernist *auteur*, abreast of all the most salient philosophical and technical concerns affecting literary production in the period immediately before and after World War II.

Sean Pryor's essay 'Making Evil, with Flann O'Brien' treats determinism and ethics and their relationship to narrative and character. In its consideration of how O'Brien inverts traditional theological and philosophical concepts of sin, it strikes notes that resonate throughout this collection, including the idea of transgression, and how modernist conceptions of subjectivity resist calcified forms. John Attridge's 'Mythomaniac modernism: lying and bullshit in Flann O'Brien' proposes that O'Brien's linkage of fictional production to other forms of non-veridical utterance entails a critique not only of traditional ethical and religious condemnations of lying, but also of certain principles of high modernist aesthetics. Stefan Solomon shifts the emphasis to theatrical aspects of O'Brien's fiction. '"The outward accidents of illusion": O'Brien and the Theatrical' considers the influence of American playwright William Saroyan on O'Brien. Solomon deploys Martin Puchner's recent work on 'anti-theatrical' Modernism, contending that O'Brien's novels absorb 'the theatrical' as his plays cannot. Stephen Abblitt looks at another cardinal relationship in O'Brien's work, this time one of overweening influence. 'The Ghost of "Poor Jimmy Joyce": A Portrait of the Artist as a Reluctant Modernist' examines how O'Brien's parody of Joyce as an exemplar of high modernism is in tension with his own production of a fundamentally modernist novel in *The Dalkey Archive*. David Kelly is also concerned with the influence evoked by Joyce. His essay '"Do You Know What I'm Going to Tell You?": Flann O'Brien, Risibility and the Anxiety of Influence' analyses the humour in O'Brien as a mode of resistance to the crises of modern being, turning tropes typically associated with the traumatic loss of faith and stability in the inter-war period into matters of intense amusement.

Maebh Long's essay '*An Béal Bocht*, Translation and the Proper Name' is attuned to language, in this case the proper noun. Deploying Derridean theory, she relates how naming functions as categorization in O'Brien's work, in the context of debates on class and postcolonial identity in modernist writing, also raising issues pertaining to translation of *An Béal Bocht/The Poor Mouth*. Joseph Brooker's 'Ploughmen without Land: Flann O'Brien and Patrick Kavanagh' brings us further into Irish cultural and social history, offering a comparative treatment of O'Brien alongside his friend, the poet Patrick Kavanagh. Brooker assesses how both writers, in their markedly different yet parallel styles, 'struggled quixotically against the cant and limitations that they found in Ireland'. Dirk Van Hulle's essay 'Flann O'Brien's *Ulysses*: Marginalia and the Modernist Mind' richly deploys the archive, including the marginalia on O'Brien's copy of *Ulysses*, to examine O'Brien's relationship with Joyce from the perspective of cognitive science. Van Hulle argues that O'Brien (like Joyce and Beckett) prefigured a new model of the mind, which – in cognitive sciences – is currently being referred to as 'enactivism' or the 'extended mind'.

Baylee Brits's essay '"Truth is an Odd Number": Flann O'Brien and Infinite Imperfection' deploys scientific paradigms, in this case the preoccupation with numerology in *At Swim-Two-Birds*, in particular the numerical system of Good and Evil. She argues that numerology in the novel manifests as 'sophisticated recognitions of the speculative dimensions that literature shares with science and mathematics'. Rónán McDonald's essay '"An astonishing parade of nullity"': Nihilism and Value in *The Third Policeman*' critically assesses the question of nihilism in O'Brien's novel, in terms of its subversion of conventional value systems. McDonald argues that O'Brien's novel emerges from an Irish condition marked by particular anomalies and that although it is in dialogue with European modernist discourse, it refuses abstract philosophical diagnoses of cultural or existential malaise. Julian Murphet's essay 'Flann O'Brien and Modern Character', like Brits', also deals with mathematical tropes, in this case the 'numerical sublime' and the infinite. Murphet argues that O'Brien is one of the greatest innovators in novelistic characterization in the twentieth century, having consistently deposed the hallowed norms of modern character to allow for genuinely novel experiments in the presentation of selfhood.

Sam Dickson's '"No Unauthorized Boozing": Flann O'Brien and the Thirsty Muse' addresses the question of alcohol in O'Brien essay explores relationships between intoxication, sleep and literary creation in O'Brien's fiction, comparing O'Brien's textual versions of intoxication as an investigative, creative mode to those of his peer, Aldous Huxley, and contending that O'Brien's infirm bodies are not degenerate but offer figurations of O'Brien's uniquely modern literary regeneration. Sascha Morrell's essay 'Soft Drink, Hard Drink and Literary (Re)production in Flann O'Brien and Frank Moorhouse' compares how Flann O'Brien's *At Swim-Two-Birds* (1939) and Australian author Frank Moorhouse's *The Electrical Experience: A Discontinuous Narrative* (1974) use beer and soft drink manufacture, respectively, as conceits both for literary production and for the production of 'character'. In so doing, these texts offer challenging representations of authorial power, class relations, and the intersections between literature and commodity culture. Mark Steven's essay 'Flann O'Brien's Aestho-Autogamy' considers O'Brien's work in relation to the struggle of modernist writers to find autonomy and the need for a 'room of one's own', a struggle both complicit with material conditions and disdainful of them. He discerns in the trope of masturbation a reflection of some of these concerns, framing masturbation as a formal and narrative act that allows 'modernist literature to think through its own economic, political, and aesthetic conditions of production'. Finally, Mark Byron's 'Modernist Wheelmen' proposes the bicycle as the preeminent vehicle of the modernist literary avant-garde, with close attention to the political and existential implications of the human-bicycle dyads that O'Brien imagines in *The Third Policeman*.

1

Making Evil, with Flann O'Brien

Sean Pryor

Dic mihi, quaeso te, utrum deus non sit auctor mali.
— Augustine, *De libero arbitrio*[1]

Fiction and sin

Towards the beginning of *The Dalkey Archive*, in an underwater cave, Saint Augustine denies God's prescience. '*God has not foreknowledge*,' he explains to De Selby, Mick and Hackett: '*He is, and has knowledge*.'[2] Augustine substitutes timeless knowledge for foreknowledge because he wants to defend free will. For further reading on the subject he recommends *De libero arbitrio*, his early work on the free choice of the will. De Selby claims in response to have read all the Church Fathers, and if he has read *De libero arbitrio* he knows that Augustine explicitly attributes prescience to God: 'God has foreknowledge of everything that will be.'[3] De Selby has good reason to assume that Augustine still believes in God's foreknowledge. So either Augustine falsely denies that prescience, or, simplifying the argument of his early work, he twists one truth to affirm another. Perhaps he just has a bad memory; he certainly seems inconsistent. On the other hand, O'Brien's Augustine may not be history's Augustine, the author of *De libero arbitrio*; the underwater apparition may not be the former Bishop of Hippo at all (*CN*, 645).

---

[1] Augustine, *De libero arbitrio*, 1.1.1.1, in *Corpus christianorum series latina*, vol. 29, ed. William Green (Turnholti: Brepols, 1970), 211. See Augustine, *On the Free Choice of the Will, On Grace and Free Choice, and Other Writings*, trans. Peter King (Cambridge: Cambridge University Press, 2010), 3: 'Please tell me whether God is not the author of evil'.
[2] Flann O'Brien, *The Complete Novels* (New York: Alfred A. Knopf, 2007), 641. Hereafter abbreviated *CN*.
[3] Augustine, *On the Free Choice of the Will*, 79. See Augustine, *De libero arbitrio*, 3.3.8.34: 'deum ... esse praescium omnium futurorum'.

The conflict between free will and foreknowledge has clear and comic consequences for the plot of the novel. Is the destruction of the world, as De Selby declares, a 'prescribed doom, terrible but ineluctable' (*CN*, 672)? That would make Mick's messianic mission to save the world laughably inconsequential, or even an unwitting contribution to the world's demise. But if that doom really is prescribed, surely De Selby need not hurry it along, and perhaps Mick is actually destined, whatever mission he consciously chooses, to thwart De Selby's plan. God may not know what is to happen, but we may be sure, from the moment we turn the first page, that O'Brien does. The assurance might be false, in the sense that a writer might have made it all up as he went along, but it is at least a common assumption: we place our trust in 'the prescience of the author' (*CN*, 5). O'Brien can joke about prescribed dooms because, now that the book has been written, everything that happens to Mick and De Selby and Augustine has been scripted in advance, and neatly fenced off in the fairyland of fiction. Mick does not quite know that he is a fiction, but he does sometimes feel like 'the plaything of implacable forces' (*CN*, 758). That may be the case for any of us – whether we live in a novel by Flann O'Brien, a novel by Thomas Hardy, or the real world in which novels live. The conflict between freedom and determinism has consequences for the plot of any novel, for plot as such. The problems of free will, of a character's autonomy, of that character's involvement in a sequence of events governed by cause and effect, of the necessary determination of characters and events by historical, social, psychological, and material conditions – these problems have decisively shaped our theories of narrative and character.

The Dalkey Archive doubles the fun by rewriting real writers. Joyce and Augustine are doubly determined, by history and by O'Brien. There are, as it were, two characters jostling under the proper names James Joyce and Saint Augustine. When Augustine denies God's prescience and mocks Saint Peter, O'Brien mischievously usurps history, for Augustine's historical character ought to prescribe orthodox theology and solemn piety. We ought to foreknow Augustine's responses, at least in kind. But even as Augustine quite characteristically insists on free will, he disclaims responsibility for his actions, pleading an ineluctable prescription: '*I done what the mammy said, and everybody – you too – has to do what the mammy says*' (*CN*, 639). He blames his mother, Monica, and he blames God, for God's hand is at work in all things. That blasphemy suggests the hand of O'Brien, but Augustine's inconsistencies also register self-determination, a change of heart, the free choice of the will. That would be consistent in its own way too, since Augustine famously enjoyed a much more drastic change of heart, a conversion as momentous as Saint Paul's. The historical Augustine was himself two antithetical characters – a sinner and a saint – and O'Brien's composite ghost satirizes the total transformation of the one into the other. Thus, the author of the godly *Confessions* proves oddly unrepentant. O'Brien once praised the Bishop of Hippo, 'one of the greatest comics of the Christian era', for his 'astonishing feats in the sphere of hippocracy'.[4] Worse still, the righteous moral of Augustine's conversion is dubiously founded on fiction: '*I invented obscene feats out of bravado, lest I be thought innocent or cowardly*' (*CN*, 636). Do as I say, not as I say I did. The narrator of the *Confessions* (in both his roles), the character who debates with his friend Evodius in *De libero arbitrio* (a dialogue), and the historical figure we know from altarpieces and hagiographies was of Augustine's own making.

These gleeful inversions and conversions of fiction and history, character and identity, the made and the maker, recur when Mick meets Joyce later in the novel. But the interview with Augustine introduces a specifically theological framework for understanding character and narrative. Augustine is history's greatest Christian theorist of freedom and determinism, which he sought to reconcile through the doctrine of original sin, whereby sin is natural and unnatural, inevitable and voluntary. O'Brien makes great play with the doctrine's paradoxes. De Selby complains to Augustine that the notion of a universal Fall is preposterous and unjust, the first disobedience in the garden of Eden having happened so very long ago (*CN*, 641). Hackett protests that the 'yarn about everybody being born in original sin is all bloody bull', but Mick worries, when instructed that people turn into bicycles and bicycles into people, that such metamorphoses would contradict original sin (*CN*, 651, 679). (Presumably, bicycular atoms are innocent.) O'Brien's novels are obsessed by sin, original and otherwise – in the fact of it and our language for it, in the logic of the concept and the social history of its diverse formulations. In *The Hard Life*, Mr Collopy and Father Fahrt debate the concept's finer points while Finbarr suffers for his sins under the leather of the Christian brothers. In *At Swim-Two-Birds*, Trellis determines to write his great and daring book in order to 'show the terrible cancer of sin in its true light' and to demonstrate that 'all children were born clean and innocent': 'It was not by chance that he avoided the doctrine of original sin and the theological profundities which its consideration would entail' (*CN*, 32). In one sense it is not by chance because he has good reason; he freely chooses his beliefs. In another, because he has no choice: he has been scripted by the novel's narrator, just as he will script his characters. Trellis's denial of the

---

[4] Flann O'Brien, letter to Timothy O'Keeffe, 4 November 1962, in 'A Sheaf of Letters', *Journal of Irish Literature* 3, 1 (1974): 65–92 (81).

theological doctrine neatly and ironically betrays the original sin involved in fiction.

O'Brien's novels are obsessed by sin and yet seem to laugh at genuine ethical reflection. He satirizes the evils perpetrated by Augustine, Catholic theology, Irish Catholicism, and Irish society more broadly, but he also satirizes the concept of evil. Some say O'Brien attacks folly, rather than evil.[5] Others suggest that he substitutes epistemology for ethics.[6] He certainly deals irreverently with theological, philosophical, and legal ethics, and he does so by modelling ethics on fiction. Augustine's real sin turns out not to be lust or heresy, but making, narrating. Trellis's sin is the sin of being made, narrated. It is hard to take such sin seriously. O'Brien's art bursts evil's balloon.

Character and creation

This is not what novels are supposed to do. Recent theory celebrates the ethical nature of the novel or of narrative, though this has little to do with the representation of good or evil characters and acts. The form of the novel, critics say, establishes an aesthetics of alterity: a shifting field of relations between subjects.[7] The novel brings to life relations with the other, relations which are inherently ethical, and to do that is, by implication, an inherent good.[8] Some critics emphasize the autonomy of characters, and some will even complain when a narrative voice seems to dominate or obscure a character's thought and expression.[9] Some critics insist on the autonomy of the author, who inflicts her choices upon the reader; others stress the autonomy of language, beyond any character's or author's total control; and yet others celebrate the

---

[5] J. C. C. Mays, 'Brian O'Nolan: Literalist of the Imagination', in *Myles: Portraits of Brian O'Nolan*, ed. Timothy O'Keeffe (London: Martin Brian & O'Keeffe, 1973), 77–119 (93).

[6] See Chris Morash, 'Augustine ... O'Brien ... Vico ... Joyce', in *Conjuring Complexities: Essays on Flann O'Brien*, ed. Anne Clune and Tess Hurson (Belfast: Institute of Irish Studies, 1997), 133–42 (139); and Hugh Kenner, *Samuel Beckett* (New York: Grove Press, 1961), 37.

[7] For a summary account of the aesthetics of alterity, see Dorothy J. Hale, 'Aesthetics and the New Ethics: Theorizing the Novel in the Twenty-First Century', *PMLA* 124, 3 (May 2009): 895–905. For discussion of O'Brien's fiction and theories of alterity, see Joseph Brooker, 'Myles' Tones', in *'Is it about a bicycle?': Flann O'Brien in the Twenty-First Century*, ed. Jennika Baines (Dublin: Four Courts, 2011), 17–31 (27–8).

[8] See Adam Zachary Newtown, *Narrative Ethics* (Cambridge, MA: Harvard University Press, 1995), 7.

[9] See Brian Phillips, 'Character in Contemporary Fiction', *Hudson Review* 56, 4 (Winter 2004): 629–42 (639–40).

reader's autonomy, her free submission to the narrative, its characters and its language.[10]

That is the solemn logic of autonomy at which O'Brien's satire takes aim. The narrator of *At Swim-Two-Birds* may propose that a reader should 'regulate at will the degree of his credulity', and that characters 'should be allowed a private life, self-determination and a decent standard of living' (*CN*, 21) – but 'allowed' rather gives the game away. Augustine insists that, though God is 'the creator of all natures', this does not make him the creator 'of all acts of will'.[11] So to speak, he determines our self-determination: he makes us free. But for Kant it is 'totally incomprehensible to our reason how beings can be *created* to use their powers freely'.[12] ('Of all those German daddies,' Myles na Gopaleen muses, 'Kant was the grand-daddy.')[13] By this logic, ethics and creation are incompatible. Characters, authors, and readers are all created beings, and creation obeys the phenomenal realm's principle of causality. (Conflating real people and fictional people under the category of the created is part of the fun: Myles also recommends the problem of causality as a subject for 'boisterous discussion at Christmas Night parties'.)[14] Neither Trellis nor the Pooka can legitimately be held responsible for his actions. 'The characters of a novel are beings that are shut up, prisoners,' writes Emmanuel Levinas. It is not that 'the artist represents beings crushed by fate', but that 'beings enter their fate because they are represented'.[15] Ordinarily we regulate our credulity and allow that a novel's characters have in fiction the freedom we have, or believe ourselves to have, in fact. O'Brien impishly suggests that we are in fact as fictive and unfree as a character.

Ethical language is emptied by this shift. Trellis can intend to present 'a man of great depravity and a woman of unprecedented virtue' (*CN*, 32) but

---

[10] See Wayne C. Booth, 'Why Ethical Criticism Can Never Be Simple', in *Mapping the Ethical Turn: A Reader in Ethics, Culture, and Literary Theory*, ed. Todd F. Davis and Kenneth Womack (Charlottesville: University Press of Virginia, 2001), 16–29; Dorothy J. Hale, *Social Formalism: The Novel in Theory from Henry James to the Present* (Stanford: Stanford University Press, 1998), 221–2; and Dorothy J. Hale, 'Fiction as Restriction: Self-Binding in New Ethical Theories of the Novel', *Narrative* 15, 2 (May 2007): 187–206 (190).
[11] Augustine, *Concerning the City of God against the Pagans*, trans. Henry Bettenson (London: Penguin, 2003), 193; and Augustine, *De civitate dei contra paganos*, 5.9.130-32, in *Corpus christianorum series latina*, vol. 47, ed. B. Dombart and A. Kalb (Turnholti: Brepols, 1955).
[12] Immanuel Kant, *Religion within the Boundaries of Mere Reason and Other Writings*, trans. Allen Wood and George Di Giovanni (Cambridge: Cambridge University Press, 1998), 144 (6: 142).
[13] Myles na Gopaleen, 'Only a Letter', *Irish Times*, 30 July 1953, 4.
[14] Myles na Gopaleen, 'A First Claus?', *Irish Times*, 24 December 1956, 6.
[15] Emmanuel Levinas, 'Reality and its Shadow', in *Collected Philosophical Papers*, trans. Alphonso Lingis (Dordrecht: Kluwer Academic, 1993), 1–13 (9–10).

the vice and the virtue seem meaningless. That Furriskey turns out not to be the wickedest of villains is not to his credit, for that is the narrator's doing, just like Trellis's intention. The situation becomes especially preposterous when, having discovered that sleep suspends Trellis's powers, Furriskey and Peggy 'arrange to lead virtuous lives, to simulate the immoral actions, thoughts and words which Trellis demands of them' (*CN*, 58). The verbs bestow false agency and the adjectives have no content. This senselessness is funny. O'Brien's comedy thrives on what seem to be immoralities – brutal murders, grotesque violence, systematic oppression, rape, theft, adultery – but can an action be immoral in itself, without being the act of an autonomous agent? An inevitably evil character, a man who is by nature depraved, is less like an ethical subject than a personification, an allegorical figure like Sloth or Pride or Sin itself. The trouble with any sober allegory of evil is that at some level the allegorical figure has no choice.[16] Thus, for all that the Pooka wreaks havoc, neither he nor his actions are really evil. 'My name, said the Pooka, with an apologetic solicitude, is Fergus MacPhellimey and I am by calling a devil or pooka' (*CN*, 104). The *calling* is a vocation but also a naming and a making, and the making is a creating and a compelling. The same is true for the Good Fairy, who is, so to speak, not at all good because he is made good: 'My correct name is Good Fairy, said the Good Fairy. I am a good fairy' (*CN*, 102). Proper name, identity and common noun converge: the meeting of word, character and category dispels ethics with ontology. (This is neatly ironic, for the word *fairy* derives from *Fata*, the name of the Fates who dictate our lives. Conversely, their name transforms the past participle *fatum*, that which is said, into those who do the saying.) In *The Poor Mouth*, the same principle satirizes social and historical conditioning, the sense of 'predestined failure' produced in the Irish by English prejudice and oppression.[17] Call every boy Jams O'Donnell and he will by vocation be a Jams O'Donnell.

For Aristotle, in contrast, character is precisely ethical being. Aristotle models fiction on ethics. He argues that ethical virtue (*ēthikē aretē*) is the product of habit (*ethos*). This does not mean that virtue arises in us by nature; if it did, it could not be praiseworthy.[18] (Augustine makes the same point about Lucifer: 'if the Devil is a sinner by nature, there can really be no

---

[16] See Andrew Escobedo, 'Allegorical Agency and the Sins of Angels', *ELH* 75 (2008): 787–818.

[17] Declan Kiberd, *Inventing Ireland: The Literature of the Modern Nation* (London: Vintage, 1996), 511.

[18] Aristotle, *The Nichomachean Ethics*, ed. and trans. H. Rackham, 2nd edn, Loeb Classical Library (Cambridge, MA: Harvard University Press, 1934), 2.i.1-2, 3.i.1 (70–1, 116–17). Aristotle goes on to argue that virtue and vice become permanent. Once you have become an unjust person, your character is fixed (3.v.13–14; 146–9).

question of sin'.)¹⁹ Instead, virtue arises within us and virtue is a choosing state (*hexis proairetikē*); it is a habit or character we develop and which then governs our choices.²⁰ Thus, in the *Poetics*, Aristotle defines character (*ēthos*) as that which reveals choice (*proairesis*).²¹ The word *ēthos* means both ethical character and *dramatis persona*, as does the English *character*. The lexical and the logical overlap is ripe for O'Brien's metafictional satire. The Pooka assures Shorty, Slug, and friends that they can trust the Good Fairy, that the Good Fairy is foreknowable, because he is 'of unimpeachable character' (*CN*, 138). Sure enough the Good Fairy soon betrays him, yet the Pooka was unwittingly right: you can hardly impeach the Good Fairy for being himself. It is nonsense to wish, as Trellis does, to create 'a depraved character' (*CN*, 57), for the *dramatis persona* would have no hand in acquiring the habit of depravity.

O'Brien extends his satire on character, comically and perversely, by parodying the materialism whereby objective circumstances determine ethical character. When Brinsley objects to the narrator's draft because his characters seem indistinguishable, and then insists on 'the importance of characterization in contemporary literary works of a high-class, advanced or literary nature', the narrator reduces characterization to physiognomy:

Head: brachycephalic; bullet; prognathic.
Vision: tendencies towards myopia; wall-eye; nyctalopia.
Configuration of nose: roman, snub; mastoid. (*CN*, 159)

Physical form determines subjectivity: the obstinacy of a bullet-head, the folly of short-sightedness, the imperial bearing of a roman nose. When Furriskey, Lamont and Shanahan bring Trellis to trial they first condemn him on these very grounds: 'He looks a right ruffian. . . . He looks a very criminal type, I must say' (*CN*, 192). But while O'Brien often invokes the logic of physiognomy, by which the physical determines the metaphysical, he also has the laws that govern the physical realm break down. The 'impossible' atomic theory of both *The Third Policeman* and *The Dalkey Archive* thoroughly confuses matter and spirit. Bicycular atoms may be born innocent, but in the end a bicycle can be hung for its crimes (*CN*, 314). When the Pooka punishes Trellis his body is subjected to laughably impossible abuse, and in 'addition to his person' – for his person is his personality, his body his character – his room is 'the subject of mutations unexplained by any purely physical hypothesis . . . nor did the

---

[19] Augustine, *City of God*, 446; Augustine, *De civitate dei*, 11.15.
[20] Aristotle, *Nichomachean Ethics*, 2.vi.15 (94–5).
[21] Aristotle, *Poetics*, ed. and trans. Stephen Halliwell, and other works, Loeb Classical Library (Cambridge, MA: Harvard University Press, 1999), 1450b.

movements of the room conform to any known laws relating to the behaviour of projectiles' (*CN*, 174). The freakish suspension of physical causality is as much a torture to Trellis as the boils on his back.

The Pooka can do this to Trellis, his author, because he exercises 'strange powers', but he only has those powers as a character. 'The vocation of the pooka,' he explains, is to punish 'such parties as are sent to me for treatment by Number One, which is the First Good and the Primal Truth' (*CN*, 105). His vocation is voiced by someone else, the narrator. He is instructed and determined by his true god, an author above and beyond poor Trellis. Conversely, you might say that Trellis usurps and perverts that god's role as maker, and so deserves his diabolical treatment. When we turn in this way from characters to authors, the relation between ethics and ontology takes on a new aspect. Augustine is quite clear about the fact that God's creations are good, for God is a good author, the consummate artist, and the first cause: 'There can be no better author than God, no more effective skill [*ars*] than his word, no better cause than that a good product should be created by God, who is good.'[22] This is an ontology of ethics: being and the good converge. Peggy and the Pooka are, by this logic, equally and naturally good. And since for Augustine God is good, being is good, and evil is contrary to God, evil has no positive being: 'to this highest existence, from which all things that are derive their existence, the only contrary nature is the non-existent.'[23] The heretical alternative is the Manichean postulate of a second god who makes evil. But since the underwater Augustine condemns '*the Manichean dualism of light and darkness, good and evil*' (*CN*, 642), and since *The Dalkey Archive* and *At Swim-Two-Birds* have but one author, perhaps instead O'Brien's surprisingly orthodox fiction is an ethical good not through an aesthetics of alterity, but through benevolent poesis in the tradition of God.

Narration and guilt

If good is conformity to the nature God has made, and evil is revolt against that good nature, it may be good for characters to do seemingly bad things, to obey their maker whatever that maker may ask.[24] Abraham would have been quite right to sacrifice Isaac, but Furriskey's rebellion for the seeming good is wrong. This logic founds ethics not, for instance, on obedience to a

---

[22] Augustine, *City of God*, 453; Augustine, *De civitate dei*, 11.21.
[23] Augustine, *City of God*, 473; Augustine, *De civitate dei*, 12.2.
[24] Augustine, *On the Free Choice of the Will*, 100: 'Every vice, in virtue of the fact that it *is* a vice, is contrary to nature'; Augustine, *De libero arbitrio*, 3.13.38.133.

moral law discerned by reason, but on the relation between a creature and its creator. In the short story that sowed the seed for *At Swim-Two-Birds*, the novelist narrator creates 'a rank waster and a rotter', McDaid, part of whose villainy is to be 'a dyed-in-the-wool atheist'.[25] When McDaid rebels, the narrator punishes him by sending him to a prayer-meeting, but far from suffering punishment, McDaid stays to pray. That is to say, McDaid substitutes a venial atheism for a mortal one: he switches allegiance from his immediate maker, the professedly devout narrator, to God, his maker's narrator. In *At Swim-Two-Birds*, as the hierarchies of fiction are increasingly blurred and characters owe allegiance to competing authors, the ethical relation of creature and creator produces a kind of satiric polytheism. When Shanahan and friends, authored by Tracy, have a showdown with Red Kiersay's cowboys, authored by Henderson, they are like the warring tribes of polytheistic ancient Palestine. Sublunary authors are, after all, not much like the orthodox Judaeo-Christian deity. That God is omniscient and omnipresent, while Trellis relinquishes 'absolute control' as soon as he falls asleep (*CN*, 31).[26] God creates 'all things from nothing [*de nihilo*]'; the very breath of life, he himself is uncreated.[27] An author merely modifies prefabricated materials; an author is at best a tube to pipe the breath of life. All authors are, in this sense, plagiarists. On trial for his life, Trellis is accused of plagiarizing Tracy, but then Tracy and Henderson simply hire their characters, just as Trellis hires Finn MacCool (*CN*, 39, 51, 57).

Nevertheless, our making is comparable to God's. God creates all things from nothing and he himself has no cause. Correspondingly, 'nothing causes an evil will' and the will, as Myles na Gopaleen defines it, 'is an impulse originating *ex nihilo*'.[28] You could say that that is why we – as authors rather than as characters – are ethically responsible. If Trellis is made to make a depraved character, the guilt is the narrator's. Thus, when the narrator explains to Brinsley that Furriskey will be 'so bad that he must be created *ab ovo et initio*' (*CN*, 32), it only betrays his own villainy and confusion. If Furriskey

---

[25] Flann O'Brien, 'Scenes in a Novel' (1934), in *Myles before Myles: A Selection of the Earlier Writings of Brian O'Nolan* (London: Grafton Books, 1988), 78–9.
[26] Perhaps O'Brien had been reading the Psalms. On the one hand: 'he that keepeth Israel shall neither slumber nor sleep' (Ps. 121.4); on the other hand: 'Awake, why sleepest thou, O Lord?' (Ps. 44.23). In a draft of the novel, Peggy explains to Furriskey that 'Trellis's powers of omniscience and omnipresence . . . are withdrawn when he falls asleep'. See Flann O'Brien, typescript with holograph corrections of *At Swim-Two-Birds*, Flann O'Brien Papers, Harry Ransom Humanities Research Center, Box 1, Folder 1, 91. The corresponding passage is at *CN*, 58.
[27] Augustine, *On the Free Choice of the Will*, 6; Augustine, *De libero arbitrio*, 1.2.5.13.
[28] Augustine, *City of God*, 477; Augustine, *De civitate dei*, 12.6; and na Gopaleen, 'Only a Letter', 4.

was hatched from an egg, the egg was laid by the narrator. (Horace counsels poets not to begin the story of the Trojan War *ab ovo*, with the hatching of Leda's eggs, but *in media res*.[29] O'Brien's narrator indulges culpably in not one but three beginnings.) As authors, we are responsible for the will that acts upon and refashions the materials we are furnished with. Here, too, O'Brien comically models ethics on fiction, for the act of narration, of fashioning those materials, risks the sin of self-love: the subjugation of others and the reinvention of oneself. O'Brien's first four novels are in the first person, and though his narrators are different in many ways, each is an objectionable piece of work. He once labelled Finbarr, the narrator of *The Hard Life*, 'a complete ass'.[30] The unnamed narrator of *The Third Policeman* is 'a heel and a killer' (*CN*, 405). The wretched Bonaparte O'Coonassa puts on the 'poor mouth' to exculpate himself and cultivate sympathy. Even in *The Dalkey Archive*, O'Brien's free indirect discourse satirizes Mick's attempts to narrate himself out of guilt and into virtue: 'Gradually an equanimity of mood descended on him. His mission was simple and honourable, his primary object the redemption of his soul. What was wrong with that? Nothing' (*CN*, 782). What is wrong with that is the attempt to remake oneself. Mick sins against the truth that his motives are compromised and, more fundamentally, against the truth that he is not his own maker.[31]

Narration thus becomes a dream of autonomy and, as Terry Eagleton observes, 'Pure autonomy is a dream of evil.'[32] By this logic, language reduces the shifting field of ethical relations to a map of the subject's dominions. Myles gives free rein to this dream in an early 'Cruiskeen Lawn' column:

> man is merely an objective phenomenon, a private hallucination of my own, not so much my faithful subject as my priceless object, my personal anonymentity, my household inanimity. Yet this inert and homemade... being, albeit incapable of initiating any meritorious action, can sometimes, by sole virtue of my approval, please. ('Me' understood.) [Myles's ellipsis][33]

---

[29] Horace, *Ars poetica*, 147–8, in *Satires, Epistles and Ars poetica*, trans. H. Rushton Fairclough, rev. edn, Loeb Classical Library (London: William Heinemann, 1929), 462.
[30] Flann O'Brien, letter to Mark Hamilton, 20 February 1961, in 'A Sheaf of Letters', 78.
[31] Strangely, O'Brien commented that all the characters in *The Dalkey Archive* 'are intended to be obnoxious, particularly the narrator' (letter to Cecil Scott, in 'A Sheaf of Letters', 86). Perhaps by the narrator he meant Mick, the protagonist. Perhaps instead he meant the third-person narrative voice: the noxiousness even of impersonal telling. In that case Mick might be blameless, made and betrayed by such unscrupulous use of free indirect discourse.
[32] Terry Eagleton, *On Evil* (New Haven: Yale University Press, 2010), 12.
[33] Myles na gCopaleen, 'Cruiskeen Lawn', *Irish Times*, 5 October 1945, 2.

Authors of all genres benevolently exercise this power over both their materials and their readers. 'The novel, in the hands of an unscrupulous writer,' warns the insufficiently scrupulous narrator of *At Swim-Two-Birds*, 'could be despotic' (*CN*, 21). When readers freely submit to the *Confessions* – at least to the *Confessions* written by O'Brien's unorthodox apparition – they swallow a pack of lies, and the lies are tremendously powerful. We only know of Augustine's mother, his wives and his misspent youth because he tells us about them, and we only know what he chooses to tell us. He chooses the lessons we are to learn and to live by. Hypocrisy is hippocracy (*Hippo* + *kratos*, power or authority) when telling tall tales empowers the Bishop of Hippo. In contrast, Hackett contends that the Church has unjustly condemned Judas because Judas left no written record, or because that record was maliciously suppressed (*CN*, 665). It is as if only silence speaks of innocence, and even speaks of vilification. Authorship would then mean authority, the culpable domination of the other, and authorship would then mean falsity, the self-serving pretence of virtue and the vice of self-deluding fiction.

Take the opening sentence of *The Third Policeman*, whose narrator Keith Hopper calls an 'egocentric solipsist':[34]

> Not everybody knows how I killed old Phillip Mathers, smashing his jaw in with my spade; but first it is better to speak of my friendship with John Divney because it was he who first knocked old Mathers down by giving him a great blow in the neck with a special bicycle-pump which he manufactured himself out of a hollow iron bar. (*CN*, 223)

This is less like a confession than the tale of some unrepentant sinner deep in the *Inferno*. It begins with what is effectively a boast. Not everybody has been privileged to hear my remarkable story. The sentence quickly displaces responsibility by tracing a chain of cause and effect. It was Divney who did it, really: Divney dealt the first blow and Divney made the murder weapon. In fact, manufacturing the bicycle pump displaces that great blow. The story proves remarkable, not because an old man was brutally murdered, but because Divney made the pump from such unlikely materials, and did it all by himself. One man's success displaces the joint crime, and credit for the pump displaces guilt for the killing.

In a sense, not even the narrator really knows how old Mathers was killed, for he does not understand what killing means. Or you could say he culpably refuses to acknowledge the meaning of life and death. This is somewhat

---

[34] Keith Hopper, *Flann O'Brien: A Portrait of the Artist as a Young Post-Modernist*, 2nd edn (Cork: Cork University Press, 2009), 121.

ironic, since, when he dies, he does not understand that he dies. Two pages later he makes a kind of confession: 'it was for De Selby I committed my first serious sin . . . my greatest sin' (*CN*, 225). But the words are empty; they register no change of heart. Even when, at the end of the novel, the narrator has escaped hanging for a crime he did not commit, he thinks again of finishing the crime he failed to commit: stealing the black cashbox. Neither his words nor his actions give evidence of genuine ethical reflection. If it is 'better' for the narrator to tell the story this way, that is because it seems easier or more comfortable for him. Denis Donoghue argues that the murder 'is accompanied by no sign of guilt or scruple: the ethical issue is disposed of in silence'[35] – and that silence is offered to the reader's judgement. The reader's encounter with the other seems ethical after all. We can justly judge the evil narrator. We can see that his decision to speak 'first' of the friendship matches Divney's 'first' blow. The tale is as guilty as the deed.

To blame Divney and the bicycle pump is to misrepresent the truth about oneself, but it matters whether that falsity is free or determined. In order to engage ethically with the narrator, we need to allow him a degree of autonomy. To be evil, he really does need to *decide* to exculpate himself. Yet throughout the novel he, too, is the plaything of implacable forces. He repeatedly describes a strange lack of agency: 'I went forward mechanically, swung the spade over my shoulder and smashed the blade of it with all my strength against the protruding chin' (*CN*, 232; cf. *CN*, 237, 239, 369, 395, 398). That makes sense neither as an excuse nor as a boast. It is ethically blank. Much later, having escaped the police and seemingly free, the narrator returns to old Mathers's house for no good reason: 'I think I had made up my mind to go . . . when some influence came upon my eyes and dragged them round till they were again resting upon the house' (*CN*, 381). Consciousness and agency separate: 'If I had given (or had been able to give) unrestricted rein to either fear or reason I should have turned my back forever on this evil house. . . . But there was some other thing interfering with my mind' (*CN*, 385). If character is a choosing state, therefore, the narrator is not a character. Identity is soon reduced to bodily momentum: 'My feet carried my nerveless body unbidden. . . . My mind was completely void' (*CN*, 402). And that momentum is narrative. Consciousness of unconsciousness is as close as the narrator comes to an understanding that, in the story he tells and in the telling of his story, he is being narrated.[36]

---

[35] Denis Donoghue, 'Introduction' to Flann O'Brien, *The Third Policeman* (Normal: Dalkey Archive, 1999), xi.

[36] 'As a character, [the narrator] wavers between metafictional self-consciousness and "realist" passivity' (Hopper, *Flann O'Brien*, 92).

So little that the narrator says or does makes sense as deliberate good or evil. It is not that he exercises free will, nor that he succumbs to a logical sequence of cause and effect. The influences and interferences that compel the mechanism are unnamed and inexplicable. He suffers sheer determination, a kind of terrifying cosmic whim. Narration's dream of autonomy reveals pure heteronomy. It is conventional to conceive of narrative necessity and a character's freedom operating in inverse proportion. The more a character exercises her freedom, the more arbitrary the narrative; the more the narrative is governed by cause and effect, the more the character is determined. But the narrator in *The Third Policeman* seems least a free agent when his actions are most inexplicable. That makes ethics all but impossible. Such moments appear throughout O'Brien's novels. In the dénouement of *The Poor Mouth*, Bonaparte happens to notice an unidentified stranger and, 'without any volition on my part, my gaze remained on him' (*CN*, 487). This ought to be his redemption, the discovery of his long lost father, a reward for all the evils he has suffered – but it is only an accident. And in any case the man is probably not his father; the man simply has the same name, Jams O'Donnell. That is to say, both men have merely been called, have been named and determined. The narrator's misadventures, whether comic or tragic, are the machinations of fate. He narrates *The Poor Mouth* having been imprisoned for a crime he did not commit and having committed plenty of other crimes. Justice is incidental. 'Tis amazing how fate drives us in this life from the bad act to the good one and back again,' the Captain philosophizes, blithely confusing ethics and determinism (*CN*, 451).

The strangest and most arbitrary event in *At Swim-Two-Birds* is not the gleeful *deus ex machina*, the burning of Trellis's book, but the previous paragraph:

> I went slowly up the stairs to my room. My uncle had evinced unsuspected traits of character and had induced in me an emotion of surprise and contrition extremely difficult of literary rendition or description. My steps faltered to some extent on the stairs. As I opened my door, my watch told me that the time was five fifty-four. At the same time I heard the Angelus pealing out from far away. (*CN*, 214)

This ought to be a climax of confession, aptly accompanied by the call to prayer: for having misunderstood and misrepresented my uncle, for the sin of authorship, I ask forgiveness. But like the uncle's good will, the narrator's contrition is perfectly surprising. The one induces the other, we are told, but by some unknown law of induction. The result is so difficult to render because it is the fact of being rendered. It is a negative image of free will: the entirely unsuspected event, which undoes the authorial pretension to divine prescience and beneficent autopoiesis. 'O'Brien refused to believe that the writer recreates the world,' suggests Colm Tóibín, 'but instead he set out to show that the world re-creates the writer.'[37] Only God begets himself.

It must be complete

So O'Brien's art bursts good's balloon, too. Within the fairyland of fiction neither good nor evil exists. Outraged by what Myles calls 'the Smut Board', otherwise known as the Censorship of Publications Board, O'Brien routinely satirizes the ethical judgement of literature.[38] The editor of *The Poor Mouth* explains that he has censored all the 'improper subjects' in Bonaparte's original text (*CN*, 409) – an odd statement, considering the subjects that remain. Trellis recognizes that a 'purely moralizing tract' would attract no readers, and so fills his book with 'plenty of smut' (*CN*, 31). Disowning *Ulysses*, Joyce brands it 'that dirty book, that collection of smut', and righteously contemns its true authors: 'Muck-rakers, obscene poets, carnal pimps, sodomous sycophants, pedlars of the coloured lusts of fallen humanity' (*CN*, 760, 762). If the ethical judgement of books by their contents is laughable, it is laughable to judge narrators by their stories or writers by their books. Brian McHale writes that, however many metafictional realities a novel layers and overlaps, however self conscious the characters may be, there is always 'an absolute ontological "ceiling"'.[39] The narrator, the maker of Trellis and Furriskey and the Pooka, is blissfully unaware of Flann O'Brien (or Brian O'Nolan) and can do him no harm. But does an ontological ceiling mean an ethical one? If not, Brian O'Nolan may be as innocent as his creations, being himself created. It is as if by modelling ethics on fiction O'Nolan's novels genially justify the ways of makers to men, or at least exculpate them.

Augustine likens God to an author and creation to a poem. God would never have made men or angels, foreknowing the evil they would do, 'if he had not known at the same time how he would put such creatures to good use, and thus enrich the course of the world history by the kind of antithesis

---

[37] Colm Tóibín, 'Flann O'Brien's Lies', *London Review of Books* 34, 1 (5 January 2012): 32–6 (34).
[38] Myles na Gopaleen, 'Censorship', *Irish Times*, 9 February 1956, 8. For discussion of O'Brien, the 1929 Censorship of Publications Act, and Irish censorship more broadly, see especially Hopper, *Flann O'Brien*; and Carol Taaffe, *Ireland Through the Looking Glass: Flann O'Brien, Myles na gCopaleen and Irish Cultural Debate* (Cork: Cork University Press, 2008).
[39] Brian McHale, *Postmodern Fiction* (London: Routledge, 1987), 13.

which gives beauty to a poem'.[40] As if in emulation, Trellis looks to tell the tale of 'the timeless conflict of grime and beauty, gold and black, sin and grace' (*CN*, 32). (How beautifully antithesis, suggesting three parallel oppositions, makes gold evil and black good.) In God's creation, evil is a good in relation to good itself, and there can be no evil without good. Good precedes and redeems evil, and that antithetical relation is beauty, though not of the same kind as the 'manifold diversity of beauty in sky and earth and sea'.[41] Perhaps, then, there was no poetry or art in Eden, just the simple beauty of the pure good.[42] But in a passage that O'Nolan cancelled from the draft of *At Swim-Two-Birds*, Trellis insists that there was no good in Eden either, for there can be no good without evil:

> Where is the man, said Trellis horizontally, that is going to tell me that good can exist side by side with good? Good and evil are complementary terms. You cannot have one without the other. Each gets its force by reason of the other and would be meaningless without the other. There was no good in the Garden till the serpent came, only negation and bathos. Therefore the devil created good.[43]

Here, mere being and sheer creation are beyond good and evil, and though God is an author, the true artist is the devil. The artist does not originate; the artist completes. Art redeems the evil it makes, putting it to the good use of beauty, so that the evil is no longer evil and the beauty not simply good. Art's balloon floats high above the realm of ethics. No less an authority than Father Fahrt explains that moral debauchery has always been 'essential to inspire great men to achievement in the arts' (*CN*, 547). One need only look at the Greeks, he reasons. 'As art must be essentially good,' Myles urges, 'so also must it be essentially evil; art, in other words, must be complete.'[44] Art's only duty is to the whole truth of the real world as we find it and make it. That world is our ontological ceiling, or, better, our historical horizon: the

---

[40] Augustine, *City of God*, 449; Augustine, *De civitate dei*, 11.18.
[41] Augustine, *City of God*, 1075; Augustine, *De civitate dei*, 22.24.
[42] Furriskey and friends know that Adam cannot have played the fiddle before the Fall, but they dubiously believe him to have sung (*CN*, 149).
[43] Flann O'Brien, typescript with holograph corrections of *At Swim-Two-Birds*, Flann O'Brien Papers, Harry Ransom Humanities Research Center, Box 1, Folder 1, 22. This passage appears early in the novel, between the close of a long speech by Finn ('in the craw of his gut-hung knickers') and Conán's reply ('Good for telling') (*CN*, 15). For further discussion of this and other cancelled passages, see Samuel Anderson, 'Pink Paper and the Composition of Flann O'Brien's *At Swim-Two-Birds*', MA Dissertation (Louisiana State University, 2000).
[44] Myles na gCopaleen, 'Cruiskeen Lawn', *Irish Times*, 5 April 1944, 3.

long and complex history of the concepts of good and evil. A rather poor historian, Father Fahrt forgets that Greek philosophies of virtue and vice are very different from Christian doctrines of good and evil. As that history proceeds those schemas are remade by the Enlightenment and unmade by Nietzsche, 'the mad German ruffian'.[45] And that history also encompasses the concepts of character and narrative with which, in the *Confessions* or *The Portrait of a Lady*, we think through good and evil. (In this sense, good and evil only exist within the fairyland of fiction, and so do we.) Flann O'Brien's devilish apostasy and profane ambition is to transcend that horizon, or at least to perch atop the wall and survey the garden. That is why he had to cancel Trellis's horizontal fable, for no one within the garden must know the whole.

---

[45] Myles na Gopaleen, 'Nagging: Cruiskeen Lawn', *Irish Times*, 2 August 1957, 6.

2

Mythomaniac Modernism: Lying and Bullshit in Flann O'Brien

John Attridge

Next to some of the lines that he struck out from the original draft of *The Waste Land*, Ezra Pound impatiently scrawled the abbreviation 'B—ll—S'.[1] Trimming the fat from Eliot's modernist masterpiece in the making meant not only excising the infelicitous and the redundant but also purging the poem of insincerity: removing anything that might vitiate its raw, modern truthfulness. Pound's terse reprimand – in which we can read both a gruff 'balls' and an exasperated 'B.S'. – epitomized a pervasive modernist structure of feeling. Modernist literary movements were morbidly sensitive to cant, fancy and other forms of phoniness, painfully aware that words were 'the great foes of reality', conscious that the tide of the 'Sea of Faith' had gone definitively out, fearful themselves of contributing to the sum of what now stood exposed as humbug.[2] The very idea of truthful propositions, Nietzsche declared in 1873, was incoherent, founded on the delusion that words denote things. Truth, on the contrary, was altogether a matter of convention, the famous

> mobile army of metaphors, metonyms, anthropomorphisms, in short, a sum of human relations which were poetically and rhetorically heightened, transferred, and adorned, and after long use seem solid, canonical, and binding to a nation. Truths are illusions about which it

---

[1] Valerie Eliot, ed., *The Waste Land: A Facsimile and Transcript of the Original Drafts Including the Annotations of Ezra Pound* (New York: Harcourt Brace Jovanovich, 1971), 31. On this annotation see Ronald Bush, *T.S. Eliot: A Study in Character and Style* (Oxford: Oxford University Press, 1984), 57.

[2] Joseph Conrad, *Under Western Eyes* (New York: Random House, 2001), 5. The receding 'Sea of Faith' is one of the melancholy observations made by the speaker of Matthew Arnold's 'Dover Beach'. See Peter Howarth's *British Poetry in the Age of Modernism* (2005) for an account of how early-twentieth-century poets sought to divest themselves of rhetorical conventions. On Eliot and 'literary honesty', see Louis Menand, *Discovering Modernism: T.S. Eliot and his Context* (New York: Oxford University Press, 1987), 13–28.

has been forgotten that they *are* illusions, worn-out metaphors without sensory impact, coins which have lost their image and now can be used only as metal, and no longer as coins.[3]

So too, for Joseph Conrad, words had been 'worn thin, defaced by ages of careless usage'; for William Carlos Williams, 'meanings have been lost through laziness or changes in the form of existence which have left words empty'; for John Middleton Murry, the 'creative writer' toils in a 'vocabulary . . . perpetually on the verge of exhaustion'.[4] The genealogy of this sentiment can be traced in what Jean Paulhan described in 1941 as literary 'Terror': the persistence in advanced literary culture since Romanticism of a fierce antipathy to rhetoric, commonplaces and all forms of verbal convention. The product of this attitude (for Paulhan a regrettable one) was a stylistic 'perpetual revolution', in which the language of poetry was jealously quarantined from the 'words', in Mallarmé's phrase, of the 'tribe'.[5] According to this version of the 'modernist paradigm', writes Jacques Rancière, 'literary modernity . . . was posited as the setting to work of an intransitive use of language opposed to its communicative use'.[6]

In this 'paradigm', literary language defines itself against the exhausted vocabulary of 'communicative' or instrumental language, and especially against the various debased or fraudulent discourses that dominate the public sphere. It is at least arguable that this hostility to public cant peaked in Britain in the aftermath of World War I, which was widely felt to have bankrupted the linguistic economy, but the general mood of disillusionment among literary elites with the public use of language continued throughout the interwar period.[7] Writing in 1938, Cyril Connolly memorably encapsulated

---

[3] Friedrich Nietzsche, *Friedrich Nietzsche on Rhetoric and Language*, trans. Sander L. Gilman, Carole Blair and David J. Parent (New York: Oxford University Press, 1989), 250.
[4] Joseph Conrad, *The Nigger of the 'Narcissus', Typhoon and Other Stories* (Harmondsworth: Penguin, 1973), 12. William Carlos Williams, *Spring and All* (Dijon: Contact Publishing Co., 1923), 20. Murry, *The Problem of Style* (1922), quoted in David Goldie, *A Critical Difference: T. S. Eliot and John Middleton Murry in English Literary Criticism, 1919–1928* (Oxford: Clarendon, 1998), 71.
[5] Jean Paulhan, *Les Fleurs de Tarbes ou La Terreur dans les Lettres* (Paris: Gallimard, 1990), 45. 'Le Tombeau d'Edgar Poe' (1876): 'Donner un sens *plus pur* aux *mots* de la *tribu*'.
[6] Jacques Rancière, *La Politique de la littérature* (Paris: Galilée, 2007), 13. 'On a donc posé la modernité littéraire comme la mise en oeuvre d'un usage intransitif du langage opposé à son usage communicatif'. For a concise overview of efforts to distinguish literary and ordinary language, see Marjorie Perloff, *Wittgenstein's Ladder: Poetic Language and the Strangeness of the Ordinary* (Chicago: University of Chicago Press, 1996), 51–5.
[7] 'It struck many commentators that the written word, in all its forms, had not come out of the war entirely untarnished; that, in fact, the written word, like the truth it purported to convey, had become one of the prime casualties of total war'. Goldie, 18.

this sentiment with his image of words as a 'currency' which 'Fleet Street' tended incorrigibly to inflate, so that 'the more honest literary bankers, who try to use their words to mean what they say, who are always "good for" the expressions they employ, find their currency constantly depreciating'.[8] Like many other commentators around this time, Connolly equated good style with honesty.

An ethics of honesty also conditioned the theoretical discourse of the modernist novel. Consider four touchstone essays from the modernist tradition. Henry James's 1884 'The Art of Fiction' proclaimed that the novel was a serious, veridical discourse, comparable to history. Serious novelists, moreover, were distinguished above all by their sincerity: 'the only condition that I can think of attaching to the composition of the novel is, as I have already said, that it be sincere'.[9] D. H. Lawrence dismissed the *conscious* sincerity of the novelist as irrelevant in 'The Spirit of Place' (1918 and 1923), but only in order to insist all the more vehemently on the deep truth of the artwork: 'out of a pattern of lies art weaves the truth. . . . Never trust the artist. Trust the tale.'[10] In 'Modern Fiction' (1919 and 1925), Virginia Woolf applied the logic of literary Terror to the creaky conventions of Edwardian realism: 'the form of fiction most in vogue more often misses than secures the thing we seek. Whether we call it life or spirit, truth or reality, this, the essential thing, has moved off, or on, and refuses to be contained any longer in such ill-fitting vestments as we provide.'[11] And in 'How It Strikes a Contemporary' (1923), Woolf approached the same predicament from a different angle, observing that modern novelists 'afflict us because they have ceased to believe. The most sincere of them will only tell us what it is that happens to himself. . . . They cannot tell stories, because they do not believe that stories are true'.[12] Here the unavailability of conventional plots is felt as a prohibition, which the 'sincere' modern writer is honour-bound to observe. (It is something like this loss of faith which explains Bernard's failure to become a novelist in *The Waves*: 'I begin to ask, Are there stories?'[13]) However different their fictional poetics in other respects, James, Lawrence and Woolf agreed that, in the push to renovate the English novel, some notion of truth was what was at stake.

---

[8] Cyril Connolly, *Enemies of Promise* (Chicago: University of Chicago Press, 2008), 11.
[9] Henry James, 'The Art of Fiction', in Leon Edel and Mark Wilson, eds, *Literary Criticism: Essays on Literature American Writers English Writers* (New York: Library of America, 1984), 64.
[10] D. H. Lawrence, *Studies in Classic American Literature* (Cambridge: Cambridge University Press, 2003), 8.
[11] Virginia Woolf, *Selected Essays* (Oxford: Oxford University Press, 2008), 8.
[12] Woolf, 29.
[13] Virginia Woolf, *The Waves* (London: Penguin, 1951), 160.

Consider, as one final exhibit in this survey, I. A. Richards's slim 1926 manifesto *Science and Poetry* (reissued in a revised edition in 1935). Richards's neo-Arnoldian tract (bearing an epigraph from Arnold himself) takes as its premise the modern ebbing of the 'Sea of Faith', and argues that poetry can perform the social and psychological functions previously assured by religion precisely because it is linguistically distinct from everyday discourses. Whereas ordinary language in a scientific age is typified by empirically verifiable propositions, the discourse of poetry consists in what Richards calls 'pseudo-statements': 'a form of words whose scientific truth or falsity is irrelevant to the purpose at hand'.[14] Like other contemporary commentators, Richards retains a moral emphasis on literary sincerity: poetry 'cannot be faked'.[15] But the theory of the pseudo-statement provides a (pseudo)scientific explanation of why poetic propositions are not required to be true in the normal way.

After Marjorie Perloff, we can see how Richards's odd book belongs to the familiar 'modernist paradigm' invoked (deprecatingly) by Rancière, in which some essential quality of poetic language is posited which separates it from ordinary language.[16] It is also continuous with the anxiety, epitomized by Pound's marginal annotation, that even this consecrated use of language is threatened by phoniness: that the debased medium of words might be irremediably contaminated with falsehood, and could, at best, yield only 'better mendacities' (as Pound put it in *Hugh Selwyn Mauberley*). Is not the idea of the pseudo-statement an expedient to rescue poetry in general from the category of bullshit – to rehabilitate the supposedly 'false' statements of poetry and show the sceptical 'mathematicians' that poetic discourse is compatible with a positivist world view?[17] In these respects, *Science and Poetry* usefully recapitulates the cluster of high modernist attitudes and practices in relation to which I would like to situate the late modernist fiction of Flann O'Brien. Literary modernism, to put it crudely, was concerned with the question of what, if anything, distinguished the language of poetic invention from everyday speech and writing, and this concern was often allied to an anxiety about whether poetic language and literary form were capable of being truthful – of conveying that 'essential thing' which Woolf did not know whether to call 'life or spirit, truth or reality'. In what follows, I aim to trace the afterlife of this quintessentially modernist preoccupation with truth and falsehood in O'Brien's fiction. Outright mendacity is a regular occurrence in the novels, but, I propose below, more central to O'Brien's

---

[14] I. A. Richards, *Poetries and Sciences* (New York: Norton, 1970), 60.
[15] Richards, 45.
[16] Perloff, 52.
[17] Richards, 58.

fictional imagination is the class of untruthful utterances that we might well call, after Richards, pseudo-statements: discourses which ostensibly resemble assertions but which do not really assert that anything is the case.

The name of Flann O'Brien is almost mythically associated with lying and fabulation. In *A Colder Eye*, Hugh Kenner makes him the mascot of a putative Irish compulsion to make things up, prefacing his discussion of 'Irish Fact' ('anything they will tell you in Ireland') with an epigraph from *The Third Policeman*: 'I considered it desirable that he should know nothing about me but it was even better if he knew several things which were quite wrong.'[18] Kenner had had first-hand experience of O'Brien's untrustworthiness: in *Dublin's Joyce* (1956) he cited an interview with Joyce's father from the 1949 *James Joyce Yearbook* which O'Brien subsequently admitted to having made up as a joke, declaring himself delighted at the success of his hoax.[19] The anecdote is emblematic of the attitudes to truth and imposture that characterize O'Brien's fiction. It suggests, for one thing, O'Brien's contempt for the rigidly factual discourses of academic knowledge, apparent in the pathetic history of Bassett, Le Clerque, De Fournier, Du Garbandier, Hatchjaw, Kraus and, still more pathetically, Henderson, their annotator, in the footnotes to *The Third Policeman*. And it exhibits O'Brien's fondness for blurring the line between such serious assertive discourses and non-assertive pseudo-statements, like jokes and fictions. As with the po-faced parody of scholarly apparatus, the best pastiches are deadpan, never admitting to being made up.

Kenner's caricature of Ireland as a nation of mythomaniacs is apt, at least, when applied to the world of O'Brien's novels, few of whose characters are altogether innocent of imposture. The narrators of the two early novels, for example, are both notable liars: in *At Swim-Two-Birds* the narrator lies to his uncle out of avarice (to extract money), idleness (to be left alone in his room) and sheer devilment (to trap Brinsley into accompanying his uncle on an evening walk), while the narrator of *The Third Policeman* lies elaborately, if naively, to Sergeant Pluck about his identity and his business at the police barracks. The feeble invention of the gold watch, he speculates, may well have entailed all his subsequent misfortunes: 'Perhaps it was this lie which was responsible for the bad things that happened to me afterwards. I had no American gold watch.'[20] When Mick Shaughnessy says of De Selby

---

[18] Hugh Kenner, *A Colder Eye: The Modern Irish Writers* (New York: Knopf, 1983), 3.
[19] On this episode see Margaret Heckard and John Stanislaus Joyce, 'The Literary Reverberations of a Fake Interview with John Stanislaus Joyce', *James Joyce Quarterly* 13, 4 (1976), 468–71.
[20] Flann O'Brien, *The Complete Novels* (New York: Alfred A. Knopf, 2007), 250. Subsequent references are to this omnibus edition and are given in the text as *TP*.

in *The Dalkey Archive* that 'he was as ready to lie as anybody on minor matters', the reader is inclined to agree that mendacity in O'Brien's fictional Ireland occurs as a matter of course.[21] In this environment, outwardly virtuous characters naturally incur the suspicion of hypocrisy, so that even so self-consciously decent a personage as the narrator's uncle is vindictively described as 'rat-brained, cunning, concerned that he should be well thought of. Abounding in pretence, deceit'.[22] 'James Joyce' laments this cynicism as an Irish national characteristic in *The Dalkey Archive*, complaining that his daily mass attendance has earned him the reputation of a 'humbug' (*DA*, 728).

A significant episode with regard to the theme of mendacity is the interview with Augustine of Hippo in *The Dalkey Archive*, which is much concerned with determining the veracity of his *Confessions*. Augustine freely admits to embroidering the debauched actions of his youth 'out of bravado, lest I be thought innocent or cowardly', and invites De Selby glibly to call him not a 'callous' but a 'holy humbug' (*DA*, 636, 639). Lying and other kinds of untruthfulness are also a motif in the reports that Augustine gives of other Catholic saints in Heaven. Peter is said to have invented a 'cock-and-bull story about Judas coming to the gate', Paul, if he is not a liar, is at least a 'blatherskite' (or blowhard) and the four St Patricks currently resident in Heaven would 'make you sick with their shamrocks and shenanigans and bullshit' (*DA*, 637–9).

O'Brien creates comical incongruity by having a Church Father talk so nonchalantly about lying. Mendacity is outlawed repeatedly in the Bible – indeed, two such Biblical interdictions are included in the digest of quotations from the Book of Ecclesiasticus in *At Swim-Two-Birds*.[23] The choice of this particular theologian, moreover, seems calculated to amplify the effect of burlesque, since Augustine was the author of two notably inflexible treatises on the subject of mendacity: 'On Lying' (395 AD) and 'Against Lying' (420 AD). These were important documents in the Western ethical tradition on untruthfulness: as Martin Jay points out, 'it was not really until St. Augustine . . . that a firm repudiation of lying was given a sustained foundation'.[24] Both tracts addressed the question of whether lying was ever

---

[21] O'Brien (2007), 732–3. Subsequent references are to this omnibus edition and are given in the text as *DA*.

[22] O'Brien (2007), 26. Subsequent references are to this omnibus edition and are given in the text as *AS*.

[23] 'A lie is a foul blot in a man. In nowise speak against the truth, but be ashamed of the lie in thy ignorance.' (*AS*, 95) These quotations are from Ecclesiasticus 20.24 and 4.25, respectively.

[24] Martin Jay, *The Virtues of Mendacity: On Lying in Politics* (Charlottesville: University of Virginia Press, 2010), 53.

justifiable, and both concluded that it was not. In contrast with this kind of black-and-white condemnation, and with the stentorian prohibitions quoted from Ecclesiasticus, the Augustine imagined in *The Dalkey Archive* is relatively down to earth. He seems equipped with a more nuanced and elastic conception of falsehood, which encompasses the various shades of untruthfulness expressed by 'humbug' and 'bullshit', and which is, on the whole, better suited to the fictional world he inhabits.

Yet although the ultimate conclusion of both Augustine's tracts is too sweeping for O'Brien's world, there are more subtle discriminations in his analysis of lying that it will be useful to recall here. As is often noted, Augustine proposes an octopartite taxonomy of liars, which does, in fact, allow him to distinguish between the moral gravity of different types of falsehood, according to whether they harm or endanger the material or spiritual wellbeing of their listeners.[25] Harry Frankfurt discusses one of these – the 'real lie', told for the sheer pleasure of falsehood – in his essay *On Bullshit*, but he curiously fails to point out that Augustine's description of these liars, as well as of the related liars who 'wish to please by agreeable speech', resembles in one important particular Frankfurt's own definition of a 'bull session'. Just as, for Frankfurt, 'it is understood by everyone in a bull session that the statements people make do not necessarily reveal what they really believe', so, for Augustine, the audience of both the 'real lie' and the lie told to be agreeable 'are in no way deceived in matters pertaining to religion or truth. . . . It suffices for them to consider that what is narrated might have happened and to maintain their faith in the speaker whom they should not rashly judge as guilty of lying'.[26] Frankfurt leaves it 'as an exercise for the reader' to decide why bullshit is thought to be less odious than lying; the answer, surely, is that many species of bullshit are not actually deceptive, occurring in situations akin to Frankfurt's bull session where, as Augustine says, the audience may just tactfully suspend their disbelief, without fear of being duped. It seems likely that more instances of bullshit than Frankfurt allows occur in situations like the bull session, where no one is deceived. In any case, any reader of O'Brien's fiction would do well to keep the related concepts of bullshit and of sociable lying in mind, for they are central, not only to his representation of social intercourse, but also to the celebrated theory of the novel put forward in *At Swim-Two-Birds*.

---

[25] 'Now, in these eight types, one sins less seriously as he tends toward the eighth and more seriously as he turns toward the first.' Augustine, 'On Lying', *Treatises on Various Subjects*, trans. Mary Sarah Muldowney (New York: Catholic University of America Press, 1952), 109.

[26] Harry G. Frankfurt, *On Bullshit* (Princeton: Princeton University Press, 2005), 36; Augustine, 79.

In a passage commonly taken to signal O'Brien's inscription *avant la lettre* in the culture of postmodernism, the narrator denounces the genre for 'frequently inducing the reader to be outwitted in a shabby fashion and caused to experience a real concern for the fortunes of illusory characters'. Instead, he proclaims, 'a satisfactory novel should be a self-evident sham to which the reader could regulate at will the degree of his credulity' (*AS*, 21). This passage rejects the principle of verisimilitude that accompanied the rise of the realist novel in the eighteenth and nineteenth centuries, and more particularly the anti-rhetorical, Flaubertian ethos of authorial self-effacement traced by Wayne C. Booth in *The Rhetoric of Fiction*.[27] Above all, as John Cronin notes, it flouts the heightened emphasis placed on truth and sincerity by modernist authors like James, Lawrence and Woolf.[28] In this respect, the narrator's theory of the novel resembles Frankfurt's bull session and Augustine's sociable lies: discourses whose audience voluntarily regulate their credulity so as not to be deceived.

We find another allusion to the peculiar truth status of fictional utterances in *The Third Policeman*. When the narrator of that novel reminds Sergeant Pluck that his namelessness is supposed to render him immune to legal sanction, and that therefore his proposed execution is illegitimate, Pluck counters this argument by asserting that, by the same token, there can be no objection to hanging such a legal nonentity. 'Anything you do is a lie,' he reasons, 'and nothing that happens to you is true' (*TP*, 311). This self-reflexive moment conforms to the doctrine of fiction announced by the narrator of *At Swim-Two-Birds*. By alluding archly to the fact that, insofar as the narrator of *The Third Policeman* is a fictional character, any actions attributed to him are indeed ontologically null, O'Brien reminds us that novels do not assert the truth status of their utterances. The various mechanisms of fictional verisimilitude induce readers to suspend disbelief and read stories as if they were true, but this suspension of disbelief is founded on a fragile contract. To dispel the contract of verisimilitude, it is necessary only to call to mind that the narrators of fictions are not, in fact, constrained to observe the constraints of plausibility, but can, rather, flout them at any moment, exploding the contract of readerly fiction. Pluck's cunning assertion that the narrator is in fact outside the realm of legal dispute thus alludes pointedly to the paradoxical truth status of fiction: the laws that appear to regulate fictional verisimilitude are merely conventional; ultimately, the actions of fictional characters are not accountable to any binding rule. At the same time, however, the paradoxical

---

[27] Wayne C. Booth, *The Rhetoric of Fiction* (Chicago: University of Chicago Press, 1983), 91–8.
[28] John Cronin, *The Anglo-Irish Novel: 1900–1940* (Belfast: Appletree Press, 1990), 176.

structure of the policeman's epigram indicates that fictions are not strictly assimilable to lies. There is a slight solecism in asserting that anything one *does* is a lie: evidently, lying pertains to speech and writing rather than action. Similarly, Pluck also seems to concede that events do happen to the narrator, even if these events are technically untrue. These nonsensical phrasings capture something important about the truth status of fictional utterances in O'Brien's universe. O'Brien's metafictional flourish displaces the act of lying from author to character – what the character does is a lie – thus disarming the logic of veriditarian moral censure. In accordance with the theory of fiction put forward in *At Swim-Two-Birds*, O'Brien reminds us that the units of action that comprise fictional narratives – Roland Barthes's proairetic code – are by definition untrue, but that the authors of these lie-actions are not, for all that, liars.

The passage cited above from *At Swim-Two-Birds* is well known, but it is less often noted that the narrator's definition of the novel associates it with a host of other common speech acts in O'Brien's fiction which occupy the intermediate zone between lying and telling the truth. O'Brien illustrates the continuity between the discourse of fiction and other non-deceptive untruths by means of the frame tale, which allows him to dramatize fictional narration as a form of sociable undergraduate wit. As Carol Taaffe points out, O'Brien's 'model of the writer at work is not the bard alone in his cell, but the raconteur at large in the pub'[29]: the narrator's inventions thus take their place alongside other public, non-serious language games, like making puns, swapping 'obscene conundrum[s]' (*AS*, 50) or evolving facetious theories, as Michael Byrne does on the subjects of bed and sleep. Indeed, the analogy between privately circulated fictions and this last form of discourse is made clear in the scene at Byrne's flat, where they are juxtaposed as equivalent intellectual *jeux d'esprit*. Like jokes and facetious theories, these fictions are not overtly distinguished from serious statements, the narrator telling Brinsley that 'I was talking to a friend of yours last night . . . I mean Mr Trellis' (*AS*, 34–5), and Brinsley introducing Trellis into conversation at Byrne's by asking 'Wasn't Trellis another great bed-bug?' (*AS*, 99). In this way, they are integrated with a host of other kinds of everyday speech which resemble assertions but which are not intended and are understood not to intend to assert beliefs.

J. L. Austin began his 1955 William James lectures by complaining that 'It was for too long the assumption of philosophers that the business of a "statement" can only be to "describe" some state of affairs, or to "state

---

[29] *Ireland through the Looking-Glass: Flann O'Brien, Myles na gCopaleen and Irish Cultural Debate* (Cork: Cork University Press, 2008), 35.

some fact," which it must do either truly or falsely.'[30] Perhaps the principal polemical purpose of Austin's lecture series, later published as *How to Do Things with Words*, was to demonstrate the paucity of this conception, and to deflect philosophical attention away from this classical problem of truth and falsehood and towards the interactive complexities of actual speech situations. In a similar fashion, the picture of language-use that O'Brien draws in *At Swim-Two-Birds* emphasizes just how often ostensibly assertoric utterances turn out not to be serious assertions. In counting the novel as one such discourse, O'Brien's response to the question of literary truth bears comparison to Richards' theory of 'pseudo-statements'. Like Richards, O'Brien lets literature off the hook by defining fiction as a non-serious discourse. The distance that O'Brien has travelled away from the heroic age of literary modernism, however, can be measured by the fact that he does not couple this admission with an Arnoldian belief in the pseudo-statement's moral utility. Whereas for Richards, writing in the immediate afterglow of high modernism, the pseudo-statement seemed a way of salvaging poetry as a bulwark against scepticism and anomie, O'Brien uses the same premise to disembarrass novels of this responsibility: 'self-evident sham[s]' cannot be surrogate belief structures. Moreover, far from seeing this as an essential distinguishing feature of poetic discourse, O'Brien portrays it as an ordinary property of language, akin to such casual speech acts as agreeable lying, bullshit and joking.

Examples abound in O'Brien's fictional world of utterances that are not supposed to be taken seriously, and which are, nonetheless, not stigmatized as lies. O'Brien provides a cultural heritage for contemporary Dublin bullshit, for example, in the fantastic exaggerations of Finn MacCool. As Declan Kiberd notes, Finn MacCool's fustian alludes parodically to contemporary renderings of Irish myth, 'an exaggerated imitation of the Victorian translatorese into which Standish H. O'Grady put the stories of *Silva Gadelica*'.[31] In its deployment of conventional untruths, however, it also bears comparison with the more prosaic kinds of bullshit that circulate among O'Brien's UCD students and his working men and women. Like facetiousness and other jokes, the tradition of hyperbole exemplified by MacCool's preposterous bombast is untrue without being mendacious, sustained by the same kind of contract that Augustine describes in his description of sociable lying.

Another species of discourse characterized by non-assertoric utterance in O'Brien's fiction is the commonplace. Indeed, this kind of speech emerges

---

[30] J. L. Austin, *How to Do Things with Words* (Cambridge, MA: Harvard University Press, 1975), 1.
[31] *Irish Classics* (London: Granta, 2000), 506.

as the archetype of the pseudostatement, quasi-phatic utterances, closely related to bullshit, serving to pass the time of day rather than communicate information. The fullest record of O'Brien's unerring ear for cliché are the 'Cruiskeen Lawn' columns for *The Irish Times*. One series, the 'Cathechism of Cliché', was explicitly devoted to compiling 'a unique compendium of all that is nauseating in contemporary writing', but this same bilious sensitivity to cliché is apparent in many other pieces as well: in the cloying platitudes recited by the Plain People of Ireland, for instance ('People do say that the German language and the Irish language is very guttural tongues').[32] Clichés are an important trope in *At Swim-Two-Birds*, which contains, indeed, several idioms later reprised in the column. The oral idioms and banalities employed in the columns by characters like the Plain People of Ireland and Myles's loquacious bus-stop acquaintance, for example, are mirrored in an *embourgeoisé* form by the narrator's uncle. Like the bus-stop pest, the uncle employs the locution 'do you know what I'm going to tell you' to puff up banal or trite announcements, such as his solicitous remark to Brinsley that 'there is a very catching cold going around. Every second man you meet has got a cold' (*AS*, 27). His conversation, when it does not consist in *bona fide* adages ('First come, first called') (*AS*, 29), ('Friendly advice no wise man scorns') (*AS*, 161) and folk Catholicism ('There is a special crown for those that give themselves up to that work') (*AS*, 28), is characterized by this kind of anodyne avowal, and by repetition ('Tell me this, do you ever open a book at all?') (*AS*, 11). It is, perhaps, this conventional and iterative quality that leads the narrator to amuse himself by surreptitiously classifying his uncle's speech according to the figures of classical rhetoric.

The closest approximation of the mechanical, recitative oral discourses mocked in the newspaper column, though, is provided by Trellis's creatures Shanahan, Lamont, Furriskey and Peggy. The comically genial confabulations around the Furriskey hearth consist almost entirely in exchanges of received ideas, with each unassailably fatuous withdrawal from the store of common knowledge or common opinion being met either with *a priori* recognition or reimbursement in the same currency. Furriskey nominates the voice as the original musical instrument, Lamont asserts that 'the fiddle is the sweetest of the lot', Furriskey rejoins that 'the piano is far and away the most . . . useful', Lamont concurs that 'everybody likes the piano' (*AS*, 150–2), and so on; each move in the repartée is incorrigible because effectively meaningless. Interspersed with these opinions are other kinds of statement that are similarly immune to refutation. These include apocryphal anecdotes, like

---

[32] Flann O'Brien, *The Best of Myles*, ed. Kevin O'Nolan (Normal, IL: Dalkey Archive Press/ Illinois State University, 1999), 105, 202.

Sergeant Craddock's prodigious long jump (*AS*, 86–7), and garbled allusions to history and literature, like the description of Paganini as a 'great fiddler, a man by the name of Pegasus' who made a deal with the devil (*AS*, 153). Like much of the uncle's speech, these ostensibly assertive utterances do not behave like assertions, as O'Brien's staging of a dialogue around them makes plain: in this context, for these speakers, it would be inappropriate to assess the truth-content of any given assertion, precisely because these statements are commonplaces of one kind or another, second-hand views that have been heard before.

Commonplaces in the novel behave, in fact, like fiction and Augustine's agreeable lies: although they may not be true, they are, in some sense, non-serious, and hence non-deceptive. In order to function properly, John Searle observes, assertions must 'not be obviously true to both the speaker and the hearer in the context of utterance'.[33] Conversely, the failure to fulfil this condition is one of the essential characteristics of a commonplace. The answer to the rhetorical question 'Do you know what I'm going to tell you?' is inevitably 'yes', even when the particular information imparted is, in a trivial sense, new. The pervasiveness of commonplaces, clichés and cant in 'Cruiskeen Lawn' and *At Swim-Two-Birds* both underline O'Brien's sensitivity to the rhythms of ordinary speech and illustrate his particular sense, akin to Austin's point in *How to Do Things with Words*, that assertoric sentences account for only a fraction of what happens in everyday conversations.

In a fascinating essay on the 1917 Spectra poetry hoax and the magazine *Others*, Suzanne W. Churchill asserts pithily, 'Modernism loves a lie.'[34] A preoccupation with masks, hoaxes, role-playing, pseudonymity and other forms of imposture does undoubtedly characterize some kinds of modernist culture. At the same time, we have seen, certain strains of Anglo-American literary modernism took very seriously their duty to fight cant and bombast and create a truthful poetic idiom. Although superficially opposed, each of these tendencies in modernist culture yet rests on the same binary model of truth and falsehood: literature is either true, in some sense, or it is false, and to be shunned. In light of O'Brien's work, however, and of the analyses made by philosophers like Austin, Searle and Frankfurt, it seems necessary to adopt a more nuanced schema, and to recognize the many shades of untruth that proliferate both in literature and in everyday discourse. O'Brien

---

[33] John Searle, 'The Logical Status of Fictional Utterance', *New Literary History* 6, 2 (1975), 322.
[34] 'The Lying Game: *Others* and the Great Spectra Hoax of 1917' in Suzanne W. Churchill and Adam McKible, eds, *Little Magazines and Modernism: New Approaches* (Aldershot: Ashgate, 2007), 177.

was highly sensitive to these grey areas separating outright lies from truth claims. His fine, Joycean ear for spoken language led him to record, satirically but meticulously, the many uses of language that exist in these grey areas: facetiousness, hyperbolic story-telling, recycled platitudes, jokes and so on. As we have seen, this same sensibility energizes O'Brien's metafictional imagination. Like Augustine's sociable lies and some forms of bullshit, fiction rests on a tacit contract between author and reader that enables false statements to be construed as if they were true. The ethos of story-telling put forward in *At Swim-Two-Birds*, and alluded to again in the lie-actions of *The Third Policeman*, certainly parts company with the fictional truthfulness espoused by, for instance, Henry James and Virginia Woolf, as Cronin points out. But at the same time, O'Brien does not simply embrace mendacity as an alternative to truth. He is, rather, alert to the paradoxical situation of fiction as an ambiguous discourse, unbeholden to truth but also distinct from falsehood. Ludwig Wittgenstein advises us, 'Don't take it as a matter of course, but as a remarkable fact, that pictures and fictitious narratives give us pleasure, absorb us. (This means: puzzle over it).'[35] Distinct both from the quasi-mythical high modernism that loves truth, and the subversive counter-modernism that loves a lie, it is perhaps the distinction of O'Brien's late modernist project to puzzle over this question with new intensity. Dispensing with the taboos of Flaubertian impersonality, O'Brien's irreverent self-reflexivity does not dispel Wittgenstein's puzzle but rather formulates its paradox more starkly. His grasp of speech acts as social and institutional, meanwhile, brings a new set of conceptual tools to this puzzle, which O'Brien imagines using the ambiguous, negotiable model of bullshit and sociable lying rather than the binary of truth and mendacity.

---

[35] Ludwig Wittgenstein, *Philosophical Investigations*, trans. G. E. M. Anscombe, P. M. S. Hacker and Joachim Schulte (London: Basil Blackwell, 2009), 150.

3

'The Outward Accidents of Illusion': O'Brien and the Theatrical

Stefan Solomon

In 1939, American author William Saroyan made his way to Dublin, where he was met by one of his transatlantic admirers, Flann O'Brien. Fashionable for his recent exploits in the short story mode, Saroyan would go on to win the Pulitzer prize for his 1940 play, *The Time of Your Life*, about the fortunes of an odd assortment of characters gathered together one day in a San Francisco saloon. O'Brien, who had become fast friends with Saroyan during his trip, thought highly of the play, writing to his fellow author, 'it is what we here call the business. It is fearfully funny.'[1] Some years later, O'Brien could only deign to refer to Saroyan's work as 'whimsical material',[2] but at the turn of the decade, the chain of influence was palpable. Judging by the existing correspondence between the two, Saroyan's value for O'Brien resided chiefly in the way he could 'make ordinary things uproarious and full of meaning and sentiment', as well as the American's ability to make himself 'appear saner than everybody else merely by being crazy'.[3] With the conviction that Saroyan was capable, within the play form, of inverting the subordination of banality to 'freshness', O'Brien was inspired to convert *The Third Policeman* into 'a crazy Saroyan play', offering as his reason the fact that 'the only good thing about it is the plot'.[4]

And, even after it was completed (though not yet published), O'Brien was still trying to adapt his second novel into a play. In June 1942, he wrote the co-founder of the Gate Theater, Hilton Edwards, that he had an idea

---

[1] Brian O'Nolan to William Saroyan, 14 February 1940, cited in Anthony Cronin, *No Laughing Matter: The Life and Times of Flann O'Brien* (London: Grafton Books, 1990), 99.
[2] Cronin, *No Laughing Matter*, 99.
[3] Ibid., 99.
[4] Brian O'Nolan to William Saroyan, 14 February 1940, cited in Cronin, *No Laughing Matter*, 100. Saroyan famously borrowed from O'Brien the title for one of his plays, *Sweeney in the Trees* (1939), the discarded working title of *At Swim-Two-Birds*.

for a play about 'horrible concepts of time and life and death that would put plays like *Berkeley Square* into the halfpenny place'.[5] But while this never eventuated, he was able to see a few of his dramatic projects through to fruition on the stage: *Thirst*, a short sketch that played at the Gate in Christmas that year (and again at the Theatre Royal a few months later); *Faustus Kelly*, which ran for 2 weeks at the Abbey in January 1943; and finally, in March, an adaptation of Karel and Josef Capek's *Insect Play*, now called *Rhapsody in Stephen's Green*, which showed for five nights at the Gaiety Theater. By all accounts, O'Brien's exploits in the theatre represented only marginal improvements on the sales of his first two novels, but where those novels eventually succeeded in gaining a receptive audience, his plays have never been held in the same esteem.

To try and account for this critical disparity, I want to suggest that modernist theatre by the beginning of World War II had well and truly undergone what Martin Puchner has called an 'anti-theatrical' revolution, and could no longer console itself with the kind of eccentric, character-based drama that was the staple of someone like Saroyan. With respect to what Mikhail Bakhtin has referred to as the 'novelization' of all other genres, I want to propose that there is something less remarkable about O'Brien's plays as compared to his novels, because the latter were capable of realizing more comprehensively the project of the former. The distance between O'Brien's plays and his somewhat more dramatic novels is almost that between Joyce's *Exiles* and the 'Circe' episode in *Ulysses*. And as we see with Joyce, while the dramatic form could still make itself keenly felt in modernist novels over the first half of the twentieth century, drama as a form was altered irretrievably, so that for O'Brien to elevate his accomplishments in *At Swim-Two-Birds* and *The Third Policeman* onto the stage would have been no mean feat.

In the history of the literary arts, the novel would eventually emerge triumphant as that most voracious of genres, satisfying its appetite by subsuming all other genres into itself. In the stomach of the novel, the epic, lyric, and dramatic meet, and the heterogeneous voices of all and sundry are given expression against the backdrop of a comprehensively detailed world. Dramatic dialogue might appear capable of achieving this totality of voices in a manner more explicit than the novel, but Bakhtin argues otherwise. On the one hand, he contends, drama is absolutely monologic – it may have a multitude of voices, represented in dramatic dialogue, but is not by definition dialogic, because it only ever has access to one world. It 'permits only one, and not several, systems of measurement', thereby denying the possibility of

---

[5] Cronin, *No Laughing Matter*, 132.

discrete ontological planes.⁶ On the other hand, drama is bereft of the power of a single authorial voice, the dialogue governed only by stage directions; without narrative guidance, the characters are just a cacophony of voices, as 'there is no all-encompassing language, dialogically oriented to separate languages'.⁷ If in drama, voices go centripetally awry, the novel's victory lies in its more centrifugal orchestration of those voices, allowing them to inter-animate one another under the aegis of the narrative voice.

But as Puchner has argued, the novel's rise to prominence over against its closest challengers produced at least one spectral by-product that returned with interest to haunt it throughout the twentieth century. For, as Puchner writes, if the novel was celebrated for its realization of heteroglossia, allowing a space for a cacophony of voices, the origins of that achievement were, in fact, dependent on the pre-existence of dramatic dialogue. And, as the novel increasingly incorporated dramatic dialogue, thereby augmenting its own claim to harbour a 'totality of objects', modern drama simultaneously made use of narrative elements, especially narrative diegesis. If modernist writers, especially those involved with the theatre, carried on and even intensified an abiding 'antitheatrical prejudice', it was only because of a suspicion that the theatre played a constitutive role in modernist literature.⁸

One symptom of this anxiety was the 'closet drama', which resisted representation either by minimizing action (such as Mallarmé's *Igitur* – 'addressed to the intelligence of the reader staging everything'⁹) or by committing to an exuberant overinvestment in action (as in Joyce's 'Circe' episode from *Ulysses*, which is impossible to faithfully stage, if we take Leopold Bloom's and Bella Cohen's sex changes literally).¹⁰ Under either guise, the closet drama removed stage directions from the technical restrictions of the theatre, affording them the power of a narrative voice free from embodied actors.¹¹ In so doing, it drew attention not to the players but rather to language, to the printed words on the page; Fredric Jameson points to the way that typography itself becomes an event in the 'reading play', which relies on narrative more than ever before to bind the 'discontinuous images' of the drama.¹²

---

⁶ Mikhail Bakhtin, *Problems of Dostoevsky's Poetics*, ed. and trans. Caryl Emerson (Minneapolis: University of Minnesota Press, 1984), 34.
⁷ Bakhtin, 'Discourse in the Novel', in *The Dialogic Imagination: Four Essays*, ed. Michael Holquist, trans. Holquist Emerson and Caryl Emerson (Austin: University of Texas Press, 2004), 266.
⁸ Martin Puchner, *Stage Fright: Modernism, Anti-Theatricality, and Drama* (Baltimore and London: The Johns Hopkins University Press, 2002), 1.
⁹ Stéphane Mallarmé, *Oeuvres complètes*, vol. 1, ed. Bertrand Marchal (Paris: Gallimard, 1998), 475, cited in Puchner, *Stage Fright*, 66.
¹⁰ See Puchner, *Stage Fright*, 84.
¹¹ Ibid., 66.
¹² Fredric Jameson, *The Modernist Papers* (London and New York: Verso, 2007), 148.

This emphasis on language apart from theatricality was in part an attempt to reclaim the dramatic character from its place on the stage: if character remained principally a province of the actor, and not of language, the artwork would remain dependent on the human, in the most explicit way. So if, as Puchner argues, there was a modernist anti-theatrical tradition, developed first by Nietzsche and then Benjamin, the objections raised by its disciples referred specifically to the cult of the actor – that potentially dangerous tradition that would conflate actor and character under the auspices of the 'aura'. Adhering to diegetic text as a means of evading the naturalized mimesis of the stage, brought about especially by the presence of the actor, so-called anti-theatrical drama also contributed to the death of character as such. Since acts of impersonation were deliberately foreclosed, the actor could no longer retain his position as a stable mimetic sign, signifying 'character'.[13]

Flann O'Brien turned towards theatre from quite a different direction to his modernist precursors. As a commentator on the Irish theatre, he supported neither a theatre of the people, so-designed, nor a theatre closed to the public altogether, as was the logical tendency expressed in the closet drama. Several of O'Brien's 'Cruiskeen Lawn' articles take up the long-standing problem of the Abbey audiences, albeit sardonically, and in 1938 he famously traded epistolary blows with Sean O'Faolain and Frank O'Connor over the state of Irish theatre. While O'Faolain had agitated for a move away from the Abbey's ubiquitous accent on 'Peasant Quality' or P.Q., O'Connor defended it as an attribute derived 'out of knowledge of [the Irish] people'.[14] O'Brien's solution was a happy medium: retain the peasant audience that provided the Abbey with its best material, while ensuring that they laugh only on cue.

> People who go to the Abbey nowadays simply go for entertainment, and laugh outright when something on the stage seems funny or ridiculous, notwithstanding the fury of a thousand red-faced art-stuffed boyos in the wings. God forgive them! The obvious remedy is to exclude the loutish audiences and add to the cast of each play 500 "extra" peasants, accommodating them in the stalls. The producer can then get his laugh when he wants it, and can see that it's a real laugh.[15]

And, shortly after the unsuccessful run of *Faustus Kelly* at the Abbey, O'Brien wrote – somewhat bitterly it seems – of a recent trip to the theatre:

> There was a frightfully boring play on, the stage crowded with those commonplace personalities, stock characters, and nothing but talk

---

[13] Puchner, *Stage Fright*, 16.
[14] Sean O'Faolain, 'Ideals for an Irish Theatre', *Irish Times*, 12 October 1938, 5.
[15] Flann O'Brien, 'Ideals for an Irish Theatre', *Irish Times*, 15 October 1938, 7.

talk talk. I can't remember the name of the piece and this at least is a consolation. But throughout the proceedings the audience was continually being distracted by curious rasping noises. I made some investigations during the intervals and discovered that this was the sound of the plot creaking.[16]

If he worked slightly against the grain of the traditional Abbey parlour comedy, O'Brien was nevertheless very amenable to their demands that he revise his work in line with public taste. He told producer Hilton Edwards that *Faustus Kelly* was deliberately written as an Abbey play, and was very much acting on a commercial impulse when he submitted the revised version.[17]

Whether he wrote for or against the Abbey, however, O'Brien's perception of the theatre was a far cry from the anti-theatricality of a number of modernist writers more accustomed to the demands of the stage play. As a playwright, his model was Saroyan, not Mallarmé; accordingly, the emphasis for O'Brien seems to have been on the possibilities offered by the stage for character, and not on its overshadowing within the work. His notion that 'the only good thing about [*The Third Policeman*] was the plot' assumes that its deficiency was one of characterization: without the 'dramatic collision' between characters, upon which dramatic works traditionally depended, he feared that he would only be capable of writing what he termed, 'another bum book'.[18] But perhaps the theatrical had already entered O'Brien's novel, albeit superficially, prior to his anxious confession. For while the narrator of *The Third Policeman* is no 'Playboy of the Western World', there is certainly a lineage running to the one, who smashes the jaw of old Philip Mathers with his spade, from the other – the creation of J. M. Synge – who cleaves his father's skull in twain with a loy.[19]

Keith Hopper has already drawn attention to the theatrical dimension in *At Swim-Two-Birds*, comparing the meta-theatres of Pirandello and

---

[16] Myles na gCopaleen, 'Cruiskeen Lawn', *Irish Times*, 26 February 1943, 3.
[17] See Cronin, *No Laughing Matter*, 132.
[18] Brian O'Nolan to William Saroyan, 14 February 1940, cited in Cronin, *No Laughing Matter*, 100.
[19] Aside from this derivation, Synge's was far more of a negative influence on O'Brien. Despite Synge's revisionary portrait of the British music-hall Paddy, his compatriot was (as Hirsch points out) '[e]specially galled' by the other's work: "nothing in the whole galaxy of fake is comparable with Synge," O'Brien wrote. "Playing up the foreigner, putting up the witty celtic act, doing the erratic but lovable playboy, pretending to be morose and obsessed and thoughtful–all that is wearing so thin that we must put it aside soon in shame as one puts aside a threadbare suit." O'Brien, *The Best of Myles*, ed. Kevin O'Nolan (London: Pan, 1978), 234, cited in Edward Hirsch, 'The Imaginary Irish Peasant', *PMLA* 106, 5 (October 1991): 1128.

Brecht with the similarly self-conscious metaphors of acting and playwriting involved in O'Brien's novel.[20] Although these modernist prose and dramatic works are analogous in their bid to erase the boundaries separating their own narrative, ontological and logical levels, there are certainly differences obtaining between them. While Hopper is surely correct, then, to assert the influence of Pirandello's *Six Characters in Search of an Author* – 'the perfect model for the metafictional estrangement between character and author'[21] – upon O'Brien's work, the impress of that play appears oddly to have had no noticeable effect on the actual dramatic efforts of the Irish author.[22] The kind of metafictional latitude given to the characters in *At Swim* – to the extent that those used in Dermot Trellis's novel arraign their own creator in a court of law – is categorically distinct from the inflated centrality of character in the stage play, where there exists the potential of words on the page to take on an embodied existence on the stage.

Indeed, unlike some of his modernist contemporaries, who were intrigued by the 'anti-theatrical' possibilities of the dramatic form, O'Brien seems to have conceived each of his stage plays with a mind to their performances – at the Abbey, or the Gaiety, or the Gate.[23] For his *Rhapsody in Stephen's Green*, O'Brien was already considering its appearance on stage in relation to earlier plays, describing the queen wasp in the following terms: '*For glitter and majesty she must exceed even Meriel Moore as the courtesan in "Jack-in-the-Box."*'[24] This comparison with an actor who appeared as part of the Gate Theatre's Christmas entertainment in 1942[25] was not simply motivated by the envy of that earlier show's commercial success, but perhaps just as much by the 'glitter and majesty' of Moore's actual stage presence.[26] In thinking

---

[20] See Keith Hopper, *Flann O'Brien: A Portrait of the Artist as a Young Post-modernist* (Cork: Cork University Press, 1995), 110–11.

[21] Ibid., 130.

[22] Graham Greene made this connection with *At Swim-Two-Birds* as early as 1939, in his reader's report for the publisher Longmans Green: 'We have had books inside books before now, and characters who are given life outside their fiction, but O'Nolan takes Pirandello and Gide a long way further.' Greene, 'Proof-reader's report on *At Swim-Two-Birds* for Longmans Green Ltd., 1939', cited in *A Flann O'Brien Reader*, ed. Stephen Jones (New York: Viking Press, 1978), 31.

[23] O'Brien's short sketch, *Thirst*, was performed by the Dublin University Players. See Anne Clissmann, *Flann O'Brien: A Critical Introduction to His Writings* (Dublin: Gill and Macmillan, 1975), 262.

[24] Flann O'Brien (Myles na gCopaleen), *Rhapsody in Stephen's Green: The Insect Play*, ed. Robert Tracy (Dublin: The Lilliput Press, 1994), 35. Italics in original.

[25] This variety show also included O'Brien's own *Thirst*. See Robert Tracy, 'Notes', in O'Brien, *Rhapsody in Stephen's Green*, 85n. 11.

[26] Moore was in fact cast in *Rhapsody* as 'Mrs. Cricket', when it opened on 22 March 1943. O'Brien, *Rhapsody in Stephen's Green*, 19.

theatrically, O'Brien is thinking, above all, of the way in which a character like 'the courtesan' (from Wilde's *La Sainte courtisane* of 1894–95) could leave the page, and become physically manifest in the theatre, gaining those 'outward accidents of illusion'[27] that would permit the characters of his own works to become more robust than even the plots themselves.

If, as perhaps O'Brien believed, the novel could stand to gain a greater sense of characterological intensity from the theatre, then his first full-length play certainly attempted to bear this out. In *Faustus Kelly*, the titular character sells his soul to the devil to win both election to parliament, and the hand of a local widow. Kelly's expected fall from grace is flouted when it is revealed that the devil – known as the Stranger – will not be sanctioned as a rate collector. In the final scene, when the tormentor realizes that the ins and outs of Irish public life present a fate worse than death, he leaves his prey in peace. As a character, Kelly himself is immediately recognizable as the worst kind of blustering bureaucrat. In his first appearance, he arrives late to a council meeting, and when greeted with a surprised silence, '*naturally takes [it] as a tribute to his own great importance*'.[28] Over the course of the three acts, Kelly assumes this role comfortably, and 'when he soars away on his own', as the *Irish Times* reviewer put it, he carried the play.[29]

But the play truly proves its mettle most in the inconsequential ramblings of the council chamber, which pits a 'thick western brogue' against a 'strong Cork accent' and a 'pronounced northern accent', and lets them simply talk. In fact, when this chatter gives way to the more fusty Faustian plot, the focus on the individual voice seems to detract from the play's real strengths, dominating and thus retroactively determining how we interpret the earlier scenes; the later moral implications of Faustus Kelly's bargain, securing his position as a T.D., actually come to usurp the play's best humour. When O'Brien later re-read his own play, he pondered the reason for its poor reception, suggesting that it was perhaps ahead of its time, 'oracular and prophetic' in its focus on Ireland's 'national failings', and that it had taken over a decade before 'life and facts [caught] up with it'.[30] His suggestion that an 'order to close it down'[31] came from the government was some way off the mark, as Anne Clissmann points out: 'If the play failed, it was not because the government disliked it or because the satire was too savage; it was because

---

[27] Flann O'Brien, *At Swim-Two-Birds* (London: Penguin, 2001), 25.
[28] Myles na gCopaleen, 'Faustus Kelly', *Stories and Plays* (Dublin: Hart-Davis, MacGibbon, 1973), 128.
[29] 'Abbey Theatre', *Irish Times*, 26 January 1943, 3.
[30] na gCopaleen, 'Cruiskeen Lawn', *Irish Times*, 3 April 1954, 10.
[31] Ibid., 5 July 1957, 6.

it was tedious and badly structured.'[32] Where the neophyte playwright had imagined prescience in his work, the majority of critics had instead seen a certain outmodedness, most likely owing to its failed imitation of an Abbey play.

As Clissmann writes, 'within the more rigid confines of the dramatic structure, O'Brien did not develop the discipline and the compression needed to create successful dramatic characters. His genius was expansive, so when he turned to drama his speeches were too long', and 'his essentially linguistic humours ignored the need for action on stage'.[33] Robert Tracy extends this critique, suggesting that O'Brien's early novels succeed because they are structured episodically, without regard for sustained plot or theme, but that the dramatic form presents a different problem. In a given stage play (as anticipated by the Abbey Theatre audience), the customary division of the narrative into acts and scenes routinely cohered around character-based plotlines, which tied the action together, The plot of a novel like *At Swim-Two-Birds*, however, while initially offering the student protagonist as anchor to the rest of the narrative, soon loses interest in this one character, and pursues others who are only connected with him at several removes.

In a similar manner, Tracy argues, even the strong character focus of *Faustus Kelly* cannot ensure its success after its first act, because the remainder of the play is insufficiently connected with its opening. The eponymous protagonist operates as a parodical figure, but his embodiment of the very worst of political bombast tends towards the tedious instead of the comical.[34] This is, however, somewhat redeemed at the end of the play, when only the Stranger remains on stage, stammering his final lines just as his would-be victims have done, and in similar fashion to the last broken exchanges in O'Casey's *Juno and the Paycock*.

O'Brien's more compartmentally arranged *Rhapsody in Stephen's Green* likewise succeeds only in certain places. Adapted from Karel and Josef Čapek's *Insect Play*, it retained the allegorical dimensions of the Czech original, but transposed its referents from Europe to present-day Ireland, complete with a third-act war between some thinly veiled 'ants' from the North and South of a country fearing British invasion. This addition of local colour was heralded

---

[32] Clissmann, *Flann O'Brien*, 255. O'Brien again denied the accusations leveled against his play in 1963, trying to recuperate its critical mistreatment with historical reality: 'Many people told me afterwards in strict confidence that it was a very bad play. Maybe. I personally find Shakespeare's *King Lear* unendurable.' na gCopaleen, 'The Fausticity of Kelly', *Radio-TV Guide*, 25 January 1963, cited in Clissmann, *Flann O'Brien*, 253.
[33] Clissmann, *Flann O'Brien*, 260.
[34] See Robert Tracy, 'Introduction', *Rhapsody in Stephen's Green*, 6–7.

as a clever appropriation of the earlier play's content,[35] and one critic even went as far as to conclude that in this last scene, 'the confusion of thought which exists in this country is well pointed by the dramatist'.[36] The first act centres around a swarm of bees, two of which long after the queen bee, but are eventually resigned to sting each other and so relieve themselves of their daily labour: to go on living is to go on working, they reason. In the second act, a married beetle couple consolidates their life savings – a ball of dung – while a nesting duck ruthlessly eats them, and is in turn consumed by a hungry parasite. *Rhapsody in Stephen's Green* alludes to other dramatic works, including, as it does, a drone bee whose only lines are quotes from various Shakespearean plays, and a parasite described as '*the last word in mealy-mouthed joxers*',[37] possibly a reference to Joxer Daley, a similarly parasitic character from *Juno and the Paycock*.

The form of the stage play privileges dramatic dialogue as the necessary site of human exchange, which is commonly mediated by stage direction, but not often by the stronger narrative voice that inhabits the novel. O'Brien's plays, however, work best when they interrogate this very assumption of spoken lines of dialogue as transparent expressions of characters' thoughts, and there are explicit reflections on the problems of the spoken word in each of them. In *Rhapsody in Stephen's Green*, this interest in linguistic constraint is especially pronounced. At a time when 'Revival Irish' was very much a live issue, the third act depicts the Northern Unionist ants protecting the next generation from being forced to learn Latin – 'a dad lounguage' – and this soon reveals an associated target closer to home. The battle is finally one fought over language, with the victorious Green ants wearing '*enormous gold fainnes*' as '*[w]ords and shouts that sound like Irish are heard above the din*'. When the Tramp, who guides the audience as a choric figure throughout, becomes finally fed up when a voice proclaims itself emperor of the world in an Irish he cannot understand, he '*grinds* [the voice] *to bits*'.[38] This gives way to the play's epilogue, which contains a fantastically frenetic jumble of all the characters' words, and ends as swiftly as *Faustus Kelly*.

Across the two plays, in these two cacophonous instances, O'Brien betrays some investment in dialogic exchange. But it is still, nonetheless, in his first novel that we can witness the full interpenetration of different voices across time, from the narrator's use of the *Conspectus of the Arts and Natural Sciences* to provide a description for Dermot Trellis, to his appropriation of Kelly's

---

[35] 'Gaiety Theatre', *Irish Times*, 23 March 1943, 3.
[36] Maxwell Sweeney, 'Entomology in Eire', *Irish Times*, 27 March 1943, 4.
[37] O'Brien, *The Insect Play*, 53.
[38] Ibid., 78.

'A pint of plain is your only man' into Jem Casey's later poem, 'Workman's Friend'.[39] In *At Swim-Two-Birds*, precisely because all characters fall under the jurisdiction of the narrative voice, they are allowed to paraphrase and imitate each other, their lines of dialogue functioning as sources of mutual interanimation throughout. Indeed, the scene most obviously given to a structured exchange of voices in *At Swim* is that which takes place in the courtroom, towards the end. Of this particular episode, Niall Montgomery wrote to O'Brien, 'The court scene at the end makes me say, Why Not Make It Into A Play?'[40]

A perfectly reasonable suggestion, perhaps, but there is something absolutely singular about the form of *At Swim* (as a novel) that would make a transfer to the stage very difficult. In the court room, Bakhtin's various 'systems of measurement' are all in play: Dermot Trellis's son, Orlick, writes a book in which his father is the protagonist, and that book includes the trial episode in which Trellis' characters exact revenge upon their maker. While this sequence of events is no doubt logically preposterous, Orlick himself is an ontological impossibility, since he is the product of his father's rape of one of his own characters, combining 'the plane of the author and the plane of his creation'.[41] In this scene, the wronged characters intend to convict and execute Trellis for his authorial crimes, before worrying that his demise would also signal their own, since they only exist by his hand. Joseph Brooker has written of a 'central tendency' in O'Brien's humour, namely 'the literalization of what was metaphorical'.[42] As such, the sentiment here, as elsewhere in the novel, is that the world in which authors and characters exist is physically and ontologically the same, not merely metaphorically so. The characters' dreamed revenge on Trellis would be one that results in his literal death (as well as their own), and must be so in order to follow the metafiction to its logical conclusion.

The same is true of the physical comedy in another 'theatrical' installment in an Irish novel. In Joyce's 'Circe' episode, as Martin Puchner has argued, certain biological transformations (Bloom's sex change) demand literal realization, which can only occur in the fictional world of the novel, and not onstage: 'At one moment, for example, Bello "(bares his arm and plunges it elbow deep into Bloom's vulva)" (440), a prescription that indicates graphically

---

[39] See David Cohen, 'An Atomy of the Novel: Flann O'Brien's *At Swim-Two-Birds*', *Twentieth Century Literature* 39, 2 (Summer 1993): 218.
[40] Niall Montgomery to Brian O'Nolan, 26 March 1937, cited in Clissmann, *Flann O'Brien*, 251.
[41] Rolf Breuer, 'Flann O'Brien and Samuel Beckett', *Irish University Review* 37, 2 (Autumn–Winter 2007), 347.
[42] Joseph Brooker, *Flann O'Brien* (Devon: Northcote, 2005), 34.

enough, one should think, that Bloom has actually been transformed into a woman and that he has not simply changed his clothes.'[43] In this way, the dramatic aspirations of the chapter must be preserved within the pages of *Ulysses* (although its performance has, of course, been attempted many times), and remain all the more dramatic for being so.

As for *Ulysses*, so too for *At Swim*, where the ambition is for literalization in the fictional world, and not in the theatrical world. The potential literalization of O'Brien's courtroom scene, which gives the impression – typographically – of a stage play, would no doubt detract from a complexity that is only possible within the pages of a novel. That is to say, the fact that Trellis' characters come alive in the court room, prosecuting him for his various abuses as an author, carries all the more weight because the character in a novel has no afterlife and cannot hope for a later embodiment on stage. That prolonged existence is the very promise of the play form, which proleptically endows the character with more than words alone. But the dramatic corporeality of character is exactly the type of literalization in which *At Swim-Two-Birds* does not partake, and the text thereby avoids the potentially auratic confluence of character and actor. 'Why Not Make It A Play?' Because the court room scene in O'Brien's novel is all the more potent when kept at arm's length from the drive to embodied appropriation in the Abbey Theatre.

In that respect, what emerges in this scene provides a good counterbalance to the similar sequences on offer in *Faustus Kelly*, which take place in the council chambers. In O'Brien's play, the protracted speeches – especially those of the title role – largely prohibit any action, and although there is a certain amount of energy in the exchanges of Act I, it never approaches the gymnastic shuttling between ontological and narrative planes in *At Swim*. This disparity exists primarily at the level of form: where the play requires the addition of character names to designate the speaker of each portion of dialogue, the novel is under no such obligation, but is nevertheless free to appropriate the structure of the dramatic work on its pages. Bereft of the capitalized character names that routinely accompany indented stage dialogue, those words spoken in the court scene in *At Swim*, precisely because they are not anchored, a priori, to character names, append themselves instead to O'Brien's authorial voice. It is of no small importance, too, that none of the dialogue in *At Swim* is demarcated by quotation marks, such that it manifests visually on the same typographical plane as the narrative description. In his novels, O'Brien affords the same privilege to both character and plot, but in so doing preserves the discursive power of the former. As their voices intermingle with the words of

---

[43] Puchner, *Stage Fright*, 88.

the narrator on the page, O'Brien's characters pretend to the same status as their author (and their author's author), because individual speech acts are all governed by (and accordingly rail against) the same voice.

Of course, the struggle between character and author lies at the heart of *At Swim*, and is framed by another, far more deep-lying, conflict within the work: that between the novel and the play. This debate over genre is one that Flann O'Brien seemed to have taken very seriously in his letters and journalism, and at least one character in his most famous novel seems to have approached it with the same degree of sincerity. As we see in the student protagonist's potted manifesto of the novel, the major problem with that genre lies in its propensity for strict authorial control, which is exacted on both the characters, and the reader:

> It was stated that while the novel and the play were both pleasing intellectual exercises, the novel was inferior to the play inasmuch as it lacked the outward accidents of illusion, frequently inducing the reader to be outwitted in a shabby fashion and caused to experience a real concern for the fortunes of illusory characters. The play was consumed in wholesome fashion by large masses in places of public resort; the novel was self-administered in private. The novel, in the hands of an unscrupulous writer, could be despotic.[44]

The student's division of the arts in *At Swim-Two-Birds* suggests something quite opposed to the traditional critique of the theatre. The actor personified the modernist problem with mimesis in the theatre, which could not be undone, no matter how estranged the acting may have been. But for the student, the actor formed part of a public spectacle that laid bare the artifice of the stage, making clear the 'outward accidents of illusion', an understanding that was reinforced by the 'large masses' with whom one attended the theatre. This also permitted the characters to attain a certain sense of agency, insofar as they could grow out from under their author's watchful eye, and develop against his own wishes. The student continues:

> It was undemocratic to compel characters to be uniformly good or bad or poor or rich. Each should be allowed a private life, self-determination and a decent standard of living. This would make for self-respect, contentment and better service. It would be incorrect to say that it would lead to chaos. Characters should be interchangeable as between one book and another. The entire corpus of existing literature should

---

[44] O'Brien, *At Swim-Two-Birds*, 25.

be regarded as a limbo from which discerning authors could draw their characters as required, creating only when they failed to find a suitably existing puppet.[45]

But, of course, the student's friend puts paid to this entire formulation in one sentence: 'That is all my bum, said Brinsley.'[46]

This theory is 'all my bum' in *At Swim* because the characters therein do, in fact, lead physical existences on the same plane as their creators, and so are patently *not* illusory in the way the student has reckoned them. But O'Brien seems to have taken the student's model more seriously than Brinsley, since his determination to adapt his novels as stage plays appears to have been motivated by aesthetic, as well as commercial, means. O'Brien thinks on the same epistemological plane as his protagonist, desiring to craft his 'bum book' into something that is not 'all my bum'. Of course, in attempting such a transformation, O'Brien perhaps neglects the fact that what is most theatrical about his most successful novels is the fact of their genre: by incorporating that which is made literal on the stage, these 'anti-theatrical' works of art remain their author's most enduring theatrical achievements.

[45] Ibid.
[46] Ibid.

4

The Ghost of 'Poor Jimmy Joyce': A Portrait of the Artist as a Reluctant Modernist

Stephen Abblitt

Drunken poets

On 16 June 1954, poet Patrick Kavanagh and novelist Brian O'Nolan led a small troupe of revellers around Dublin, visiting the Martello Tower at Sandycove, Glasnevin cemetery, Davy Byrnes's and 7 Eccles Street, plus many other pubs besides, reading relevant and favourite passages from *Ulysses* as they journeyed. The intention was to replicate the lively travels of Stephen Dedalus and Leopold Bloom, in celebration of the fiftieth anniversary of the day on which James Joyce chose to set the modernist masterpiece. The group also included poet and later O'Brien biographer Anthony Cronin, literary critic and magazine editor John Ryan, registrar of Trinity College, Dublin, A. J. Leventhal and dentist Tom Joyce (Joyce's cousin, the family representative).

The day began at Sandycove, with a scuffle between Kavanagh and O'Nolan, and by their arrival at the Bailey pub in the city centre, in the early afternoon, in the midst of the "Lestrygonians" episode, the pilgrimage had to be abandoned, everyone too drunk to continue, long before the group could reach their planned destination at Eccles Street, via the former brothel district "Nighttown."[1]

The respectfully disrespectful episode, the first Bloomsday celebration, unfolds now in a strange critical and discursive space somewhere between tribute and travesty, and, inadvertently, this uneasy tension between

---

[1] John Ryan, *Remembering How We Stood: Bohemian Dublin at the Mid-Century* (Dublin: Gull and MacMillan, 1975), 127.

praise and parody exhibits Flann O'Brien's persistently ambivalent attitude towards Joyce.

O'Brien's unreliable, often contradictory opinions concerning Joyce are perhaps best exemplified by the 1964 novel *The Dalkey Archive*; here, Joyce is caricatured as a humbled barman, denying his authorship of *Ulysses* and claiming complete ignorance of *Finnegans Wake*. By the provocation of a derisive and subversive laughter, O'Brien expresses a desire to exorcize the ghost of the man he lovingly, mockingly referred to as 'poor Jimmy Joyce' (who had, O'Brien claimed, abolished the King's English). But *The Dalkey Archive* is also a studied if somewhat scatological, perhaps unhinged, critique of modernism, dramatizing O'Brien's conflicted attitude towards this literary movement through its comic representation of Joyce, peripheral yet central throughout the narrative. Doubly meaningful, O'Brien's repeated parodies and hilarious disavowals of Joyce – in the newspaper column 'Cruiskeen Lawn', the essay 'A Bash in the Tunnel', and elsewhere – are surely composed for comic effect, to evoke laughter. But they also present a dotted commentary on what is at stake for O'Brien in writing after Joyce, in the wake of his high modernism, as O'Brien can neither entirely dismiss nor embrace his predecessor's art. *The Dalkey Archive* is caught out by this mocking discrepancy between its cruel caricature of Joyce and its reality as a novel fundamentally modernist. O'Brien recognizes his dependence on Joyce as indispensable antecedent and modernism as chosen style of literary production, and yet continually expresses this ferocious desire to symbolically murder the Father, decrying his life's work as obscure, elitist and masturbatory.

The very production of the novel appears compelled by this anxiety of influence. Harold Bloom famously describes an artist who broadly harbours a sense of anxiety over the ambivalent influence of an antecedent, hindered by a tendency to produce derivative and therefore weak works, yet acutely aware of the necessity, inspired by example, to forge an own original artistic vision. This influence, 'a disease of self-consciousness',[2] 'always proceeds by a misreading of the prior poet, an act of creative correction that is actually and necessarily a misinterpretation',[3] evident in *The Dalkey Archive* as this mad misrepresentation of Joyce and reductive rendering of high modernism. Presenting a portrait of the artist as a reluctant modernist, this chapter suggests that the deliberate but vital failure to exorcize the irrepressible

---

[2] Harold Bloom, *The Anxiety of Influence: A Theory of Poetry* (New York: Oxford University Press, 1973), 29.
[3] Ibid., 30.

ghost of 'poor Jimmy Joyce' is typical of O'Brien's ironic modernism – ironic because we must learn to read ironically, if we are to make significant sense of Joyce's jocoserious interjections into *The Dalkey Archive*.

On board

O'Brien proffers a deceptively doubled response to Joyce's inexorable legacy in *The Dalkey Archive*. Commenting on the cultural milieu of bohemian Dublin in the middle years of the twentieth century, O'Brien's friend Niall Sheridan asserts that Joyce 'was in the very air [they] breathed'.[4] Similarly, but far more portentously, Cronin claims in his biography of O'Brien, *No Laughing Matter*, that 'the figure of Joyce hung over . . . [O'Brien's] life like a sort of cloud from which the apocalyptic vision could come or had come'.[5] Ronald L. Dotterer too suggests O'Brien wrote 'in Joyce's shadow'[6] – although, drawn toward the discursive cultivation of the otherworldly connotations implied by Cronin, I prefer the metaphor of the ghost. Ontologically uncertain, disturbing both sensory perception and intellectual intuition, the ghost is difficult to grasp, as it 'does not belong to the order of knowledge'.[7] It is a 'borderline creature, an insider as well as an outsider'[8] which, undecidable, remains 'neither present not absent, neither dead nor alive',[9] and so can neither adequately be mourned nor exorcized. Joyce's placement in *The Dalkey Archive* is wholly spectral, hauntological even: he is properly neither dead nor alive, neither present nor absent. Writing on his own relationship with Joyce, Jacques Derrida claims that each time he commits words to paper 'Joyce's ghost is coming on board',[10] and the same

---

[4] Niall Sheridan, *Myles: Portraits of Brian O'Nolan*, ed. Timothy O'Keeffe (London: Martin, Brian and O'Keeffe, 1973), 39.

[5] Anthony Cronin, *No Laughing Matter: The Life and Times of Flann O'Brien* (Dublin: New Island, 2003), 176.

[6] Ronald L. Dotterer, 'Flann O'Brien, James Joyce, and *The Dalkey Archive*', *New Hibernia Review* 8, 2 (2004): 54.

[7] Colin Davis, '*État Présent*: Hauntology, Spectres, Phantoms', *French Studies* 59, 3 (2005), 376.

[8] Derek Attridge, 'Ghost Writing', in *Deconstruction is/in America: A New Sense of the Political*, ed. Anselm Haverkamp (New York and London: New York University Press, 2005), 225.

[9] Davis, '*État Présent*', 373.

[10] Jacques Derrida, 'Two Words for Joyce' (trans. Geoffrey Bennington), in *Post-Structuralist Joyce: Essays from the French*, ed. Derek Attridge and Daniel Ferrer (Cambridge: Cambridge University Press, 1984), 149.

sentiment pervades *The Dalkey Archive*: untouchable and evasive, Joyce's ghost is still always already on board – and O'Brien is ambivalent about how ethically to respond.

The diffidence of the author

Robert Martin Adams suggests that various stylistic and formal characteristics of his work 'mark O'Brien as a *post*-Joyce, if not wholly *propter*-Joyce, writer'.[11] O'Brien comes in the wake of Joyce, comes after and succeeds Joyce (he is post-Joyce), and also remains near to or close to Joyce, writing because of or on account of Joyce, through or by means of Joyce (these are the three meanings of the Latin *propter*: near, because of, and through) – by means of the vast new territories opened by the epochal modernist. Opposition also suggests proximity: 'To be against (opposed to) is also to be against (close to, in proximity to) or, in other words, up against.'[12] O'Brien is against and up against Joyce: the oppositional conflict is visible in his repeated irreverently parodic writings about Joyce, but a specific closeness is evident as his literary output remains thoroughly modernist, engaged in this strange immanent critique of literary modernism – so much of which remains on the surface, and in lieu of any substantial critical engagement reductively cites and re-cites the proper name 'James Joyce' as symbol or synecdoche of an entire cultural movement.

A few brief incidents encapsulate this ambivalent attitude towards Joyce. In March 1939, O'Brien published his first novel, the comic bildungsroman *At Swim-Two-Birds*. He sent a copy to the nearly blind Joyce, then living in Paris, with an inscription on the flyleaf referring to 'plenty of what's on page 305', directing Joyce to the phrase 'diffidence of the author'. O'Brien seeks an altercation, to provoke a famous literary feud – but he is disappointed. This game of rivalries is one Joyce will not play. Instead, the ailing Joyce gave the novel his generous approval, describing O'Brien as 'a real writer, with a true comic spirit'.[13] O'Brien's response to such praise was dismissive: 'When Samuel Beckett met O'Brien in Dublin and passed on Joyce's praise, O'Brien had already had enough of the Joycean debate, and reportedly snarled: "Joyce, that refurbisher of skivvies' stories!"'[14] O'Brien fearlessly, obsessively

---

[11] Robert Martin Adams, *AfterJoyce: Studies in Fiction after Ulysses* (New York: Oxford University Press, 1977), 190.
[12] Jonathan Dollimore, *Sexual Dissidence: Augustine to Wilde, Freud to Foucault* (Oxford: Clarendon Press, 1991), 229.
[13] Quoted in a letter from Niall Sheridan to Timothy O'Keeffe, dated 4 March 1960.
[14] Keith Hopper, *Flann O'Brien: A Portrait of the Artist as a Young Post-Modernist* (Cork: Cork University Press, 2009), 41.

struggles to stage a 'rebellion against an older rebel'[15] – but the rebellion goes unfinished as he proves incapable of decisively breaking from Joyce.

As with many of his writings on Joyce, O'Brien's reaction to Joyce's praise of *At Swim-Two-Birds* is highly performative. Nothing O'Brien said or did or wrote about Joyce remains untainted by a comic flair and a particularly Joycean love of punning wordplays, a general linguistic *jouissance*, where often the pure pun is the motivation for writing rather than the clear conveyance of any specific meaning. The result is that we can never be too certain of O'Brien's beliefs, and find ourselves second guessing authorial intention – a kind of self-concealment through jocular obfuscation. There are close to one hundred references to Joyce in O'Brien's 'Cruiskeen Lawn' newspaper columns, consisting of attacks of varying degrees of seriousness and mock-callousness, regularly referring to 'poor Jimmy Joyce'. Often appearing simply to flesh out a pun, 'Joyce was said to be a wilfully obscure writer, or even an incoherent one, whose experiments had been destructive of the English language.'[16] He is depicted as 'a semi-demented genius whose books were great fun for the initiate but had not much extension into life', who 'wound up by writing a private language', and whose writings, 'though impressive for their obsessional quality, were onanistic and could even be taken as an example of the futility of artistic endeavour'.[17]

The essay 'A Bash in the Tunnel' most fully and colourfully expresses O'Brien's compulsively antagonistic attitude towards Joyce. O'Brien relates a tale allegedly told him by a stranger in a pub, about a man trapped in a railway carriage, humorously scrutinizing the position of the artist in Ireland:

> Funny? But surely there you have the Irish artist? Sitting fully dressed, innerly locked in the toilet of a locked coach where he has no right to be, resentfully drinking somebody else's whiskey, being whisked hither and thither by anonymous shunters, keeping fastidiously the while on the outer face of his door the simple word, ENGAGED?
>
> I think the image fits Joyce: but particularly in his manifestation of a most Irish characteristic – the transgressor's resentment with the nongressor.[18]

This cheeky, jeering derision serves as engaging story-telling, with wonderful literary flair, but the persistence of this spectre of Joyce in O'Brien's writing serves a greater purpose than just comic effect.

---

[15] Dotterer, 'Flann O'Brien, James Joyce, and *The Dalkey Archive*', 55.
[16] Cronin, *No Laughing Matter*, 172.
[17] Ibid., 173.
[18] Flann O'Brien, 'A Bash in the Tunnel', in ed. Claud Cockburn, *Stories and Plays* (New York: Viking Press, 1973), 206.

Joyce is not dead at all

These skirmishes with Joyce's legacy – Bloomsday 1954, the response to *At Swim-Two-Birds*, the 'Cruiskeen Lawn' columns, and 'A Bash in the Tunnel' – serve to lay the foundation for a more sustained confrontation in *The Dalkey Archive*. In a letter to Gerald Gross dated 10 September 1962, O'Brien mentions the origin of Joyce's characterization in this novel, complete with a statement of his dissatisfaction with Joyce, and with the repeated critical comparisons eagerly drawn between the two writers:

> Ignorant reviewers have messed me up with another man, to my intense embarrassment and disgust, and he will be another character. I mean James Joyce. I'm going to get my own back on that bugger. (I suppose you know that, like Hitler, Joyce isn't dead at all. He is living in retirement and a sort of disguise at Skerries, a small watering-place 21 miles N. of Dublin. He has been trying to screw up enough courage to join the Jesuits.)

Later, in a letter to publisher Cecil Scott, dated 6 January 1964, O'Brien suggests that 'James Joyce has been dragged in by the scruff of the neck'. The claim appears thoroughly disingenuous, because the *The Dalkey Archive* is a very explicit and public outlet composed by O'Brien to examine Joyce's potent influence over his own literary career.

Amidst the digressive and episodic narrative of *The Dalkey Archive*, Joyce is brought back to life – or, precisely, found, rediscovered, for he never really left. 'Strong poets keep returning from the dead,'[19] and none appear stronger, for O'Brien, than Joyce. Gathered in a pub, witnessing a conversation between our protagonist Mick Shaughnessy and Dr Crewett, we learn of Joyce's survival. He is 'a man back from the grave, armed only with the plea that he had never gone there, yet hiding under a name unknown in a little town'.[20] Piecing together this alternate fictional biography, we learn that Joyce spread the news of his own death, and that he later left Zürich and continued living in France until forced to flee towards the end of World War II, losing contact with his wife and family in the process, escaping to London before returning home to Ireland. Mick quickly decides he must find and meet Joyce. Crewett questions his motivations, and Mick responds with this expression of a naïve desire to find out the truth: 'I believe the

[19] Bloom, *The Anxiety of Influence*, 140.
[20] O'Brien, *The Dalkey Archive* (London: Harper Perennial, 2007), 98.

picture of himself he has conveyed in his writings is fallacious. I believe he must be a far better man or a far worse' (96). He wants to write 'a real book about Joyce': 'I've read some of the stupid books written about Joyce and his work, mostly by Americans. A real book about Joyce, springing from many long talks with him, could clear up misunderstandings and mistakes, and eliminate a lot of stupidity' (ibid.). Obtaining Joyce's location from Crewett, Mick travels to Skerries, where he finds 'Dublin's incomparable archivist' (124) working as a barman in a pub, incognito really only because it so defies belief and expectation. Is this the real Joyce, playing the part or having lost his mind, or is this another man masquerading as Joyce? This question, so central to the narrative, remains unanswered. Mick, however, decides this must be the real Joyce, putting his faked death down to a desire to escape the notoriety that enveloped his literary career. This Joyce clearly wishes to be disassociated from the works attributed to him: 'I've had things imputed to me which – ah – I've had nothing to do with' (125). *Dubliners* is not all his own work but a strained collaboration with the future senator Oliver St John Gogarty, who refused to have his name on the title page, claiming it would ruin his reputation as a doctor. *Ulysses* is a 'dirty book', 'a collection of smut', 'artificial and laborious', 'pornography and filth and literary vomit, enough to make even a Dublin cabman blush', as well as a practical joke played on him by 'an American lady in Paris by the name of Sylvia Beach', who fell in love with him and wanted to make him famous (165–7). *Finnegans Wake* is simply an old Irish folk song, and signifies nothing more for its supposed author. Joyce claims his 'real work has hardly appeared at all yet' (125); this consists of 'mostly pamphlets for the Catholic Truth Society of Ireland . . . on marriage, the sacrament of penance, humility, the dangers of alcohol', and 'a biographical piece on Saint Cyril' (165–6). O'Brien takes his revenge on Joyce, whose literary pretensions are humbled, his reputation revealed to be just that, his achievements and ambitions as a writer erased. He has lost his art, and in place of a literary career, this Joyce wants to join the Jesuits, where he eventually ends up, mending the father's underclothes, which are 'perpetually in a state of near collapse' (182), for want of any more practical skill to offer. Throughout this novelistic parody – a direct, lampooning revenge, incomparable to Joyce's elaborate parodies of Malory, Defoe, Swift, Sterne, Dickens and others in the 'Oxen of the Sun' episode of *Ulysses* – the reader develops the clear image of an anxious and resentful author, and observes an amusing comic critique, but one too often lacking in any serious engagement with its subject, instead coming across as a hollow outburst of infantile aggression.

Remember me!

'A wholly irrecuperable intrusion in our world', Joyce's ghost represents an 'ethical injunction'[21] for O'Brien, commanding, like the ghost of Hamlet's father: 'Remember me!'.[22] *The Dalkey Archive* is primarily a raucous comic novel, but it is also an act of remembrance, a commemoration, and a staging of an ethical aporia. What does it mean to act responsibly towards the spectral Joyce in staging this remembrance? In a eulogy to his friend Roland Barthes, Derrida speaks these words: 'to keep alive, within oneself: is this the best sign of fidelity?'[23] This survival (*sur vivre*, living-on) is the living's responsibility towards the dead. It occurs in our reading *and* writing, Joyce surviving not only by his humorous (mis)remembrance and resurrection in *The Dalkey Archive*, but also through our critical engagements with and responses to his literary legacy.

No laughing matter

Kant defines laughter principally as 'an affection rising from the sudden transformation of a strained expectation into nothing'.[24] O'Brien parodies Joyce as a rather sad and artless man, humbled, thoroughly the opposite of the James Joyce portrayed in both popular and scholarly culture, as the novel makes a mockery of his life and his literary works. We are meant to laugh, and we do, because it is quite clever and really very funny. We laugh primarily because the depiction of Joyce does not match up to our own image of that man. But O'Brien's humorous treatment of Joyce is not only the evocation of laughter by this riotous inversion. Theorizing the mechanics of humour as social and cultural critique, Bergson suggests that with every burst of laughter 'the whole thing threatens to break down, but manages to get patched up again'.[25] Laughter is subversion – but it always steps back from the brink, harmoniously reinstates order in the end. Deploying humour as critique, O'Brien's comic inversion is also subversion: the signifier 'Joyce' (spectre, legacy, influence, aesthetic) is toppled, his literary works

---

[21] Davis, '*État Présent*', 373.
[22] William Shakespeare, *Hamlet* (London: Penguin, 1980), I.v.91.
[23] Derrida, *The Work of Mourning*, ed. Pascale-Anne Brault and Michael Naas (Chicago and London: University of Chicago Press, 2001), 36.
[24] Immanuel Kant, *Critique of Judgment*, trans. J. H. Bernard (New York: Hafner Pub. Co., 1951), 117.
[25] Henri Bergson, *Laughter: An Essay on the Meaning of the Comic*, trans. Cloudesley Brereton and Fred Rothwell (New York: Dover Publications, 2005), 49.

disparaged as an irrelevant, onanistic self-indulgence which even he derides and disowns. Disavowed even by this fictional Joyce, literary modernism appears exhausted, an elaborate joke best forgotten – except for certain of its devices evidently central to *The Dalkey Archive* itself. For this novel is far more complex than the inversion and subversion of Joyce and modernism by way of parody. In 'A Bash in the Tunnel', O'Brien comments on Joyce's use of humour: 'Humour, the handmaid of sorrow and fear, creeps out endlessly in all Joyce's works. He uses the thing, in the same way as Shakespeare does but less formally, to attenuate the fear of those who have belief and who genuinely think that they will be in hell or heaven shortly, and possibly very shortly.'[26] Humour attenuates fear in those who have belief. The question is what does O'Brien fear, and what does he believe in? He fears and believes in Joyce, fears his debt to Joyce's innovative aesthetic styles and forms, fears he could never live up to the responsibility – and so packages it as this infantile, shallow, scatological satire.

Unsuspected common loyalties

Early in *The Dalkey Archive*, Joyce is brought into proximity with the other great villain of the novel, the philosopher and mad scientist De Selby. He plans to end life on earth by destroying its atmosphere, eliminating the element of oxygen using a substance named DMP, and Mick heroically takes it upon himself to save the world by stopping its manufacture. And this apocalyptic endeavour ultimately fails – though through no work of Mick's. Mick mentions De Selby to Joyce in conversation, describing both men as great pioneers, suggesting he arrange a meeting. The meeting never takes place, but shortly afterward Mick ponders the potential intellectual correspondences between the two madmen: 'Would they coalesce in some quiet and fruitful way, or clash in murderous disarray?' (131):

> Would Joyce and De Selby combine their staggeringly complicated and diverse minds to produce a monstrous earthquake of a new book, something claimed to supplant the Bible? De Selby could easily produce the incredible materials, perhaps with the help of angels, while Joyce could supply the unearthly skill of the master-writer. . . .
>
> Two elderly men, of giant intellectual potential, who had run wild somewhat in their minds might, in coming together, find a community of endeavour and unsuspected common loyalties. (133)

---

[26] O'Brien, 'A Bash in the Tunnel', 208.

The two men do have something in common; De Selby is some sort of Joycean twin or double, a doppelgänger similarly incomprehensible and obscure, commonly ignored simply so as to salvage the sanity of humanity. Upon pondering their common loyalties, Mick decides the two men could not possibly get along, owing mostly to De Selby's misanthropic destructive master-plan. But is this not Joyce's master-plan too? De Selby hopes to destroy reality. Has Joyce not done the same? Joyce's high modernism stands to decimate the very prospect of reality in literature, proving the thorough inadequacy, the sheer falsity, of any representational realism in art. From the standpoint of the literary realists who preceded him, Joyce's work represents aesthetic annihilation, as the reader violently and apocalyptically witnesses an epochal shift from a meaning inherent in the object to one produced by the perception of the subject – a shift most famously noted by Barthes through his theorization of the writerly text.[27] Through his doubling with the mad scientist De Selby, Joyce is obliquely characterized as an undecidable figure, and also as the bringer of semantic annihilation, harbinger of the death of absolute truth, interpretative certitude, capitalized Meaning, all transcendental signifiers. This is epitomized in *The Dalkey Archive* by the narrator's – and the author's – blank refusal to present the reader with a definitive, realist and above all objective portrait of either De Selby or Joyce. We are left swimming, flailing, arms waving wildly, to interpret the actions and intentions of both men. We are left unable to decide if De Selby is what he says he is, and is capable of what he says he is, and to decide if this Joyce is first the real Joyce, and then if he truly did not write *Ulysses* and *Finnegans Wake*, and has no idea of the literary achievements promulgated in his name, and truly does want to become a Jesuit, or is really just playing the role to escape his own fame and notoriety. We are never given enough information to make these decisions; the true nature of meaning, the objective and absolute truth, whatever such terms might mean after Joyce's semantically explosive literary modernism, remains undecidable. Interpretative certitude – the exhaustion of this text's semantic resources – is forever promised as Mick valiantly quests for answers (manifested most clearly in his desire to write this elusive 'real' book about Joyce), but it is always delayed, never delivered. This undecidable characterization of Joyce – Is he real? Has he lost his mind? Is his ignorance of his literary career feigned? – is all part of an ironic commentary on the evidently elusive nature of reality after the playfully disordered, excessive, chiasmic literary modernism of which he, Joyce, is made exemplary.

---

[27] Roland Barthes, *S/Z*, trans. Richard Miller (New York: Hill and Wang, 1974).

An ironic modernism

To appreciate O'Brien as a reluctant modernist, we need to learn to read ironically. This ironic modernism is beautiful modernist enterprise precisely because it relies exclusively on the perceptiveness of the reading subject, 'reading ironically means, in complex ways, not taking things at their word; it means looking beyond standard use and exchange to what this or that might *really mean*'.[28] Meaning is (at the very least) doubled as, subverting conventional realist expectations of the ready availability of evident and certain knowledge, irony posits an incongruity or discordance between the literal or presented meaning and the intended meaning. Beneath O'Brien's standard use of so many comedic, parodic and satirical elements in his characterization of Joyce (a literal interpretation of the novel's wandering narrative), this portrait of Joyce as a humbled and artless barman and prospective Jesuit that is at once a brutal parody *and* a loving comical depiction of a literary forefather who clearly means everything to O'Brien, we can also perceive other, more private, subversive meanings concerning O'Brien's relationship to Joyce as a writer, and his reluctance to neither break away from nor fully embrace a modernism of which Joyce will always be the exemplar. O'Brien's ironic modernism is clearly on display: there is a powerful, unmistakeable ironic discrepancy between his repeated disavowals of Joyce's modernism, and his obvious dependency on the advances made by this literary movement, his production of a novel employing an assortment of modernist techniques, styles, forms and hermeneutics. These two positions, ironically, do not need to be reconciled – luckily, because they cannot be. Instead, this ironic 'doubleness of meaning'[29] perfectly expresses O'Brien's conflicted attitude towards Joyce's modernism: on the narrative surface it is an irrelevant and onanistic self-indulgence which deserves to be laughed at wholeheartedly, but at a more fundamental level it is also the basis of O'Brien's own art form, inescapably generating the very possibility of his excessive, digressive, highly performative writings, the puns, wordplays and linguistic slippages evident in his fiction and also his newspaper columns and literary criticism. Deriding and embracing Joyce, O'Brien is not simply saying one thing while meaning another, but saying one thing and meaning it, while also, excessively, saying and meaning something else too. His animosity towards Joyce and his dismissals of literary modernism also displays his love of Joyce and his homage to literary modernism. Ironically, *The Dalkey Archive* is both tribute and travesty.

---

[28] Claire Colebrook, *Irony* (London and New York: Routledge, 2004), 3.
[29] Ibid., 10.

O'Brien, unabashed, in the tunnel

Despite his oft-stated disdain for a frustrating critical tendency to read fictional characters as autobiographical representations of their authors, it is tempting to read Mick Shaughnessy's final words on Joyce as passing directly from the snarled lips of O'Brien, perhaps tempering his more outlandish repudiations of the exemplary modernist: 'Joyce, Mick said in the end, wherever he is and however he feels, was in his day a great writer' (191). Despite everything – despite the endless parodies and put-downs, the angrily hilarious ranting, and his final caricature as an artless barman – Joyce remains for O'Brien a great writer never to be forgotten but always remembered, a ghostly influence never to be exorcized, and his literary modernism remains an essential element of O'Brien's own art. But, deliberately, consciously, conflicted and caught between praise and parody, tribute and travesty, devotion and derision, unabashed, O'Brien remains a reluctant modernist.

5

'Do You Know What I'm Going to Tell You?': Flann O'Brien, Risibility and the Anxiety of Influence

David Kelly

Do you know what I am going to tell you? Many readers will recognize that somewhat inane query as one of Brian O'Nolan's favourite pieces of Dublinese, and as Myles Na Gopaleen he sprinkled it liberally through the pages of *Cruiskeen Lawn* over his years as a columnist for the Irish Times. But as Flann O'Brien he relished it, too, and in *At Swim-Two-Birds* he gave it to the student-protagonist's uncle to use in one of his brief and discomfiting ventures into the student's bedroom, interrupting his conversation with his good friend Brinsley. It is used as a prefatory query which adds an air of conspiratorial importance to the exchange, or pompous self-importance to the interlocutor in this case, as he inquires of Brinsley: 'Do you know what I'm going to tell you, there is a very catching cold going around.' 'Description of my uncle', adds the student: 'Rat-brained, cunning, concerned-that-he-should-be-well-thought-of. Abounding in pretence, deceit. Holder of Guinness clerkship the third class'.[1] The first time we hear the phrase, however, it is in altogether more genial circumstances, and it prefaces one of the most memorable lines in the entire O'Brien oeuvre: as the student lifts his first ever pint of porter to his lips, his good friend Kelly offers the view: 'Do you know what I am going to tell you ... a pint of plain is your only man.'[2]

In either case it is funny, but to get back to the point, as it happens, in a sense you, dear reader, *do* know what I am going to tell you, because there are certain expectations about what we might have to say about this much-beloved author. It is not just that many of us enjoy revisiting our favourite moments, but also that our themes and perspectives are defined in advance by what O'Brien wrote and how he wrote it, as well as by what

---

[1] Flann O'Brien, *At Swim-Two-Birds* (London: Hart-Davis MacGibbon, 1960), 40.
[2] Ibid.

has subsequently been said about it, so there can be a sense of going over old ground when it comes time to reconsider the case of Flann O'Brien. In this regard it seems to me that my position is not unlike that of the writer in the modern period, who felt the burden of literary tradition and literary precursors weighing heavily upon her or him, having been preceded by and, in a way, robbed of originality by what had already been said and written, other texts and other writers – but, of course, this is precisely one of the central themes taken up by O'Brien. It bothered Joyce as well, and his textual avatar, Stephen Dedalus, had very high aspirations to escape the snares of a burdensome past – personal, literary and cultural – in order to get on with the business of creating the uncreated conscience of his race:

> Welcome, O life, I go to encounter for the millionth time the reality of experience and to forge in the smithy of my soul the uncreated conscience of my race.[3]

Despite Stephen's ardent if melodramatic desire for unprecedented creative power, Joyce's pun on 'forge' in that famous sentence, with its implication of both creation and counterfeiting, is enough to tip the wink to the knowing reader that his struggle was with an inescapable history, and he was destined to wrestle with the problematics of originality and artifice, the problematics of forgery, all his textual life. That is why we next see him, after the lofty final longings of *A Portrait of the Artist as a Young Man*, back on earth in the Martello tower with stately, plump Buck Mulligan, bemoaning his fate (personal, literary and cultural) in that sullen manner of his:

> – Look at yourself, he said, you dreadful bard.
> Stephen bent forward and peered at the mirror held out to him, cleft by a crooked crack, hair on end. As he and others see me. Who chose this face for me? This dogsbody to rid of vermin. It asks me too.
> – I pinched it out of the skivvy's room, Buck Mulligan said. It does her all right. The aunt always keeps plainlooking servants for Malachi. Lead him not into temptation. And her name is Ursula.
> Laughing again, he brought the mirror away from Stephen's eyes.
> – The rage of Caliban at not seeing his face in the mirror, he said. If Wilde were only alive to see you.
> Drawing back and pointing, Stephen said with bitterness:
> – It is a symbol of Irish art. The cracked lookingglass of a servant.[4]

---

[3] James Joyce, *A Portrait of the Artist as a Young Man* (Harmondsworth: Penguin, 1960), 253.
[4] James Joyce, *Ulysses* (Harmondsworth: Penguin, 1968), 12–13.

But if Wilde were only alive a little longer, he might have encountered a rather similar figure in a not altogether dissimilar situation (indeed, one who also found his body to be verminous, and not in any metaphorical sense), but one who had grasped something that clearly eludes the existentially distressed and rather self-pitying Stephen here: the importance of not being quite so earnest. The student of *At Swim* tells us:

> The washstand had a ledge upon which I had arranged a number of books. Each of them was generally recognized as indispensable to all who aspire to an appreciation of the nature of contemporary literature and my small collection contained works ranging from those of Mr. Joyce to the widely read books of Mr. A. Huxley, the eminent English writer. (12)

It is part of the problem Stephen had, the burden of the cultural past that weighs heavily upon one's own originality and artistic ambition, although here it is compounded by the additional presence of Joyce himself, as well as that notorious novel-within-a-novel writer, Mr A. Huxley. It might well be enough to induce that peculiarly Romantic anxiety of influence Harold Bloom first brought into scholarly focus as post-Romantic modernism drifted towards the postmodern. 'The strong poet peers in the mirror of his fallen precursor,' writes Bloom,

> and beholds neither the precursor nor himself but a Gnostic double, the dark otherness or antithesis that both he and the precursor longed to be, but feared to become.[5]

And yet there is little evidence of anxiety and even less of Gnostic doubling here, as the student rather blithely finds a place for himself amid the words of others, casually making his own mark on, and in, the mirror the artist holds up to nature in a moment of literal self-reflection at that book-burdened washstand:

> The mirror at which I shaved every second day was of the type supplied gratis by Messrs. Watkins, Jameson and Pim and bore brief letterpress in reference to a proprietary brand of ale between the words of which I had acquired considerable skill in inserting the reflection of my countenance. (12)

---

[5] Harold Bloom, *The Anxiety of Influence: A Theory of Poetry* (Oxford: Oxford University Press, 1973), 147.

Of course one might have to deal with other cultural pressures, too, such as those supplied in more fluid form by Messrs. Watkins, Jameson and Pim, and they might get the better of you; but even under this less cerebral influence, with a bit of skill and a talent for adaptation, our narrator still manages to assert a certain original artistry:

> I opened wide my windpipe and made a coarse noise unassociated with the usages of gentlemen.
> I feel very bad, I said.
> By God you're the queer bloody man, he said.
> I was down in Parnell Street, I said, with the Shader Ward, the two of us drinking pints. Well, whatever happened to me, I started to puke and I puked till the eyes nearly left my head. I made a right haimes of my suit. I puked till I puked air.
> Is that the way of it? said Brinsley.
> Look at here, I said. I arose in my bed, my body on the prop of an elbow.
> I was talking to the Shader, I said, talking about God and one thing and another, and suddenly I felt something inside me like a man trying to get out of my stomach. The next minute my head was in the grip of the Shader's hand and I was letting it out in great style. O Lord save us. . . .
> Here Brinsley interposed a laugh.
> I thought my stomach was on the floor, I said. Take it easy, says the Shader, you'll be better when you get that off. Better? How I got home at all I couldn't tell you.
> Well you did get home, said Brinsley.
> I withdrew my elbow and fell back again as if exhausted by my effort. My talk had been forced, couched in the accent of the lower or working classes. Under the cover of the bed-clothes I poked idly with a pencil at my navel. (39)

That last image is wonderful: the writer reflecting on the degree to which he is himself the creator of an aesthetic effect induced by a prior discourse on the one hand – the accents and phrasing of 'the lower or working classes' – but induced equally by comic self-invention on the other – the student's parodic adaptation of that discourse – all figured idly in the idle poking at the navel with a pencil, probing the origins of text and self, and musing on where one begins and ends. And I would point out here that these concerns for originality, forgery, generative capacity and the discursive construction of the self, all of which are at stake here, are not only at play in *At Swim* – although its structure of novel-within-novel-within-novel, its array of writers tugging at creative control of the narrative, and its preoccupation with characters invented (through 'aestho-autogomy') or borrowed for the occasion, are all clearly meant to foreground these sorts of textual and indeed existential issues. They are there too in O'Brien's other early novels, in such things as the vocation of the narrator of *The Third Policeman*, an exegete of the works of another – a derived and wholly dependent authorial position in which any claim to originary textual authority is radically questioned. 'I knew that if my name was to be remembered,' the anonymous exegete tells us, 'it would be remembered with de Selby's'.[6] Quite so. And then there is Bonaparte O'Coonassa in *The Poor Mouth*, who drops his own newborn child in astonishment at this unlikely evidence of his own generative capacity; Bonaparte, who repeatedly claims it is his intention to record 'some testimony of the diversions and adventures of our times . . . for those who succeed us because our types will never be there again nor any other life in Ireland comparable to ours who exists no longer'.[7] And yet we discover that the destiny of the Corkadoraghans is apparently recurrent, with episode after episode having already been written down in 'the guid books', to which Bonaparte frequently refers, to say nothing of books such as Thomas O'Cronin's *The Islandman*, which stands behind this text much as Joyce does behind *At Swim*.[8]

What is it like to feel this kind of cultural or literary weight? What is it like to be so keenly aware of illustrious and potentially overshadowing precursors, of walking in the path of those who have gone so imposingly before? Well, as it happens, for the scientifically interested and the empirically minded, a film exists showing Flann O'Brien literally walking that path, and I believe if we study this footage we might get an answer to that question. It is a brief filmic record of the very first Bloomsday,[9] when Flann O'Brien and a few of his friends decided to retrace the steps of Leopold Bloom around Dublin town, which can be viewed here: http://www.youtube.com/watch?v=A0gNNWHmj9Q. And do you know what I'm going to tell you? – although O'Brien looks a little unsteady, I suspect this is more the result of the influence of Messrs Watkins, Jameson and Pim, rather than any anxiety of influence from elsewhere. In fact, although it is not unlikely that he later made a right haimes of his suit, he looks to be enjoying himself.

He looks to be enjoying himself, too, in three of the funniest novels in or out of the English language. And while I do not want to suggest that O'Brien

---

[6] Flann O'Brien, *The Third Policeman* (London: MacGibbon and Kee, 1974), 9.
[7] Myles na Gopaleen, *An Beal Bocht*, translated as *The Poor Mouth* by Patrick C. Power (London: MacGibbon and Kee, 1975), 11.
[8] 'The like of us can never be again' was O'Cronin's sad refrain.
[9] Or second, if we include Leopold's day in 1904.

does not take things seriously, I do want to suggest that he had an almost unique faculty for finding things funny. And it is *what* he found funny that fascinates me. Because if he found it funny when people asked the question – 'do you know what I'm going to tell you?' – he was equally amused when you *did* know what he was going to tell you, or at least a version thereof, when precursors like Joyce or O'Cronin, *The Cattle Raid of Cooley* or the story of *The Frenzy of Sweeney*, laid out the terrain in advance so that he could step parodically through while raising but comically parrying matters central to our conception of the crises of modernity, like the fraught situation of the modern writer, this whole dilemma of authorial originality amid the weight of the past, which opens onto the larger crisis of modern subjectivity itself, adrift amid the determining and indifferent forces of history and culture.

What's more, he found it just as funny when people *did not* know what they were going to tell you, although they thought they *did*. Because that is also the case of the narrators of the first three novels – each of whom, importantly, takes the trouble to write to us. This is one of the defining features of O'Brien's work at this time, and indeed is one of the defining aspects of his comic approach, which reflects that fundamentally modernist concern with the mutual implication of narrative meaning and narrational circumstance of a kind explored most fully by the likes of Conrad, James, the stream of consciousness writers and so on. Except here there is this surprising insistence on the writtenness of the record, and not just the presence of the consciousness behind it. And funnily enough this is most insistently the case in the most unlikely circumstance, that of *The Third Policeman*, with a dead author who nevertheless still manages to produce a text with all of the material appurtenances of the book, including an elaborate scholarly apparatus conducting intricate debates with others in the field of de Selby studies, while the main narrative continues on its own increasingly unexpected path – most unexpected, of course, to the writer, when the extraordinary discovery that he is dead shocks him into the next circle of hell, which goes round and round like that wheel on the bike of the parish postman who, with every bump on the cobbled roads of Ireland, is becoming a little less a man, and a little more a bicycle.[10] Things take a funny turn indeed. 'I think the idea of a man being dead all the time is pretty new,' O'Brien famously wrote to William Saroyan about this novel with its logically impossible provenance. And then he added: 'When you are writing about the world of the dead and the damned where none of the rules and laws (not even the law of gravity) holds good, there is any amount of scope for back-chat and funny cracks.'

---

[10] 'Hell Goes Round and Round' was one possible title the deep revolving O'Brien mused on in the writing of this novel.

So, even when it comes to the grim matter of death itself – 'our last personal end', as the student reflects on the matter in *At Swim* – it is the comic possibilities of the situation that most intrigue him.

I would make the point, though, that the scriptive and narrative situation of the exegete is shared with his brother writers in the other early novels – each of them finds themselves in states they were not aware of, and indeed in narratives they were not aware of, and in fact producing books they were not intending to. The exegete wants to publish the de Selby Index, but bedevilled by the process of writing we get this dizzying season in hell instead. The student of *At Swim* sets out to impress us with three entrances into a fiendishly involved novel but ends up telling us the unlikely story of his own coming of age and his reconciliation with his uncle: 'Description of my uncle', he concludes, with an unlooked for maturity: 'simple, well-intentioned; pathetic in humility; responsible member of large commercial concern'. 'I went slowly up the stairs to my room,' he continues, in a tone of unaccustomed personal and literary perplexity:

> My uncle had evinced unsuspected traits of character and had induced in me an emotion of surprise and contrition extremely difficult of literary rendition or description. My steps faltered to some extent on the stairs. As I opened my door, my watch told me that the time was five fifty-four. At the same time I heard the Angelus pealing out from far away. (312)

After the opening bravura of three separate beginnings, indicating unexampled literary potency, in the end time is out of joint and creative powers falter. Like Trellis musing on the function of art as he walks up the stairs behind his cleaning woman, muttering '*Ars est celare artem*', the student appears ultimately to find himself wondering whether, at bottom, the effect of his own art has been to unknowingly conceal – but from himself – his own part in it. He did not set out to write a *bildungsroman*, but there you are – all we do get of the novel he tells us he intended to write is discontinuous and fragmented and even physically lost in part. Similarly, Bonaparte O'Coonnassa specifically writes in order to produce a testament of Corkadoragha and its denizens because 'their like will not be there again', but he ends up telling us the biographical tale of Jams O'Donnell and the recurrent life of colonial subjection that begins in squalor and ends in 'the jug', like his father before him, and his before him. Despite their best intentions, none of these writers can quite produce the book they wanted to, and in time the exegete, the student and Bonaparte will all discover that, as Brinsley observes in *At Swim*, 'the plot has [them] well in hand' (139).

But, as I said, O'Brien finds these sorts of things funny, and this is a sensibility much at odds with his time and its general mood of apprehension, disillusion and anguish. With the high modernists we tend to read this as part of the working through of a general cultural distress arising from a traumatic loss of faith and cultural stability: the shifting sands of modernity and the devastations of war that undermined the firmer footing of an older order of things. But the same tropes and techniques that figured there as emblems of that distress are re-worked in O'Brien as matters of intense comic amusement. If Joyce and the moderns found it necessary to take on Homer and the entire western literary canon as a problem for their own artistic creativity, O'Brien was faced with the seemingly superadded futility of working in the shadow not only of that same canon but of those moderns as well. Yet this is not registered with any sense of dismay or anguish: as the student insists, these are, after all, 'spare-time' literary activities, recreative in every sense of the term, pastimes not central to the business of living, as they are with others. To be the young Stephen Dedalus wrestling in the shadow of St Stephen and Icarus with the problems of cultural inheritance and artistic aspiration is one thing, but to be the next student in line, beset with similar insecurities but watching your friend spewing buff-coloured puke over a too-zealous inquirer on Rousseau – well, it is hard to take oneself quite that seriously. (On the other hand *The Third Policeman* and *The Poor Mouth* are literally pastimes, as Bonaparte, in 'the jug', has all the time in the world to write his story, and the exegete all the time out of it.) And it is not just finding things funny – it is finding *these things* funny: not just the plight of the hapless modern writer, but a human condition that includes a crisis of subjectivity, an absence of free will, a subjection to powerfully determining cultural forces, and a potentially malevolent metaphysical destiny. Even Ireland's colonial history becomes grist to the comic mill in *The Poor Mouth*, although this is tempered more by the sardonic than the risible, and the target appears to be an amalgam of postcolonial piety and hypocrisy, as well as deluded sentimental Celtic fantasy.

So what O'Brien found funny was not what others found funny at the time – the time of the socially committed O'Casey (Sean, not Jem), the withdrawn and linguistically unreachable Joyce, the emergent, existentially brooding Beckett. And this is a problem: it just does not sit well with cultural models of modernism whose centre of gravity – in every sense – is something like *The Waste Land*, or *The Trial*, or *Heart of Darkness*, or any of those wonderful angst-ridden signature texts of a modernism we all grew to know and love. It is this that makes one wonder whether the shift from the Eliots and Kafkas and even Joyces to O'Brien represents a kind of generational shift away from those who experience trauma – the shock of the new, and all that

that entailed in the early years of the twentieth century – to those who simply deal with it (even *comically* deal with it) because it has become manageably familiar. Certainly O'Brien's comic exploration of such modernist tropes as textual fragmentation, the metaleptic vertigo of narratives inside narratives, the dizzying logic of endless repetition and *reductio ad absurdum*, and the profound destabilizations and subversions of authority and subjectivity that these imply, seems to indicate a different sensibility from those that went before, or at the very least a fundamental attitudinal change, which appears to be something like a comically inspired accommodation to the modern condition. And that there is some kind of shift is registered most fully in the ways in which literary criticism has come to handle O'Brien – the difficulty it has with locating him among the moderns, and its tendency to gather him into the postmodern camp. This might be extraordinarily well argued by writers like Keith Hopper in his *A Portrait of the Artist as a Young Postmodernist*, or shrewdly observed, as in Declan Kiberd's view that O'Brien 'was an experimentalist who was way ahead of his time: only after his death did his readers learn how to become his contemporaries'.[11] What is more, it is certainly not without interest that it was Jorge Luis Borges – that great pivotal figure in the shift from the modern to the postmodern, the first exponent, in John Barth's phrase, of 'the literature of exhaustion' – who first recognized something of the peculiar genius of O'Brien, which consisted in part in understanding the inventive potentiality of the situation of the modern writer, even when destined to rehearse an inescapable cultural inheritance. Was it this that gave the Argentine librarian the idea for his Pierre Mennard, the quintessential postmodern writer whose work illuminates the astonishing *novelty* of repetition, even without difference? Perhaps, but in any case I wonder whether the perceived need to categorically make something of O'Brien's humour just may have occluded the humour itself.

So in the end I would like to suggest that the writings of this successful public servant in de Valera's deeply conservative Irish state – written at a time when much of the countryside was still without electricity and the economy was largely rural agrarian – are less reflective of the cultural logic of late capitalism than they are the effect of Flann O'Brien's innate faculty for finding things funny. And I suspect that it is this that our cultural models have most trouble with. Modernism, postmodernism – these are constructions that quickly recruit the text to a regime of meaning of one kind or another, depending on how we put them together in the first place, but we might do well to use the most uniquely gifted comic writer of the mid-twentieth century to open up those constructions, rather than use them to explain and

---

[11] Declan Kiberd, *Irish Classics* (London: Granta Publications, 2001), 517.

constrain him in one way or another. For the irony of this situation is that O'Brien appears to have achieved illuminating perspectives on the nature of modern life through a comic understanding which our later age could only arrive at with an almost studied humourlessness. It is no easy task, of course, to engage seriously with the comic without either looking po-faced or making a great haimes of it, so one would need to fortify oneself appropriately for the task and find the right conceptual ground on which to undertake the work, to which end it might well do to bear in mind Brian O'Nolan's personal view that there is no such thing as a *large* scotch, and that no argument need be taken too seriously if it is based on licensed premises.

6

An Béal Bocht, Translation and the Proper Name

Maebh Long

An Béal Bocht tells the story, from birth to incarceration, of Bónapárt Ó Cúnasa, resident of Corca Dorcha in the Gaeltacht of the West of Ireland. There, in the unending rain, poverty and lust for potatoes he lives a harsh parody of the life described in Gaeltacht autobiographies and Revivalist writing. As Myles once wrote in the *Cruiskeen Lawn*, Synge, Gregory and Yeats 'persisted in the belief that poverty and savage existence on remote rocks was a most poetical way for people to be, provided they were other people',[1] and so *An Béal Bocht* works to strongly critique the simultaneous idealization and abandonment of the native Irish speaker by pushing this 'poetic' way of life to a *reductio ad absurdum*, presenting a carnivalesque stretching of tendencies, difficulties and prejudices to histrionic, hyperbolic conclusions. It was, as O'Nolan described it,

> an enormous jeer at the Gaelic morons here with their bicycle clips and handball medals but in language and style was an ironical copy of a really fine autobiographical book written by a man from the Great Blasket island of Kerry (long dead and now uninhabited) and translated into English under the title *The Islandman* by the late Robin Flower of the British Museum.[2]

An Béal Bocht depicts what might be called a tragi-farcical repetition of an anachronism: as Ireland attempted to create a sense of national identity, the Gaeltacht was understood through a form of ancestor worship, where living ancestors act in keeping with a past that the descendants create, and then

---

[1] Myles na gCopaleen, *Cruiskeen Lawn*, *The Irish Times* (hereafter CL), 4 October 1954.
[2] Brian O'Nolan (hereafter BON) to Timothy O'Keeffe (hereafter TOK), of MacGibbon and Kee, 27 February, 1960. Brian O'Nolan Papers, Special Collections Research Center, Southern Illinois University Carbondale. Hereafter SIUC.

despise for being out of date. Thus, in *An Béal Bocht*, the inhabitants of Corca Dorcha are treated either as just Neanderthal miscreants, or as Neanderthal miscreants who hold some anthropological and linguistic interest. Irish is confused by a visiting linguist with the grunting of a drunken pig – a confusion which gets him a PhD – the poorest man in the village has his water bottle broken by a visitor from Dublin because it belies his charming Gaelic poverty, and visiting *Gaeligoirí* hold a *feis ceoil* in which the starving Irish speakers dance to their deaths. The inhabitants of the Gaeltacht are treated by the rest of Ireland as humanoid animals, or proto-humans, to the extent that Bónapárt asks his grandfather

> *An bhfuilir cinnte . . . gur daoine na Gaeil?*
> *Tá an t-ainm sin amuigh orthu, a uaislín . . . ach ní fritheadh deimhniú riamh air. Ní capaill ná cearca sinn, ní rónta ná taibhsí, agus ar a shon sin is inchreidte gur daoine sinn.*[3]

Sean O'Casey described the novel as having 'the swish of Swift's scorn . . . bred well into the genial laughter of Mark Twain. It is well that we Gaels should come to learn that Gaels do not live by Gaelic alone, though, of course, no Gael can really live without it.'[4] It was, in short, 'a vicious bite at the hand that never fed it.'[5]

On the first, last and only day of Bónapárt's schooling, the vicious schoolmaster asks him his name: '*dhírigh sé méar fhada bhuí orm, agus dúirt*: "Phwat is yer nam?"' (*ABB*, 25).[6] One of his classmates whispers that the English-speaking teacher wants Bónapárt's name, and so Bónapárt proudly recites his name and a list of predecessors. But in response the schoolteacher beats him on the head with an oar, screaming 'Yer nam . . . is Jams O'Donnell!' (*ABB*, 25). Leaving Bónapárt on the floor in a pool of blood, the teacher turns to each student in the class, giving each a violent beating and informing each

---

[3] Myles na gCopaleen, *An Béal Bocht nó an Milleánach* (Dublin: Mercier Press, 1999), 90. Hereafter cited in text as *ABB*. Translations given in footnotes, and taken from Flann O'Brien, *The Poor Mouth* (London: Flamingo, 1993) unless otherwise stated. *The Poor Mouth* is referred to in citations as *TPM*.
  'Are you certain that the Gaels are people?'
  'They've that reputation anyway, little noble, . . . but no confirmation of it has ever been received. We're not horses nor hens; seals not ghosts; and in spite of all that, it's unbelievable that we're human' (*TPM*, 100). This is an example of problematic translation in Power. The final clause, a translation of *is inchreidte gur daoine sinn* should read 'it's *plausible* that we're human', as *inchreidte* does not mean 'unbelievable'.
[4] Sean O' Casey to BON, 2 April 1942, SIUC.
[5] Ibid.
[6] 'he directed a long yellow finger at me and said "Phwat is yer nam?"' (*TPM*, 30).

that his name is Jams O'Donnell. Barely surviving the day, Bónapárt returns home, where he asks his mother what happened. She says:

> Bhí sé riamh ráite agus scríofa go mbuailtear gach tachrán Gaelach ar an gcéad lá scoile dó toisc na dtuigeann sé an Béarla and gall-leagan a ainm féinig, agus nach mbíonn aon mheas ag aoinne air toisc é a bheith Gaelach. Ní bhíonn aon ghnó eile ar scoil aon lá riamh ach an bualadh sin agus an tseafóid chéanna ar Jams O'Donnell. (*ABB*, 27)[7]

The first day of schooling in Corca Dorcha is dedicated to teaching the boys the foreign form of their names. And regardless of what their names might be in Irish, in English they are all simply Jams O'Donnell. When Bónapárt is later accused of a murder he may or may not have committed – in O'Brien's texts there are never any wholly innocent victims – the policeman asks him for his name in English. And so Bónapárt gives it in English: Jams O'Donnell. He is then sent before a judge and tried. In English. As Jams O'Donnell. In *An Béal Bocht* Irish is other to the law, and its speakers must bow to the decrees of a legal system wholly beyond their understanding. Bónapárt can only speak Irish, a language unrecognized by the English-language judicial system, and he is, therefore, forced to act simply as a silent, partial presence, a body there to satisfy the writ of *habeas corpus* but not partake or defend himself. Justice, outside of language, wholly translatable and universal, is here absolutely anglophile and Anglophone, and, therefore, not justice at all. For the English speaker there is the law, but for the Irish speaker there is only prison, only the restriction of a language other to legality and right. The enactment of a trial is sufficient to ensure that justice is done, and thus the *process* of law is privileged.

If Irish is outside the law, Irish names are also outside it; in order for the law to prosecute this external other, he must be renamed, given a marker that enables animalistic life to be included within the law, as a legal entity if not an individual. 'Jams O'Donnell' is an institution under which a member of the excluded set of Irish speakers can be (partially) included within the law. Bónapárt is given an English name, a name naming the physical presence of a silent entity who can be tried as an adult, but entitling him to no more. He is, therefore, not subject but *object* located inside and outside the law; it functions around him, including and excluding him. The proper name 'Jams O'Donnell' is thus not given to mark identity or individuality.

---

[7] 'It was always said and written that every Gaelic youngster is hit on his first school day because he doesn't understand English and the foreign form of his name and that no one has any respect for him because he is Gaelic to the marrow. There's no other business going on in school that day but punishment and revenge and the same fooling about Jams O'Donnell' (*TPM*, 34).

'Jams O'Donnell' denotes simply the *category* or *genus* of 'male, Irish-speaking peasant'. In English the inhabitants of the Gaeltachts do not have individual proper names, but are designated simply by a generic term. If Kafka's man from the country cannot pass through the open gate to the Law, it is nonetheless his gate, his doorkeeper, all in his name. For Bónapárt there is merely a gate for Jams O'Donnell, as neither the doorkeeper nor the law itself deigns to speak his language. He is not before the law, he is *beneath* the law; beneath its notice as an individual but nonetheless under its control.[8]

If 'Jams O'Donnell' means every male, Irish-speaking peasant, then it may masquerade as a proper name, but it very clearly functions instead as a common noun. A proper name, as Derrida writes, has 'no meaning, no conceptualisable and common meaning', and when pronounced 'can designate [*viser*] only a single, singular individual, one unique thing'.[9] As proper names 'designate individuals who do not refer to any common concept', proper names do not mark a particular category.[10] In *An Béal Bocht* we witness the categorizing of a people through an improper proper name, that is, a common noun masquerading as proper name. Derrida, writing on the name of God, writes that there are doubts about the name when it 'risks to bind, to enslave or engage the other ... to call him/her to respond even before any decision or deliberation, even before any freedom'.[11] Elsewhere Derrida writes that 'Mastery begins ... through the power of naming, of imposing and legitimating appellations'.[12] As Brian Friel's *Translations* demonstrates, the cultural transposition of the proper name is never a process free from ideology or the imposition of a hierarchy. When Owen, the schoolmaster's son, returns to Bailebeag, he is accompanied by two Englishmen there to create an English-language map of the region and thereby officially rename the country. Owen, who works as a translator for the men, has his own name translated? mispronounced? anglicized? into 'Roland' by them. When the villagers point out the Englishmen's mistake, Owen says, 'Owen – Roland – what the hell. It's only a name. It's the same me, isn't it? Well, isn't it?'[13] The

---

[8] An extended reading of Jams O'Donnell in relation to the law can be found in Maebh Long, *Assembling Flann O'Brien* (London: Bloomsbury, 2014). The rest of this chapter adds to sections on translation and the proper name found in that text.
[9] Jacques Derrida, 'Who or What Is Compared? The Concept of Comparative Literature and the Theoretical Problems of Translation', trans. Eric Prenowitz, *Discourse* 30, 1–2 (2008): 36.
[10] Derrida, 'Who or What', 36.
[11] Derrida, 'Sauf le nom', in *On The Name*, ed. Thomas Dutoit, trans. John P. Leavey, Jr. (Stanford: Stanford University Press, 1995), 84.
[12] Jacques Derrida, *Monolingualism of the Other, Or, The Prosthesis of Origin*, trans. Patrick Mensah (Stanford: Stanford University Press, 1998), 39.
[13] Brian Friel, *Translations*, *Plays 1* (London: Faber and Faber, 1996), 408.

answer is unambiguously 'no'. Owen and Roland are not the same person, and even if a proper name is changed into a proper name a violence is done. When a proper name is changed into a common noun, however, individuality and subjectivity are wholly denied. In *An Béal Bocht* we see a violent act of naming which works to bind and enslave, but does so by naming without giving a name worthy of the name.

When speculating on Jams O'Donnell Bónapárt says *'féach gur fónta an fear é O'Donnell and an líon sin clainne aige'* (*ABB*, 27).[14] To delimit and limit the speakers of the Gaelic mother tongue, they are given the improper name of a father who does not exist, and are forced to inherit his indigence and exclusion. The idea of inheriting nothingness is found in O'Brien's *The Third Policeman*, in which the nameless narrator, having forgotten his name after death, reports the loss of a gold watch at the barracks. When confronted by a man personifying lack – he has no name and no bicycle – the policeman says: 'I was once acquainted with a tall man . . . that had no name either and you are certain to be his son and the heir to his nullity and all his nothings.'[15] Nameless, the inheritor of nothingness, the narrator is outside the law: 'If you have no name you possess nothing and you do not exist and even your trousers are not on you although they look as if they were from where I am sitting. On the other separate hand you can do what you like and the law cannot touch you' (*TTP*, 64). But when he is about to be hanged for a murder he did and did not commit, and he protests that he is outside the law, the sergeant responds:

> "For that reason alone . . . we can take you and hang the life out of you and you are not hanged at all and there is no entry to be made in the death papers. The particular death you die is not even a death (which is an inferior phenomenon at the best) only an insanitary abstraction in the backyard, a piece of negative nullity neutralized and rendered void by asphyxiation and the fracture of the spinal string. If it is not a lie to say that you have been given the final hammer behind the barrack, equally it is true to say that nothing has happened to you."
>
> "You mean because I have no name I cannot die and that you cannot be held answerable for death even if you kill me?"
>
> "That is about the size of it," said the Sergeant. (*TTP*, 105)

Namelessness creates ontological aberrations and difficulties in proving the correct functioning of the law. And so when dealing with people who have been designated sub-human you bestow upon them not a proper name denoting singular subjects, but a common noun denoting a set. There is no

---

[14] 'isn't O'Donnell the wonderful man and the number of children he has?' (*TPM*, 31).
[15] Flann O'Brien, *The Third Policeman* (London: Harper Perennial, 2006), 59. Hereafter cited in text as *TTP*.

Jams O'Donnell and yet everyone is Jams O'Donnell, named as the other for momentary and partial inclusion within the law. The name thus operates as a synonym for the Irish speaker, for Blasket-man, for islander, and thereby takes an indefinite article – I am *a* Jams O'Donnell. There is no grand, tragic defiance in the active embracing and declaration of the name – 'I am Jams O'Donnell' as 'I am Spartacus' – just a passive acceptance of the undesired and general designation of proper-name-as-common-noun – 'I am (a) Jams O'Donnell.' For the inhabitants of Corca Dorcha individual identity is irrelevant. They are not real people, nor even characters in a (realist) novel, but archetypes in a parodic farce lambasting the treatment of Irish speakers. In O'Brien's last completed novel, *The Dalkey Archive*, his protagonist is given the name often used as a slur against Irish Catholics – Mick – and women's decisions to retain maiden names is used to imply corruption and dissolution in *The Hard Life* and *Slattery's Sago Saga*. Naming is never an innocent act. While as Myles he may joke about it – 'people hostile to the historic language of this land always called it "Gaelic" not "Irish." I think that is a point that might be taken up with the Gaelic League'[16] – O'Nolan was aware of the power of the name.

In *An Béal Bocht*'s chapter on the *Gaeligoirí* Bónapárt writes that the visiting 'Gaelic Morons' were more Gaelic than the Gaels, as they were nameless. Lacking names and surnames they are free to give themselves titles that arise from nature:

> Bhí bua eile acu nach raibh againne riamh anall ó chailleamar an fíor-Ghaelachas – bhíodar go léir gan ainmneacha gan sloinnte, ach teidil bhreátha glactha acu agus féin-bhaistithe orthu ón spéir agus ón aer, ón bhfeirm agus ón stoirm, ón bpáirc agus ón gcearc. Bhí fear ramhar toirtiúil mallbhogtha ann le haghaidh liath lodartha, a chuma air go raibh sé idir bhásanna ag dhá ghalar mharfacha, agus is é teideal a thug sé air féin ná 'An Nóinín Gaelach'; duine bocht eile a raibh toirt agus fuinneamh luchóige ann, thug sé air féin 'An Tarbh Teann'; an tríú duine a bhí ciúin ceansa neamhurchóideach, thug sé air féin 'An Pocán Meidhreach', d'ainneoin nár phoc sé aoinne riamh agus nach raibh sé meidhreach. (ABB, 44)[17]

---

[16] CL 3 November 1944.
[17] 'They had yet another distinction which we did not since we lost true Gaelicism – they all lacked names and surnames but received honorary titles, self-granted, which took their style from the sky and the air, the farm and the storm, field and fowl. There was a bulky, fat, slow-moving man whose face was grey and flabby and appeared suspended between deaths from two mortal diseases; he took unto himself the title of *The Gaelic Daisy*. Another poor fellow whose size and energy were that of a mouse, called himself *The Sturdy Bull*' (TPM, 52). The third man is not included in the translated version, but, using my own translation, it reads: 'the third person was quiet, meek, harmless, and he called himself "The Frisky Blow" but he'd never hit anyone and wasn't frisky'.

The 'natural' namelessness of the Irish is supplemented by a prosthetic title, self-chosen and self-appointed, which reflects not the attributes of the individual, but the traits he wished he had. Thus a grey, deathly man can be a lively daisy, a weak wretch can be a bull, and a shy, inoffensive soul can be a lover and a fighter. The absence of a name enables wish-fulfilling, contradictory titles whose inappropriateness is funny – there is a *Fód Móna* (Sod of Turf), *Popshúil Mairnéalach* (Popeye the Sailor), *Chiaróg Eile* (Other Beetle) – and also serves to mock *An Craoibhín Aoibhinn* (the Pleasant Little Branch), the name taken by Douglas Hyde.[18] More fundamentally than this, however, it reinforces the non-native speakers' treatment of the Gaels as antiquated, anachronistic and improper. Names in Irish, they suppose, are not proper names but always titles or sobriquets that relate to a characteristic – real or imagined – of an individual. In other words, the Irish are always already nameless, and requiring the addition or imposition of a name-as-category-type. There is never an attempt to give the Irish speakers a proper name – they are associated always with superficial descriptors and categories.

Translation and the name

The difficulty of naming in O'Brien's works is compounded by the difficulty in naming him. Is he Brian O'Nolan, Brian Ó Nualláin, Myles na gCopaleen, Myles na Gopaleen, Lord Nolan of Santry, Flann O'Brien, George Knowall, John James Doe, An Broc, Brother Barnabas, Count O'Blather, or any of the other names he harassed his own alter egos under in *The Irish Times*? If, as he wrote regarding *An Béal Bocht*, 'Every genuine copy bears the name, "Myles na gCopaleen,"'[19] then how do we read the translation – *The Poor Mouth* – given that the cover proudly displays the name of Flann O'Brien? Further complicating the movement between the Irish proper name and the English common noun is Power's translation of *An Béal Bocht*, in which the names of places and people are altered. While the anglicization of Irish proper names has a long history, the decision to alter names within a literary text is, while not without precedent, extremely problematic. Why, in a text so engaged – parodically and earnestly – with the treatment of the Irish language, would the translation present proper names according to English spellings and English equivalences?

---

[18] Declan Kiberd, *Inventing Ireland: The Literature of a Modern Nation* (London: Vintage Books, 1996), 501–2.
[19] CL 12 December 1941.

The most sympathetic answer is that Power merely continued O'Brien's mode of naturalizing foreign names. The majority of first names in *An Béal Bocht* are not Irish names – Sitric is a Norse name, Micheálangaló and Lánardó are both Italian, Feardanand is originally Germanic and Bónapárt is a French surname – but O'Brien transcribes them according to Irish phonetic rules, and thereby assimilates the ignored and destitute in Corca Dorcha into a wider history of empires and aristocratic culture. In sharp contrast to their poverty and plebeian vulgarity are their names, appellations that universalize their plight, invert histories of imperial oppression and mock the concept of a stable, isolated Irish identity. Arguably, when Power translates the text, he continues this trait of transcribing names, and spells them according to the rules of the language of the text, in this case English.

When O'Nolan translated Brinsley MacNamara's play *Margaret Gillan*, one of the major issues was the proper name/title. In letters between the publishers and O'Nolan different names were suggested; Maighréad Gilion, Maighréad Gillan, Máiréad Gilion were proposed, while O'Nolan became quite heated in making the distinction between Maighréad Ní Ghilleáin (this would imply that she was unmarried) and Maighread Bean Uí Ghilleáin (this implies that she was married).[20] When discussing the translation of *An Béal Bocht* Evelyn O'Nolan showed concern regarding the transition of names between languages, writing to O'Keeffe that 'Power translates "Corca Dorcha" as "Corkadoragha." Somewhere Brian himself referred to the same place as "Corkey Dorkey" which is much better.'[21] Similarly, when Kevin O'Nolan wrote to Evelyn to comment on possible translators for the text he criticized the early attempt made by Maurice Kennedy, focusing in particular on Kennedy's odd translation of the name of Bónapárt's townland – *Lios na bPráiscín* (the fort of the apron) – as 'The Mound of Mashed Potatoes'.[22] Much work was done on finding a translator that could capture the 'verve and "go" of Brian's Irish',[23] but even Power's was not deemed perfect, Kevin O'Nolan writing that 'the translation [Power's] is a little too easy going. It is not always faithful in detail and though this may not always matter there is danger of overlooking small points.'[24] This is particularly clear in the list of the titles taken by the *Gaeligoirí*. Power mistranslates some, excludes others

[20] Letters May 1943 between O'Nolan and Sean McLallan. O'Nolan publically comments on his irritation on this point in a *Cruiskeen Lawn* article on 31 October 1953.
[21] Evelyn O'Nolan (hereafter EON) to TOK 28 November 1969. Flann O'Brien Papers, MS.1997.027, John J. Burns Library, Boston College. Hereafter BC.
[22] Kevin O'Nolan to EON 29 November 1969, BC.
[23] EON to TOK 22 October 1969, BC.
[24] Kevin O'Nolan to EON 29 November 1969, BC.

and adds ones that O'Brien never included in either the MS or published versions of *An Béal Bocht* – 'The Gluttonous Rabbit', and 'The Headache', for example (see appendix for a full list). Interestingly, in the MS version of *An Béal Bocht* Jams O'Donnell does not exist, as the common noun all male children are re-named with is *Jams Gallagher*. Jams Gallagher is a play on James Gallagher from Máire's (Séamus Ó Grianna) novel *Mo Dhá Róisín*, in which a pupil learns of his official name – James Gallagher – for the first time when he went to school.

The difficulty of translating *An Béal Bocht* is not restricted to decisions on names. As the text contains English, Irish and phonetically mixed transliterations of the two, the movement between languages is complicated. For example, the shock of the phonetically transcribed 'Phwat is yer nam?' in the Irish text is lost in English. In the Irish text the *Gaeligoir* with whom the Seanduine speaks regarding the loss of the students in Corca Dorcha speaks in Irish, but in Irish spelt according to English phonetic rules: '*Nee doy lom goh vwill un fukal sin* "meath" *eg un Ahur Padur*' (*AB*, 42) [Lit: 'I don't think that Father Peter has the word "decline"']. And when the Seanduine dismisses him in frustration, his Irish is suddenly transcribed through English too, presumably in mockery of the man's accent: 'Nawbocklesh, avic' (*AB*, 42) ['Don't worry about it, son']. Not only is O'Brien's use of transliteration and phonetics multifaceted – this is found too in the *Cruiskeen Lawn* articles on what he called Corkadorky – a certain complexity lies in his idiosyncratic use of Irish. Thus an anonymous reader's report for *An Béal Bocht* states:

> I can quite safely assert that in an experience of sixty years this is quite the craziest piece of Irish I have ever seen. What most surprises me is the self-assurance of its author – a man who demonstrates twenty times on every page that he is the veriest tyro in the Irish language. For want of knowledge he cannot begin, or continue or finish a sentence properly. Constructions such as he writes have never before been seen in Irish, and one earnestly hopes that nothing of the kind will ever be repeated.[25]

While not everyone agreed with such a harsh assessment, O'Brien himself was very resistant to translations of his Irish texts, writing 'I don't think there is any point about translating stuff I have written in Irish into English. The significance of most of it is verbal or linguistic or tied up with a pseudo

---

[25] Reader Report, unnamed and undated (presumably 1941) for *An Béal Bocht*, BC.

Gaelic mystique and this would be quite lost in translation'.[26] Translation did, however, fascinate him, and he spoke of the possibility of translating the translations of some of his later texts. Timothy O'Keeffe joined in the idea of linguistic play, speculating in a letter to O'Brien on Gregory's mode of writing: "'Lady Gregory would translate the French text into English, and after the English had been put into Irish by a native writer, the Irish text would be translated back into English by Lady Gregory." Doesn't that ring a bell?'[27]

The mixture of names within *An Béal Bocht*, the presence of two languages within the novel(s), the innovative structures and the problems of translation create a polylingual and multicultural cacophony, a post-Babelian complexity. As Derrida writes in 'Des Tours de Babel', the tower of Babel falls and the single, universal tongue or idiom is made multiple when God, in his jealousy of the power of the tribe of Shem, creates linguistic confusion by speaking his name. The tribe of Shem wished to make a name for themselves, to be positioned and protected by a common name and a tower; a linguistic and non-linguistic signifier. Against this single tongue, single tower and single name – the name 'Shem' means 'name', and names the desire or aspiration for a universal language – God speaks his name, 'Babel' which comes from the Hebrew 'Bavel' meaning 'confusion'. Shem and God, name and confusion; both are proper name and common noun, and both name a certain linguistic undecidability and doubling. A common noun can be translated as it refers to a general concept, but a proper name exists outside translation, as it does not refer to a conceptual generality, and does not, therefore, strictly belong to the language in which it operates: 'personal proper names cannot be translated. They are sometimes adapted, in pronunciation or transcription . . . but they cannot be translated'.[28] Proper names do not mean, proper names do not describe or signify attributes, proper names cannot, therefore, be translated. A proper name is not a proper part of language. It can be spelt in different ways, and pronounced in different ways, but not translated. And yet it is precisely around proper names and that propriety/impropriety that *An Béal Bocht* investigates different modes of translation and control.

The story of Babel, the tale of the origin of linguistic diversity, of the confusion of tongues, stems from a speech act itself confused between names and nouns, the proper and the common. This complicated locutionary act brings about the possibility of translation – to enable interlingual

---

[26] BON to TOK 27 February 1960, SIUC.
[27] TOK to BON 26 May 1965, SIUC.
[28] Jacques Derrida, 'Who or What', 36.

communication – and its impossibility – idioms will never exactly correspond. The impossible necessity of translation is played out in every version of the story: how does one convey the double meaning of Babel, the intralinguistic translation between proper name and common noun already at play within the name itself? To translate it, as Derrida explains in *The Ear of the Other*, by 'confusion' is to translate a proper name into a common noun. Thus, he argues, the story of Babel is the story of an imperative: people are condemned to translate, and to begin with an act of impossible translation, that of a proper name. The tower is brought down by a speech act that is a double act of naming: a naming of God, and a naming of the act, that of confusion itself. The locutionary act self-refers as name (a proper name exhausts itself in referring to a singular individual) and yet that self-referential naming operates within the realm of the common noun to instigate a performative act: in uttering the name (of confusion) confusion reigns. The proper moves towards the common and the double speech act becomes a double bind as God instigates the necessity of translation by uttering his proper and untranslatable name, whose power of confusion lies in its (intralingual) translatability as a common noun. As Derrida says, 'this desire is at work in every proper name: translate me, don't translate me'.[29] The name becomes a mark of non-belonging, an absence within a language. Even though language is not possible without the name – 'what would a language be without the possibility of calling by a proper name?'[30] – it does not belong to the language, and 'consequently it can properly inscribe itself in a language only by allowing itself to be translated therein, in other words, *interpreted* by its semantic equivalent'.[31]

What then, occurs in the alternations between names within *An Béal Bocht*, and between *An Béal Bocht* and *The Poor Mouth*? What is the relation between Bónapárt Ó Cúnasa and Jams O'Donnell? What is the relation between Bónapárt Ó Cúnasa and Bonaparte O'Coonassa? Do we see impossible translations, problematic alterations or legitimate equivalences? Remaining first of all within the Irish text, *An Béal Bocht* is about impossible, reductive and controlling instances of translation: the movement from Bónapárt Ó Cúnasa to Jams O'Donnell is an act of inexecutable and violent translation, one in which the alteration of the signifier instigates a radical shift in the signified. *Bónapárt* is a singular subject in possession of an untranslatable proper name, but *Jams O'Donnell* is a homogeneous object within the law labelled by a translatable common noun. The 'translation' from

---

[29] Jacques Derrida, *The Ear of the Other: Otobiography, Transference, Translation*, ed. Christie V. McDonald, trans. Peggy Kamuf (New York: Schocken Books, 1985), 102.
[30] Jacques Derrida, '*Des Tours de Babel*', *Acts of Religion*, ed. Gil Anidjar, trans. Joseph F. Graham (Routledge: New York, 2002), 109.
[31] Derrida, 'Babel', 109–10.

Irish to English creates a wholly different signified. English cannot recognize the untranslatable individual and proper name that is Bónapárt, all it can see is the translatable common noun that is Jams O'Donnell. That is, in English there is no Bónapárt; he does not exist and cannot be seen.

This movement is complicated when *An Béal Bocht* is translated into English, and everything, even untranslatable proper names, become altered. Within *The Poor Mouth*, the movement from Bónapárt Ó Cúnasa to Bonaparte O'Coonassa may simply have been intended to be an uncomplicated *transcription* that enables non-Irish speakers to pronounce Irish names, but its operation as *translation* is impossible to ignore. If a text that establishes that a subject in Irish becomes no more than object in English is translated into English, and the very site of the point of opposition – the proper name/common noun – becomes a site of translation/transcription, then an undeniable performative contradiction is created. The tension between the language in which the text is written – Irish – and the language of education, biopolitical control and the law – English – is lost when the entire text is written in English, and particularly if the names are altered. The name which marks a locus of singularity – albeit a name not 'originally' Irish – cannot mark the same degree of difference from Jams O'Donnell when it is already in the same language/phonetics as Jams O'Donnell. The vital linguistic distinction and shock of the eradication of the name in the native tongue is lost.

Bónapárt – in Irish – is a playful parody of the Irish-language characters of the West of Ireland autobiographies, and a harsh satire of the representations of Irish speakers in (predominantly) English texts. Bonaparte – in English – is still a parody and a satire, but a parody of the *translated* autobiographies, and a satire whose proximity to that harshly mocked is radically increased. In other words, the distance between satirically representing an Irish stereotype, and *being* a stereotype, is drastically reduced when read in English. Within the context of English, Bonaparte is, even prior and separate to being named 'Jams O'Donnell', too much a stereotype, too much a stage character, too much a farcical repetition to be anything but a common noun designating a concept. In English, the language through which Irish-speakers are understood as anachronistic and inferior, *Bónapárt/Bonaparte is always already Jams O'Donnell*. Bonaparte is not the direct and simple *equivalent* of Bónapárt, the same signified in a different language, but a wholly different mode of stereotype. While Bónapárt cannot be translated, Bonaparte *can*, as despite its connotations of grand conquest and ambition, within *The Poor Mouth* it operates as Jams O'Donnell, or Paddy, or 'Mick', and *means* Irish stereotype. While names are of untranslatable individuals in Irish, in English they are markers of translatable category types.

An Béal Bocht, Translation and the Proper Name

Appendix: Alterations to titles between *An Béal Bocht* (MS and published versions) and *The Poor Mouth*. (Note: The list in the MS of *The Poor Mouth* is the same)

Original MS	Published Text (*ABB*)	Published Translation (*TPM*)
Cat Chonnacht (Connacht Cat)	Cat Chonnacht	Connacht Cat
Uan Orighialla (16 clock a meadhchai) (Lamb of Oriel (16 stone Mikey))	An Circín Donn	The Little Brown Hen
An Préachán Péacach (The Gaudy Crow)	An Capall Dána	The Bold Horse
An Géigín Bréige (The Imitation little Branch/Goose)	An Préachán Péacach	The Gaudy Crow
Roisín an tSléibhe (Roseen of the Hill)	An Ridire Reatha	The Running Knight
Goll Mac Mórna (Goll Mac Morna)	Roisín an tSléibhe	Roseen of the Hill
An Fhuiseog Spéire (The Skylark)	Goll Mac Mórna	Goll Mac Morna
An Spideog (The Robin)	Popshúil Mairnéalach	Popeye the Sailor
An Babhta Damhsa (The Bout of Dancing)	An tEaspag Íseal	The Humble Bishop
An tUltach Beadaigh (The Bandy Ulsterman)	An Lonn Dubh Binn	The Sweet Blackbird
An Sionnach Seang (The Slim Fox)	Tuirne Mháire	Mary's Spinning-wheel
An Cat Mara (The Sea Cat)	An Fód Móna	The Sod of Turf
An Crann Géagach (The Branchy Tree)	Babaró	Baboro

(*Continued*)

Appendix (Continued)

Original MS	Published Text (*ABB*)	Published Translation (*TPM*)
An Ghaoith Anair (The West Wind)	*Mo Chara Droma Rúisc*	My Friend Drumroosk
An Muimhneach Measardha (The Temperate Munsterman)	*An Maide Rámha*	The Oar
An Buidéal Buidhe (The Yellow Bottle)	*An Chiaróg Eile*	The Other Beetle
Liam Mairnéalach (William the Sailor)	*An Fhuiseog Spéire*	The Skylark
An tUbh Donn (The Brown Egg)	*An Spideog*	The Robin Redbreast
Ochtar Fear (Eight Men)	*An Bata Damhsa*	The Bout of Dancing
Tadhg Gabha (Tim the Blacksmith)	*An tUltach Beadaí*	The Bandy Ulsterman
An Coileach Corcordha (The Purple Rooster)	*An Sionnach Seang*	The Slim Fox
An Stuicín Eorna (The Little Stack of Barley)	*An Cat Mara*	The Sea-cat
An Tuiseal Tabharthach (The Dative Case)	*An Crann Géagach*	The Branchy Tree
Airgead Geal (Bright Silver)	*An Ghaoith Anair*	The West Wind
An Mac Breac (The Speckled Fellow)	*An Muimhneach Measardha*	The Temperate Munsterman
An-Fear-Is-Fearr-i-nÉirinn (The Best Man in Ireland)	*An Buidéal Buí* (The Yellow Bottle)	[missing]
	Liam Mairnéalach	William the Sailor

Appendix (Continued)

Original MS	Published Text (*ABB*)	Published Translation (*TPM*)
	An tUbh Donn [The Brown Egg]	The White Egg
	Ochtar Fear	Eight Men
	Tadhg Gabha	Tim the Blacksmith
	An Coileach Corcra	The Purple Cock
	An Staicín Eorna	The Little Stack of Barley
	An Tuiseal Tabharthach	The Dative Case
	Airgead Geal	Silver
	An Mac Breac	The Speckled Fellow
	An-Fear-Is-Fearr-i-nÉirinn	[missing]
		The Headache
		The Lively Boy
		The Gluttonous Rabbit
		The High Hat
		John of the Glen
		Yours Respectfully
		The Little Sweet Kiss

7

Ploughmen without Land: Flann O'Brien and Patrick Kavanagh

Joseph Brooker

After Brian O'Nolan's death, the poet Patrick Kavanagh would remark that there was no one left to talk to in Dublin. The tribute is surprising, as their relationship was not one of intimate confidences. But it indicates mutual respect. John Ryan records: '[O'Nolan] was one of the few writers in whose company [Kavanagh] was completely at ease; his respect for him was complete; he was his peer; like himself he had chosen the tougher going, the thinner air of Upper Parnassus, Dublin 14.'[1]

This essay is a comparative study of O'Nolan and Kavanagh, written in the conviction that O'Nolan can be illuminated by such juxtaposition with his peers: the writers with whom he shared pub tables as well as a historical situation. Insofar as we are pursuing a more intensive, historically informed understanding of O'Nolan, we would still benefit from close studies of him in relation to his university friends Denis Devlin, Brian Coffey, Niall Sheridan, Niall Montgomery, and figures from the press, notably his long-standing editor R. M. Smyllie. If O'Nolan (1911–66) has a distinct niche in literary history, though, it is as part of a mid-century Dublin scene in which the two other most prominent figures are Patrick Kavanagh (1904–67) and Brendan Behan (1923–64). This milieu has been documented notably by two men who were also part of it: Anthony Cronin (b.1928) in *Dead as Doornails* (1976) and *No Laughing Matter* (1989), and John Ryan (1925–92) in *Remembering How We Stood* (1975). Ryan's subtitle, 'Bohemian Dublin at the Mid-Century', summarizes the scene, though any Flann O'Brien scholar knows that the author's relation to bohemianism was vexed. Kavanagh and O'Nolan belonged to the generation of writers who quite self-consciously followed Joyce and Yeats, above all, and the Irish Literary Revival more generally. Both were literary heirs to political independence, ambivalent recorders of the

---

[1] John Ryan, *Remembering How We Stood: Bohemian Dublin at the Mid-Century* (Dublin: Gill and Macmillan, 1975), 127.

Free State. More than any of O'Nolan's Dublin peers, Kavanagh was also a major writer.

I will first outline the facts of their parallel careers. I will then move chronologically through certain points of comparison, exploring significant likenesses and differences. The aim is to illuminate both writers, and to open ground for further research.

Two Northerners

Brian O'Nolan and Patrick Kavanagh were both from Ulster. O'Nolan's Strabane, Co. Tyrone, is on the far western border of what in 1922 became Northern Ireland. Kavanagh's Inniskeen, Co. Monaghan, is also on the border, on the Republic's side. No such border existed till Kavanagh reached adulthood, but he and O'Nolan were both to some degree outsiders to the capital city where they would spend the bulk of their lives and win a measure of fame. O'Nolan was moved to Dublin as a child of 11. Kavanagh came later. He was a small farmer before he was a poet. In 1931, in an episode of literary legend, he walked 80 miles from Monaghan to Dublin to visit George Russell (whose alias was AE), the editor of the *Irish Statesman* who had already published some of Kavanagh's earlier works. His first collection *Ploughman and other Poems* (1936) and the novel *The Green Fool* (1938) both appeared before he finally settled in Dublin in August 1939. If O'Nolan's arrival in Dublin roughly coincided with the publication of *Ulysses*, Kavanagh's Dublin life dates from around the publication of *At Swim-Two-Birds*. Indeed, the two were yoked together that year when the AE Memorial Fund prize of £150 was given to Kavanagh – but with a special prize of £30 also given to *At Swim*. This was, not entirely wittingly, the first public recognition of the two writers' centrality to a literary generation.

Dublin circa 1940 was a small capital. Its literary scene was naturally far smaller still. The city's insularity was increased, from 1939 to 1945, by the Emergency, though war did bring some new visitors, spying (like Kavanagh's friend John Betjeman) or hungry for steak. In this context, poets, novelists and critics tended to be at least aware of each other's existence, across the city or across a pub. Certain public houses were favoured by writers. The Palace Bar on Fleet Street was convenient for the nearby *Irish Times*, and was a focal point of literary Dublin at least until the newspaper's editor R. M. Smyllie moved his informal court to the Pearl Bar around the corner. The Palace was the setting of Alan Reeve's cartoon *Dublin Culture*.[2] The picture shows

---

[2] The picture is reproduced on the centre pages of Ryan, *Remembering How We Stood*.

three dozen Irish men of letters (no women), many of them now little remembered. R. M. Smyllie dominates the centre. O'Nolan and Kavanagh are better known today than anyone else in the picture. They are pictured as adjacent: a standing Kavanagh waves his large hand almost across O'Nolan's face. In Reeve's picture, Kavanagh and O'Nolan appear intimately part of the same crowd. From this time they shared a profoundly bibulous literary culture in which paths crossed, rumours spread and insults or jokes could be hurled from one side of a bar to another.

Summer 1940 was the golden hour of the letter-column controversies that O'Nolan and friends cooked up in the *Irish Times*.[3] One controversy followed directly from a book review by Kavanagh, who also closed the affair with a final reflection. Here, then, O'Nolan and Kavanagh directly addressed each other – though the directness is vitiated by O'Nolan's entirely characteristic recourse to verbal disguise. The controversy would be significant for literary history, as it prompted Smyllie to employ O'Nolan as Myles na gCopaleen: an engagement that would last the next quarter-century.

By this time the first and finest two Flann O'Brien novels were written. *An Béal Bocht* (1941; translated as *The Poor Mouth* in 1973) arrived a year into the *Cruiskeen Lawn* years; the following year Kavanagh published *The Great Hunger*. These two texts stand as two of literature's major critical responses to independent Ireland, specifically the sociology and ideology of its rural life. O'Nolan's play *Faustus Kelly* (1943) was another response, which Kavanagh attended at the Abbey Theatre; he would later claim to view it as O'Nolan's finest work.[4] So too was Sean O'Faolain's journal *The Bell*, for which both men wrote. John Ryan edited its sprightly successor *Envoy*. He persuaded Kavanagh to write a monthly diary for the magazine from 1949 to 1951, and the poet also contributed his bitter ditty 'Who Killed James Joyce?' to the special Joyce issue of 1951 which was at least nominally edited by O'Nolan. *Envoy* was based in Grafton Street; the literary scene partly shifted to McDaid's pub nearby. Kavanagh – notionally symbolizing the muse – joined the pioneering Bloomsday cortège which O'Nolan and Ryan organized in 1954. The event signalled the writers' wish to pay homage to Joyce, and to claim a certain lineage from him, whatever their ambivalent relations to him.

By this time Myles' columns could be more splenetic and satirical; the mood chimed with the 13-week run of *Kavanagh's Weekly* in early 1952, to which O'Nolan contributed. Both men remained angry with aspects of

---

[3] For a discussion of these see Joseph Brooker, *Flann O'Brien* (Tavistock: Northcote House, 2005), 23–6.
[4] See Anthony Cronin, *No Laughing Matter: The Life and Times of Flann O'Brien* (London: Grafton, 1989), 134.

Ireland. Events of the 1950s swung Kavanagh's mood. Critically ill after a disastrous legal case, in spring 1955 he recuperated by the Grand Canal and commenced a self-conscious literary renaissance, founded on his gladness still to be alive. O'Nolan experienced his own late revival, notably with two later novels. Kavanagh attended O'Nolan's funeral in 1966, and died the following year.

Such is the historical outline. Let us now retrace our steps and consider certain of these episodes in more detail.

Ploughmen and potatoes

Kavanagh's early poetry is pastoral. It describes nature and agriculture in the Monaghan countryside. 'Ploughman', first published in 1930, voices the experience of a farmer in the field:

> I turn the lea-green down
> Gaily now,
> And paint the meadow brown
> With my plough.
>
> I dream with silvery gull
> And brazen crow.
> A thing that is beautiful
> I may know.

The poem's alternating lines of three and two stresses are a distinctive pattern. The regularity enhances the sense of the ploughman's repetitive activity, in which he enters a kind of agricultural trance. He 'dreams' with a passing gull, experiences 'quiet ecstasy / Like a prayer' in the 'Tranquillity' of the field. Kavanagh's ploughman is beatific, to the point where ploughing is a religious experience: 'O heart / That knows God!,' he concludes.[5]

Three years later, O'Nolan published his playlet *The Bog of Allen*, in UCD's student magazine *Comhthrom Féinne*.[6] The skit describes 'Allen Bogg's hovel in the middle of the Bog of Allen': 'a typically Irish household', where 'All the bed-clothes, including the blankets, are made of Irish poplin.' The text

---

[5] Patrick Kavanagh, 'Ploughman', in *Collected Poems*, ed. Antoinette Quinn (London: Allen Lane, 2004), 6–7.
[6] 'The bog of Allen', in Flann O'Brien, *Myles before Myles*, ed. John Wyse Jackson (London: Grafton, 1988), 40–3.

amplifies Irishness ('the Wearin' o' the Green is a strict rule in the house') to a surreal degree: 'Below on the floor is a primitive rack, made of bog-oak, for torturing leprechauns who will not divulge where the Crock of Gold is hidden.' The primary target of this parody is John Millington Synge and the perceived domination of the Abbey Theatre by his work and its imitators. O'Nolan's cooing nativist dialogue – 'Anish, now, musha'; 'Beggorah'; 'Ochone!' – signals that Synge is in his sights. But the earliest Kavanagh belongs, broadly speaking, to the bucolic attitude satirized here: unsurprisingly, as he was initially under the wing of the romantic and ruralist George Russell. Animals were central to Kavanagh's farming life, and recur through his early poetry, including the whole poem 'Plough-Horses': 'The tranquil rhythm of that team / Was as slow-flowing meadow stream.'[7] A recurring joke of 'The Bog of Allen' is the appearance of animals on stage. 'In the corner is a bed with a white sow in it' (a forerunner of the pigs in *The Poor Mouth*), and the play ends with six cows sinking the house into the bog. The intimacy of human and farmyard animal is farce in O'Nolan where it is a living, inspiring reality to Kavanagh.

The first relation to be posited between Kavanagh and O'Nolan, then, is a simple enough duality. The poet and the jester, the country and the city, sincerity and irony, reverie and comedy: this pattern can describe the contrast between many of the two writers' works. It is also a significant duality within much modern Irish literature in general: from, say, Lady Gregory and the romantic Yeats against the urban and textualist Joyce, to Beckett's division in 1934 of Irish poets into 'antiquarians and others',[8] and even to the relation between loamy Heaney and ludic Muldoon. It was reconfirmed in the *Irish Times* controversy of 1940, which commenced with Kavanagh's review of a rural novel, but gathered momentum when the newspaper published his poem 'Spraying the Potatoes' on 27 July. The poem vividly recalls a scene of agricultural labour. Kavanagh specifies strains of potato stalk: 'The Kerr's Pinks in a frivelled blue, / The Arran Banners wearing white.' The speaker works with 'barrels of blue potato-spray' and a 'knapsack sprayer', a modicum of technology that is set in a languorous rural realm, a 'headland of July':

> And over that potato-field
> A lazy veil of woven sun.

The poem centres on agricultural work, but also dazzlingly renders rural beauty, scattered with colours and foliage that becomes personified: roses

---

[7] Patrick Kavanagh, 'Plough-Horses', *Collected Poems*, 26.
[8] Samuel Beckett, 'Recent Irish Poetry', in *Disjecta: Miscellaneous Writings and a Dramatic Fragment*, ed. Ruby Cohn (London: John Calder, 1983), 70.

are 'young girls hanging from the sky', dandelions 'showing / Their unloved hearts to everyone'. The poem's close seems to dramatize Kavanagh's new distance from the countryside – 'poet lost to potato fields' – yet insists on the spellbinding powers of memory.[9]

Within 2 days O'Nolan had responded, under no less a guise than 'F. O'Brien'.

> At last, I said to myself, the Irish banks are acknowledging the necessity for hygiene. My eye had lighted on the heading "Spraying the Potatoes" and I had naturally enough inferred that our bank notes were being treated periodically with a suitable germicide, a practice which has long been a commonplace of enlightened monetary science in Australia.[10]

The supposed misunderstanding is strained, as O'Nolan has overlaid Kavanagh's evident literal meaning with a fancifully slangy one, probably with an American source. (He varies the slang definition later in the letter with his observation, not for the last time, that *Gone with the Wind* had won Margaret Mitchell 'many thousands of tons of tubers'.) His version is implicitly urban (banks) to Kavanagh's rural (farms), and crookedly idiomatic to Kavanagh's straightforwardness. The frankly emotional tone of the poem – characteristic enough of Kavanagh – makes O'Nolan's wilful misreading verge on a public insult. Drawing Kavanagh's delicate work of art into the comic cacophony of the letters page violates a generic and tonal boundary, more than the original response to Kavanagh's review had done. O'Nolan does not become much more polite in rectifying his supposed error, upon realizing 'that the heading had reference to some verses by Mr Patrick Kavanagh dealing with the part played by chemistry in modern farming':

> Perhaps the *Irish Times*, tireless champion of our peasantry, will oblige us with a series in this strain covering such rural complexities as inflamed goat-udders, warble-pocked shorthorn, contagious abortion, non-ovoid oviducts and nervous disorders among the gentlemen who pay the rent.[11]

O'Nolan now takes Kavanagh literally – but too literally. He professes to read the poem as a factual guide to farming practices, and his list of future topics places Kavanagh's poem in a series of unsavoury agricultural ills. 'Spraying the

---

[9] Patrick Kavanagh, 'Spraying the Potatoes', *Collected Poems*, 36–7.
[10] F. O'Brien, letter to *Irish Times*, 29 July 1940, reprinted in *Myles before Myles*, 207.
[11] Ibid.

potatoes' was the occasion of Kavanagh's reverie, but potato blight – though a historically resonant topic – was not supposed to be the poem's focus. O'Nolan has thus wrenched Kavanagh's art out of context; affected to miss its literal meaning; reinstated the literal meaning, but read it too pragmatically and non-aesthetically; ignored the poem's beauty and implied instead that its topic tends towards the grotesque; and done all this in a patently artificial tone, conveying an effect of insincerity equal to the sincerity suggested by Kavanagh's verse.

Some other letters also referred to the poem. Jno. O'Ruddy, apparently Niall Montgomery, scornfully asked 'What matters it if Mr Kavanagh leaves his dandelions to grow hoary-headed in his potato-beds.' Lir O'Connor replayed F. O'Brien's reading of 'potatoes' as 'good Runyon' (American slang) but 'very poor Kavanagh', and affected to doubt Kavanagh's existence. Na_2Co_3 reprised O'Brien's pedantically pragmatic reading: 'Mr Kavanagh should severely reprimand his Muse for not having consulted the Department of Agriculture's leaflet on potatoes (sent free on application) before inspiring him.'[12] It is striking that a poem that would become a staple of Irish secondary education began its public life with this transit through a hall of mirrors. A later critic of O'Nolan would interpret the whole correspondence as hostile to Kavanagh, pitting metropolitan irony against his country simplicities with the message 'You are not of our class. You have not had our education.' But Cronin denies that Kavanagh took the japes personally.[13] Of greatest interest is the response with which Kavanagh was finally allowed to bring the correspondence to a close. Only 7 years older than O'Nolan, he assumed the tone of a wise, reflective elder, shaking his head sadly at the empty energy of his comic assailants. He had wondered in his original review about 'the empty virtuosity of artists who were expert in the art of saying nothing'. His almost self-parodically characteristic phrase for such artists was 'Ploughmen without land'. O'Nolan and friends were such figures, and Kavanagh asserted that their condition was a tragedy.[14] This was one way to recast the rural / urban opposition. By this metaphor, Kavanagh's university-educated interlocutors lack the very thing that Kavanagh had possessed, and had made poetry from. By now, he too literally lacked 'land': he would spend most of his life in rickety Dublin digs. But his metaphor perhaps implied that his background had bequeathed him a poetic substance that his erudite juniors would never now gain.

---

[12] See *Myles before Myles*, 209, 212, 221.
[13] See Cronin, *No Laughing Matter*, 110.
[14] Patrick Kavanagh, letter to *Irish Times*, 7 August 1940, reprinted in *Myles before Myles*, 225–6.

Counter-pastoral

Kavanagh had thus complicated the binary opposition and turned it on his mockers. Yet the opposition, by now, was hardly so simple in any case. For one thing, Kavanagh's poetry had often shown a looseness and irreverence that stretched any simple pastoral model. The ambiguous ending of his famous 'Inniskeen Road: July Evening' –

> A road, a mile of kingdom, I am king
> Of banks and stones and every blooming thing

– is an instance, with its suggestion of exasperation at the empty countryside.[15] But the complication was deeper than this. Kavanagh had written pastoral, but by the 1940s he was no sponsor of the national self-image. He now wrote counter-pastoral. 'Stony Grey Soil' was published in the first issue of *The Bell* (October 1940), to which O'Nolan also contributed a report from the Dublin dog track. The poem strikes down the happy identification with the land found in some earlier poems. It may be taken as a retraction of 'Ploughman' a decade on:

> You told me the plough was immortal!
> O green-life-conquering plough!

The poet blames the soil of Monaghan itself for the mystification and for damaging his life – 'You burgled my bank of youth!'[16] But in his long poem *The Great Hunger* (1942) it is not merely the soil that is accused, but Irish society. The poem's fourteen sections circle the life of the potato farmer Patrick Maguire, whose life has been ruined by fear of sexuality and emotional involvement. Obeying his aged mother for decades, he has dedicated his energies to working farmland that has yielded him scant satisfaction. Kavanagh varies poetic forms, winding in and out of metres and rhyme schemes as his poem repeatedly resets its sights and formal bearings. The overall effect remains of an extraordinary, perhaps unprecedented challenge within Irish poetry: a poem that reaches at will for unlikely rhymes or sudden shifts of gear, while starkly maintaining its scorn for the country's shibboleths. The poem retains a place for lyrical appreciation of nature –

---

[15] Patrick Kavanagh, 'Inniskeen Road: July Evening', *Collected Poems*, 15.
[16] Patrick Kavanagh, 'Stony Grey Soil', *Collected Poems*, 38–9.

> Going along the river at the bend of Sunday
> The trout played in the pools encouragement
> To jump in love though death bait the hook[17]

– along with its repeated glimpses of unattainable female beauty. But the pastoral impulse, here, has been betrayed by social convention; nature's abiding bounty cannot compete with life's limitations.

The Great Hunger was contemporary with two major counter-pastorals by O'Nolan. One, of which Kavanagh could have no inkling, was *The Third Policeman*. The novel's estranged depiction of the Irish Midlands as Hell is comparable, in a sense, to Kavanagh's project, which pictures Maguire still conscious in his coffin, surrounded by 'wet clod' and opening his eyes 'once in a million years'.[18] The novel's cyclicality is also echoed in the poem, which commences with a hillside scene, tracks away from it and returns to it in the last section; and which sounds a doom-laden sense of the repetition of seasons and social rituals. More concretely still, Maguire

> ... would have changed the circle if he could,
> The circle that was the grass track where he ran.
> Twenty times a day he ran round the field
> And still there was no winning post where the runner is cheered home.[19]

The peasant, Kavanagh writes in more general terms,

> ... is tied
> To a mother's womb by the wind-toughened navel-cord
> Like a goat tethered to the stump of a tree –
> He circles around and around wondering why it should be.[20]

'Hell goes round and round,' O'Nolan had thought of calling his second novel. *The Great Hunger* does not rival its dizzying invention, but in their different ways both texts make the Irish countryside – so often revered in literature – into a place of recurrent dread.

The Great Hunger can be satirical, but is explicitly tragic. Kavanagh came to disparage the poem on this score, reckoning tragedy 'underdeveloped Comedy, not fully born'.[21] That accusation cannot be levelled at O'Nolan's

---

[17] Patrick Kavanagh, 'The Great Hunger', *Collected Poems*, 76.
[18] Kavanagh, 'Great Hunger', 88.
[19] Ibid., 70.
[20] Ibid., 86.
[21] Patrick Kavanagh, 'Author's Note' to *Collected Poems* (1964), in *Collected Poems*, ed. Quinn, 292.

second major counter-pastoral: *The Poor Mouth*. Kavanagh's quietly despairing Maguire is matched by O'Nolan's Bonaparte O'Coonassa, a peasant of open heart and low intelligence. O'Nolan's Corkadoragha, a fictional region on Ireland's Western seaboard, offers abysmal conditions to match Kavanagh's Northern countryside. Between pigs in the bed and endless rain, O'Coonassa is apt to brood upon 'the ill-luck and evil that had befallen the Gaels (and would always abide with them)'.[22] If Kavanagh's epic was the counter-pastoral inversion of a poetic mode in which he had previously been able to partake, O'Nolan's short novel was an affectionate yet devastating parody of Irish peasant memoirs. Both works debilitated the idealization of peasant life: Kavanagh's by suggesting its true pain, O'Nolan's by making a cartoon of it.

Section XIII of *The Great Hunger* strikingly shifts focus from the potato-farmer's life to those who observe him from a distance: 'The world looks on / And talks of the peasant.' Kavanagh pictures motoring tourists who 'stop their cars to gape over the green bank into his fields'. Their view differs from what we have seen thus far:

> The peasant has no worries;
> In his little lyrical fields
> He ploughs and sows[.]

For the amateur anthropologists, the peasantry remains the heart of unspoiled Ireland. This primitivist veneration sees rural life as 'the pool in which the poet dips': 'Without the peasant base civilization must die.' This external view is flatly contradicted by the rest of the poem. Kavanagh wished not only to condemn the conditions of rural life in themselves, but to indicate the mystificatory role that rural life played in versions of Ireland which were, if anything, broadcast from the city. His tourists

> ... touch the roots of the grass and feel renewed
> When they grasp the steering wheels again.[23]

Kavanagh's thought here is notably close to O'Nolan's. *The Poor Mouth*, too, while showing us the haplessness of the Gaels, most keenly satirizes the outsider's view of them. A wealthy visitor from Dublin arrives in Corkadoragha with a recording device, eager to capture Gaelic folklore before it dies out (for its like will never be there again). The locals are glad

---

[22] Myles na gCopaleen, *The Poor Mouth*, trans. Patrick C. Power (London: Flamingo, 1993), 46.
[23] Kavanagh, 'Great Hunger', 85.

to let him buy them spirits 'to remove the shyness and disablement from the old people's tongues', and do not necessarily respond by telling folk tales. The ethnographer is thrilled to take away the grunts of a pig, which is assessed in Berlin: 'they never heard any fragment of Gaelic which was so good, so poetic and so obscure as it'.[24] One joke is the provincials' merciless exploitation of the naive metropolitan. (The same point applies to the Gaelic feis, staged in a later chapter to gain money from visiting 'Gaeligores'.) Another is the idea that the pig's grunts might be taken as Gaelic, which renders the Irish peasantry close to animals. As in *The Great Hunger*, 'The peasant . . . is only one remove from the beasts he drives'.[25] But the deepest jest is that the pig's impenetrability is taken as a measure of cultural value: 'that good Gaelic is difficult but that the best Gaelic of all is well-nigh unintelligible'.[26] The outsiders seek to understand rural life, but are most impressed by it when it is most alien. The untranslatability of the peasant is the sign of his value. This makes more likely the drastic misreading dramatized more savagely in *The Great Hunger*.

Bards

Cronin makes a deeply perceptive remark about Kavanagh and O'Nolan. They shared, he notes, a 'proprietorial claim' on Ireland, 'to be asserted against politicians and other usurpers'. If this amounted to 'megalomania', then '[it] might also be thought to be something both men had derived, in however inchoate a fashion, from their bardic forebears'.[27] They felt a certain public vocation for the writer: a right to speak out and strike stances about their society, whether or not society was listening.

One practical result of this was that both men wrote reams of copy for the press and magazines. The motive was partly financial necessity. But it clearly also reflected a desire to lead public conversation. O'Nolan began with *Comhthrom Féinne*, satirizing local targets when he was also a dominant voice at UCD's Literary & Historical Society. *Blather*, which he wrote and edited with friends in 1934–35, extensively spoofed public discourse. In *Cruiskeen Lawn*, O'Nolan found a platform from which he could notionally address the whole country, though his actual readership should not be overstated. Aside from *The Bell* and *Envoy*, Kavanagh was also a regular in the

---

[24] Myles na gCopaleen, *The Poor Mouth*, 43–5.
[25] Kavanagh, 'Great Hunger', 85.
[26] Myles na gCopaleen, *The Poor Mouth*, 44.
[27] Cronin, *No Laughing Matter*, 191–2.

Irish Times; film reviewer for the *Catholic Standard*; columnist for the *Irish Press* and the *Irish Farmers' Journal*. Most strikingly, for 3 months in early 1952 Kavavagh and his brother Peter published the eight-page *Kavanagh's Weekly*: an extraordinary, loss-making investment of time and money to allow Kavanagh his own temporary outlet for still more literary and political critique. O'Nolan published in four issues too, as Myles na Gopaleen. It is telling that he used the platform to attack An Tóstal, a festival celebrating traditional Irish culture.[28] If both writers spoke to Ireland, it was never to assert Irishness: more often to deny or undercut it.

Kavanagh's Weekly was blistering about contemporary Ireland. Its first editorial described the 'Victory of Mediocrity' since the foundation of the Free State.[29] Week after week subsequently, the Kavanaghs attacked every instance they could find of corruption and mediocrity: in government, the press, cultural institutions. As Gerry Smyth observes, literary criticism was inseparable from social critique.[30] Kavanagh's fury (supported by his brother) was different from the sparkling comedy which has made Myles famous, but not so different from the more irascible polemic of Myles' later years. Both register an incredulous anger at Ireland's betrayal of itself: an ineluctable postcolonial hegemony of the mediocre and unprincipled. 'Being stupid and illiterate,' Kavanagh declared, 'is the mark of respectability and responsibility' in modern Ireland.[31] Displays of Irishness only worsened the situation. Kavanagh could make this sociologically specific, arguing that Protestants like Synge had painted on their Irishness as over-compensation for feeling foreign. But the point extended to all who now sought advancement through 'bucklepping'. In a 1947 review Kavanagh could assert that 'Ireland' was a 'myth and illusion', and that the 'Irishman' 'mystically, or poetically, does not exist'. His editors complained that his point was a sectarian one, scored against the Protestant F. R. Higgins. Kavanagh thus appended a note:

> Who wants to be an Irish writer?
> A man is what he is, and if there is some mystical quality in the Nation or the race it will ooze through his skin. . . . National characteristics are superficial qualities and are not the stuff with which the poet deals.[32]

---

[28] Myles na Gopaleen, 'How Are You Off For Tostals?', *Kavanagh's Weekly* 1, 5 (10 May 1952), 4.
[29] Patrick Kavanagh, 'Victory of Mediocrity', *Kavanagh's Weekly* 1, 1 (12 April 1952): 1.
[30] Gerry Smyth, *Decolonisation and Criticism* (London: Pluto, 1998), 105.
[31] Kavanagh, 'Victory of Mediocrity'.
[32] Patrick Kavanagh, 'The Gallivanting Poet', *Irish Writing*, November 1947, reprinted in Peter Kavanagh, *Sacred Keeper: A Biography of Patrick Kavanagh* (The Curragh: Goldsmith Press, 1979), 162–5.

As Antoinette Quinn observes, Kavanagh's position is analogous to Wole Soyinka's critique of Negritude: 'A tiger does not proclaim its tigritude.'[33] Myles na gCopaleen was equally impatient: 'I know of no civilisation to which anything so self-conscious could be indigenous. Why go to the trouble of proving that you are Irish? Who has questioned this notorious fact? If, after all, you are not Irish, who is?.'[34] Both writers would posthumously become, to a degree, icons of Ireland, familiar sights of its literary tourist industry. It is thus striking that both were ferociously critical of any self-conscious performance of nationality. The role of the twentieth-century bard was not to sing of Irishness, but to expose its more enthusiastic manifestations as a demeaning delusion.

Human comedy

Kavanagh came to spurn tragedy, claiming comedy as the true goal. He ought logically to have envied a man who could write: 'The brother says the seals near Dublin do often come up out of the water at night-time and do be sittin above in the trams.'[35] But as Seamus Heaney would remark, Kavanagh's comedy really meant 'something broader, something closer to the French *comédie humaine*' than the wit in which Myles was matchless.[36] Kavanagh would view as a turning point his recuperation from lung cancer in 1955. He now declared himself released into happy carelessness, both emotional and formal. 'Lines Written on a Seat on the Grand Canal, Dublin' is the most celebrated demonstration of this mood. Its casually imprecise adjectives ('so stilly / Greeny') and complacent repetition ('water, / Canal water preferably') complement its air of letting go (the whole poem, while relishing life, accepts the prospect of death) and modest demands (a functional bench will suffice in place of a 'hero-courageous / Tomb').[37] Kavanagh issued a stream of kindred poems which acted as their own manifestos: 'wallow[ing] in the habitual, the banal'; 'No System, no Plan', 'Let words laugh'.[38]

---

[33] Antoinette Quinn, 'Patrick Kavanagh: Poetry and Independence', in *Selected Poems*, ed. Patrick Kavanagh (Harmondsworth: Penguin, 1996), xxviii.
[34] Flann O'Brien, *At War*, ed. John Wyse Jackson (London: Duckworth, 1999), 145.
[35] Myles na gCopaleen, *The Best of Myles*, ed. Kevin O'Nolan (London: Picador, 1977), 53.
[36] Dennis O'Driscoll, *Stepping Stones: Interviews with Seamus Heaney* (London: Faber and Faber, 2008), 112.
[37] Patrick Kavanagh, 'Lines Written on a Seat on the Grand Canal, Dublin', *Collected Poems*, 227.
[38] Patrick Kavanagh, 'Canal Bank Walk' and 'Mermaid Tavern', *Collected Poems*, 224, 240.

At a stretch, Kavanagh's late 'rebirth' could be likened to O'Nolan's Indian summer, from the republication of *At Swim* to *The Saints Go Cycling In*. Both were in worsening health, both returned to successful publication. O'Nolan's first novels in 20 years were matched by Kavanagh's first new book of verse in over a decade, and by new collected editions of his prose and poetry. Yet in truth Kavanagh's late flourish was the more rewarding, and more amenable to consideration under the rubric encouraged by Edward Said, of a 'late style' which might creatively burst the banks of an earlier aesthetic.[39] His late poetry alternates sensuality, theology, everyday modernity, in an open form akin to the Beat poets he had met on a trip to the United States. '[T]he only men in America that are alive are men like Jack Kerouac,' he declared at an Illinois symposium, as roundly opinionated about a foreign country as his own.[40] The poetic result was a more productive response to the dawning Lemass era than O'Nolan managed. Kavanagh, four or five decades after the heroic phase of Irish modernism, found forms of verse that let him embrace life in a still changing Irish society. In this respect, O'Nolan's peerless parodies of pastoral did not necessarily have the last laugh. But both writers had long struggled quixotically against the cant and limitations that they found in Ireland. Profoundly different, their projects could yet be curiously parallel. As scholarship of O'Nolan becomes more historically detailed and concerned to reconstruct his cultural contexts, it can echo Kavanagh's lines:

> Gods of the imagination bring back to life
> The personality of those streets,
> Not any streets
> But the streets of nineteen-forty.[41]

---

[39] See Edward Said, *On Late Style: Music and Literature Against the Grain* (London: Bloomsbury, 2006).
[40] Quoted in James Liddy, *The Doctor's House: An Autobiography* (Cliffs of Moher: Salmon Publishing, 2004), 75.
[41] Patrick Kavanagh, 'I Had a Future', *Collected Poems*, 186.

8

Flann O'Brien's *Ulysses*: Marginalia and the Modernist Mind

Dirk Van Hulle

In a special issue of *The Review of Contemporary Fiction* devoted to Flann O'Brien, the editors Neil Murphy and Keith Hopper noted that 'the traditional view of O'Nolan as a "lesser Joyce" seems set to change'.[1] And in a piece on 'The Flann O'Brien Centenary' in *The New Yorker* of 23 September 2011, Mark O'Connell referred to Edna O'Brien's suggestion that 'along with Joyce and Beckett, Flann O'Brien constitutes our trinity of great Irish writers' – with Joyce serving as the dominant Father, Beckett as the suffering Son and Flann O'Brien as 'the shape-shifting Holy Comic Spirit'.[2] For this essay, I propose another constellation, treating Flann O'Brien as a proper star and examining the 'parallax' with Joyce and Beckett in order to measure the distance of this star. The aim is to show that Flann O'Brien, in a similar way as Joyce and Beckett, prefigured a new model of the mind, which – in cognitive sciences – is currently being referred to as the 'extended mind'. A short introduction to enactive cognition is therefore in order, before discussing this trinity of authors.[3]

Literary modernism is famous for its evocations of the fictional mind. By means of techniques such as 'interior monologue' or 'stream of consciousness', modernist texts – according to the 'critical commonplace'[4] – invite readers to 'enter' the minds of their characters. This notion of 'entering' the mind is based on a Cartesian model that presents the mind as an interior space,

---

[1] Neil Murphy and Keith Hopper, 'Editors' Introduction: A(nother) Bash in the Tunnel', *The Review of Contemporary Fiction* 31, 3 (2011): 13.
[2] Mark O'Connell, 'The Flann O'Brien Centenary', *The New Yorker*, 23 September 2011, www.newyorker.com/online/blogs/books/2011/09/the-flann-obrien-centenary-1.html.
[3] This essay develops an argument I explore in Chapter 7 of *Modern Manuscripts: The Extended Mind and Creative Undoing from Darwin to Beckett and Beyond* (London: Bloomsbury, 2014).
[4] David Herman, 'Re-Minding Modernism', in *The Emergence of Mind: Representations of Consciousness in Narrative Discourse in English*, ed. David Herman (Lincoln: University of Nebraska Press, 2011), 249.

an inside that can clearly be distinguished from an outside, based on the mind/body split. This inside/outside model has recently been questioned in cognitive sciences, notably by means of the notion of the extended mind, introduced by Andy Clark and David J. Chalmers.[5] According to this post-Cartesian paradigm, cognitive processes do not exclusively take place in the head, but in constant interaction with an external environment. This two-way interaction is regarded as a cognitive system in its own right. 'Radical enactivism' goes further and suggests that the mind is not just 'extended' but 'exten*sive*' and that 'basic minds are fundamentally, constitutively already world-involving'.[6] My suggestion is that several modernist and late modernist authors have intuitively applied this model of the 'extensive mind' in their works – suggesting that the so-called 'inward turn'[7] of twentieth-century literature is a somewhat inappropriate term. The hypothesis is that many twentieth-century writers either intuitively or consciously exploited the interaction with their books, notebooks and manuscripts to stimulate creative cognitive processes.[8] Their awareness of this mechanism, based on their own experience as thinkers on paper, is part of their view on the human mind and plays a considerable role in their methods of evoking the workings of characters' minds in their writings. To investigate this hypothesis, I propose to examine Joyce, O'Brien and Beckett's libraries and the way they can play a role in the evocation of characters' minds.[9]

Joyce and Bloom's books

On Leopold Bloom's 'two bookshelves' in *Ulysses* (1922), among the 'several inverted volumes improperly arranged',[10] there is a book called '*The Story*

---

[5] Andy Clark and David J. Chalmers, 'The Extended Mind', *Analysis* 58 (1998): 10–23.
[6] Daniel D. Hutto and Erik Myin, *Radicalizing Enactivism: Basic Minds without Content* (Cambridge, MA: The MIT Press, 2013), 137.
[7] Erich von Kahler, *The Inward Turn of Narrative*, trans. Richard Winston and Clara Winston (Princeton: Princeton University Press, 1973).
[8] Richard Menary, 'Writing as Thinking', *Language Sciences* 5 (2007): 621–32.
[9] For Joyce's library, this essay builds on research by studies such as Thomas E. Connolly's *The Personal Library of James Joyce: A Descriptive Bibliography* (Buffalo, NY: The University of Buffalo, 1955) and Patrick Gillespie's *Inverted Volumes Improperly Arranged: James Joyce and His Trieste Library* (Ann Arbor: University of Michigan Press, 1980). To examine Flann O'Brien's books, I consulted his personal library at the Burns Library in Boston College, especially his copy of Joyce's *Ulysses*. And as to Beckett's library, Mark Nixon and I studied the books that are still preserved, mainly in the author's apartment in Paris; see Dirk Van Hulle and Mark Nixon, *Samuel Beckett's Library* (Cambridge: Cambridge University Press, 2013).
[10] James Joyce, *Ulysses*, ed. Hans Walter Gabler with Wolfhard Steppe and Claus Melchior (London: The Bodley Head, 1986), 581 (episode 17, line 1358).

of the Heavens by Sir Robert Ball', which Bloom associates with the word 'parallax' (cf. infra).[11] Joyce uses parallax to make a connection between Stephen Dedalus and Leopold Bloom. They both see the same cloud from a different perspective. In both cases, the cloud serves as an environmental stimulus that sets off a series of thoughts in the fictional minds of the two protagonists. After seeing the cloud, Stephen's thoughts wander off to his mother's deathbed.[12] When Bloom sees the cloud covering the sun, this environmental circumstance immediately results in equally gloomy thoughts, but his stream of consciousness is additionally marked by an extra environmental impulse, 'a bent hag' whom he sees crossing the street. This gloomy stream of consciousness contains the phrase 'the grey sunken cunt of the world' (which will become relevant to the marginalia in O'Brien's copy of *Ulysses*; cf. infra):

> A cloud began to cover the sun wholly slowly wholly. Grey. Far.
> No, not like that. A barren land, bare waste. Vulcanic lake, the dead sea: no fish, weedless, sunk deep in the earth. . . . *A bent hag crossed from Cassidy's clutching a noggin bottle by the neck.* . . . Dead: an old woman's: the grey sunken cunt of the world.[13]

The same cloud conjures up different memories and connotations in the two protagonists' minds. Stephen sees it as a 'trivial incident'[14] followed by an epiphany, connected to a memorable phase of the mind, as he defined the notion of epiphany in Chapter XXV of *Stephen Hero* – a 'sudden spiritual manifestation, whether in the vulgarity of speech or of gesture or in a memorable phase of the mind itself'.[15] Bloom's perception of the cloud sets off a train of thought that interacts more readily with his cultural and material circumstances – in this case a bent hag crossing the street. Stephen's and Bloom's separate perceptions could be regarded as representing two different models of the mind. Stephen's (especially the younger Stephen's) perception is mainly associated with model *A: Epiphanies*; Bloom's perception generally

---

[11] Beckett's library also contains a book that shows marks of an interest in 'parallax': a copy of Pierre Rousseau's *Explorations du ciel* (1939). One of the marked pages is the one on which Rousseau explains the concept of 'parallax' as a technique to measure the distance to the moon. Beckett even tried to calculate a parallax on the back of the book (Van Hulle and Nixon, *Samuel Beckett's Library*, 207–9). His interest in parallax was most probably inspired by Joyce.
[12] Joyce, *Ulysses* (ed. Gabler et al.), 8 (episode 1, lines 248–53).
[13] Ibid., 50 (episode 4, lines 218–28; emphasis added).
[14] James Joyce, *Stephen Hero*, ed. Theodore Spencer, rev. John J. Slocum and Herbert Cahoon (London: Harper Collins and Paladin, 1991), 216.
[15] Joyce, *Stephen Hero*, 216.

shows more characteristics of model *B: The Extended Mind*. These related but distinct models will be considered in turn.

A. *Epiphanies:* In *Stephen Hero*, Stephen's definition of the epiphany is immediately followed by an example relating to the Ballast Office, which 'was capable of an epiphany', as he explains to Cranly: 'I will pass it time after time, allude to it, refer to it, catch a glimpse of it. It is only an item in the catalogue of Dublin's street furniture. Then *all at once* I see it and I know *at once* what it is: epiphany.'[16] There seems to be a discrepancy between Stephen's abstract definition of the epiphany and his concrete example. In the definition, the epiphany is characterized as a sudden spiritual manifestation. The word 'sudden' has prominence of place in the definition. In the example, the same suddenness is expressed by means of the repetition of 'at once'. But to some extent the suddenness is also undermined by this repetition of 'at once' and by the long process that precedes it. According to Scott Berkun, the effect of an epiphany is comparable to the completion of a jigsaw puzzle. The last piece of the puzzle may seem more significant than the others, because it marks the epiphanic moment, but this effect is only due to the pieces that have been put into place before. Instead of the magic moment, Berkun emphasizes 'the work before and after'.[17] Before Stephen's description of how he has the epiphany ('all at once . . . at once'), there is an intermediate explanation that seems to do more justice to 'the work before and after': 'Imagine my glimpses at that clock as the gropings of a spiritual eye which seeks to adjust its vision to an exact focus.'[18] The mind is presented here as a groping process. Instead of an epiphanic moment, the *process* or 'the work before and after' becomes more prominent. By confronting what Stephen *says he does* with what he actually *does*, applying his definition of the epiphany to his own actions, the text suggests that the epiphanic model of the mind is untenable, even while Stephen is explaining it in front of the Ballast Office, when he has to admit that the clock 'has not epiphanised yet'.[19]

B. *The Extended Mind:* Ever since Stephen employed the Ballast Office as an example, it can no longer be entirely dissociated from the notion of 'epiphany'. When Joyce refers to the Ballast Office in the Lestrygonians episode of *Ulysses*, however, he denies Leopold Bloom an epiphany:

> Mr Bloom moved forward, raising his troubled eyes. Think no more about that. After one. Timeball on the ballastoffice is down. Dunsink time. Fascinating little book that is of sir Robert Ball's. Parallax.[20]

---

[16] Joyce, *Stephen Hero*, 216; emphasis added.
[17] Scott Berkun, *The Myths of Innovation* (Sebastopol: O'Reilly Media, 2010), 8.
[18] Joyce, *Stephen Hero*, 216.
[19] Ibid., 218.
[20] Joyce, *Ulysses* (ed. Gabler et al.), 126 (episode 8, lines 108–13).

The 'ball' in 'timeball' reminds Bloom of the copy of the book by Sir Robert Ball on his bookshelves, but this does not lead to an epiphany – on the contrary. Robert Ball's popularizing explanation of parallax apparently failed to enlighten Bloom. Instead of having an epiphany, Bloom admits: 'I never exactly understood.' By now, the example that once served to illustrate the notion of epiphany (the Ballast Office) is employed to illustrate the mental 'work before and after', and with regard to evoking these workings of the fictional mind Joyce seems to have intuited the recent insights of cognitive science in terms of the 'extended' or 'extensive' mind. What is especially interesting in this context of the extended mind is that Joyce introduces a book in this nexus between an intelligent agent and the environments he navigates. Bloom's thoughts do not jump immediately from the timeball to parallax; the transition is made by the explicit mention of the book and the name of its author, *The Story of the Heavens* by Sir Robert Ball.

Flann O'Brien's copy of Joyce's *Ulysses*

The description of 'parallax' in Robert Ball's *The Story of the Heavens* follows after the introduction of Edmond Halley (1656-1742) as the astronomer who drew attention to the importance of the transit of Venus as a method of finding the distance to the sun. To understand the method, Robert Ball needs to explain the notion of 'parallax' first:

> Let us take a simple illustration. Stand near a window. . . . Place on the glass a thin strip of paper vertically in the middle of one of the panes. Close the right eye, and note with the left eye the position of the strip of paper relatively to the objects in the background. Then . . . close the left eye and again observe the position of the strip of paper with the right eye. You will find that the position of the paper on the background has changed. . . . This apparent displacement of the strip of paper, relatively to the distant background, is what is called parallax.
>
> Move closer to the window, and repeat the observation and you find that the apparent displacement of the strip increases. Move away from the window, and the displacement decreases.[21]

This description shows some resemblances with the passage in Chapter 2 of Flann O'Brien's *The Third Policeman*, where the narrator enters Old

---

[21] Sir Robert Ball, *The Story of the Heavens* (London, Paris and Melbourne: Cassell, 1892), 151–2.

Mather's house and observes: 'When I reached the floor and jumped noisily down upon it, the open window seemed very far away and much too small to have admitted me.'[22] In 'Beyond the Zone of Middle Dimensions: A Relativistic Reading of *The Third Policeman*', Charles Kemnitz reads this passage as an instruction 'in the most basic concept of relativity: Parallax'.[23] Kemnitz discusses this notion in the context of Einstein's theory of relativity, interpreting the novel as 'a literary appropriation of the language and conceptual models of relativity current during the nineteen-thirties'.[24]

Keith Hopper, however, argues that the link with Einstein reduces the complexity of 'the polyphonic composition of the post-modernist intertext'.[25] He suggests that 'O'Brien garnered his scientific knowledge of parallax from the more populist work *An Experiment with Time*, by J. W. Dunne',[26] more specifically the passage 'Nothing stays fixed to be looked at. Everything is in a state of flux . . . that you enter houses without passing through walls is, of course, one of the most commonplace of happenings in a four-dimensional world.'[27] The word 'parallax' is not mentioned in Dunne's *Experiment with Time*, but of course this does not imply that Dunne's book cannot have played a role. If anything, it implies that the intertextual composition is perhaps even more polyphonic. My suggestion is that Joyce's *Ulysses* may have played a part as well.

The personal library of Brian O'Nolan, preserved at the Burns Library at Boston College, contains a copy of the 2-volume Odyssey Press (Hamburg – Paris – Bologna) edition of Joyce's *Ulysses* (1932). The first volume is signed, first on the front flyleaf ('Brian Nolan' in blue ink, the dot on the i and the o in black ink); then in blue ink on the *faux titre* page ('Brian O Nolan / 1937'); and again on the title page, it also shows a full address in black ink: 'Brian O'Nolan / 21 Watersland Road / Stillorgan, / Co. Dublin'. This first volume contains very few marginalia, and only 'non-verbal codes',[28] for instance, a pencil mark (short horizontal line) next to 'The way of all our old industries'[29]

---

[22] Flann O'Brien, *The Third Policeman* (London: Flamingo/Harper Collins, 1993), 22.
[23] Charles Kemnitz, 'Beyond the Zone of Middle Dimensions: A Relativistic Reading of *The Third Policeman*', *Irish University Review* 15, 1 (1985): 60.
[24] Kemnitz, 'Beyond the Zone', 56.
[25] Keith Hopper, *Flann O'Brien: A Portrait of the Artist as a Young Post-modernist* (Cork: Cork University Press, 1995), 230.
[26] Hopper, *Flann O'Brien*, 232.
[27] J. W. Dunne, *An Experiment with Time* (London: Faber and Faber, 1934), 170–1. James Joyce too read Dunne's *Experiment with Time*, and the 'fourdimmansions' found their way into *Finnegans Wake* (London: Faber and Faber, 1939), 367, line 27.
[28] Heather J. Jackson, *Marginalia: Readers Writing in Books* (New Haven and London: Yale University Press, 2001), 14.
[29] James Joyce, *Ulysses* (Hamburg, Paris, Bologna: Odyssey Press, 1932), 36. See Boston College, Burns Library, catalogue; with many thanks to Amy Braitsch, Bridget Burke and Justine Sundaram.

and a pencil mark next to Mr Deasy's words 'Now I'm going to try publicity. I am surrounded by difficulties, by . . . intrigues, by . . . backstairs influence' (37; ellipses original). A vertical line is drawn next to 'He's coming in the afternoon. Her songs. Plasto's. Sir Philip Crampton's memorial fountain bust. Who was he?' – just before Blazes Boylan's name is mentioned (95). And a slanting pencil score marks the line 'Fleet was his foot on the bracken: Patrick of the beamy brow' (313).

The second volume is more heavily annotated, but it is not certain whether all the annotations are Brian O'Nolan's. Again, the same full address features on the title page of this second volume. A reproduction of 'M. Jacques Blanche's portrait of Mr. James Joyce', torn from a newspaper, is pasted onto the facing verso page. The front flyleaf (recto) shows the inscription 'B. ONolan 1942' in black ink, but also (at the top of the page) another inscription: 'MacD[onagh] / 1934' in blue black ink. Most of the annotations in this second volume are in green ink. For instance, the word *Lacus Mortis* is underlined in green ink in the following passage in the 'Oxen of the Sun' episode, mentioning the word parallax:

> Huuh! Hark! Huuh! Parallax stalks behind and goads them, the lancinating lightnings of whose brow are scorpions. Elk and yak, the bulls of Bashan and of Babylon, mammoth and mastodon, they come trooping to the sunken sea, *Lacus Mortis*.[30]

And an annotation in green ink in the bottom margin reads 'Great grey sunken cunt of the world', a reference to Bloom's thoughts when he saw the cloud covering the sun in the 'Calypso' episode (see above).[31]

There is one annotation in black ink, possibly corresponding to the black ink of the inscription 'B. ONolan 1942': in the 'Circe' episode, the

---

[30] Joyce, *Ulysses* (Odyssey Press), 434.
[31] Most of the annotations in green ink are intratextual references (often just page numbers), indicating internal correspondences and echoes in the book, as well as identifications of characters. For instance, the name of 'Lynch' is written in green ink next to the line 'I wish you could have seen my queen today, Vincent said, how young she was and radiant' (436); 'Milly' is written next to the lines '*Bold bad girl from the town of Mullingar*' (447; underlined in green ink) and '*Photo's papli, by all that's gorgeous*' (448; underlined in green ink). The name 'Penrose' (mentioned in an intervention by Virag in the 'Circe' episode, page 529) is underlined in green ink, with a reference in the bottom margin (also in green ink): 'See Molly's lovers p. 735'. There is one page on which a fuchsia colour pencil was used to make two corrections in the 'Circe' episode. On page 538, '*Kellet's*' (first line) is partially underscored and marked with the comment 'spelt wrong' in the top margin; and seven lines further down, in Bloom's intervention opening with '*(Murmurs lovingly.)* To be a shoefitter in *Mansfield*'s was my love's young dream', the word '*Mansfield*' is partially underlined and corrected: 'recte Manfield's'. The question, however, is how many of these annotations are O'Brien's (see below).

word '*Parallax!*' in Virag's intervention on page 523 is underscored with an undulating line in black ink, and the marginalia in the right margin read: 'Show this gentleman out.' The reference is to the 'Lestrygonians' episode, where the question 'what's parallax?' is followed by the sentence 'Show this gentleman the door.'[32] The paragraph from which it derives opens with a reference to the ball at the ballast office. As mentioned above, it was the homophony of the ballast office's ball and the name of the author of *The Story of the Heavens* that triggered Bloom's mind to make the connection between the timeball, Robert Ball and the notion of parallax (earlier in the same chapter).[33]

In the 'Eumaeus' episode, a vertical line (green ink) is drawn in the left margin next to Stephen's words: 'But I suspect, Stephen interrupted, that Ireland must be important because it belongs to me,'[34] which follows after his retort to Bloom: 'You suspect . . . that I may be important because I belong to the *faubourg Saint-Patrice* called Ireland for short.' One cannot exclude the possibility that these marginalia are someone else's, but whether or not the vertical line is O'Brien's, the marked passage draws attention to interests evident in his own fiction. The reversal (I belong to Ireland / Ireland belongs to me) also resembles Samuel Beckett's evocation of the 'Molloy country', Ballyba. In the manuscript of *L'Innommable* Ballyba is originally referred to with the Irish name for Dublin, 'Baile atha Cliath' (followed by the narrator's disclaimer that he cannot guarantee the correctness of the spelling).[35] The fact that Ballyba recurs in both *Molloy* and *The Unnamable* raises not only the question (as in *Ulysses*) whether the character/narrator belongs to Dublin or the other way round, but also the question of who this character/narrator actually *is*. The 'unnamedness' of the narrator is something he shares with the narrator of *The Third Policeman*. The first-person narrator of *The Third Policeman* is perhaps not unnamable, but he has 'no name'[36] and 'no pronoun' – even though he employs the first-person pronoun to say so: 'I have no pronoun.'[37] And since Beckett's characters such as Molloy, Malone, Mahood, Murphy, Mercier are referred to in *L'Innommable* as the narrator's

---

[32] Joyce, *Ulysses* (ed. Gabler et al.), 137 (episode 8, lines 571–8).
[33] Ibid., 126 (episode 8, lines 108–13).
[34] Joyce, *Ulysses* (Odyssey Press), 640.
[35] The manuscript of *L'Innommable* is preserved in two notebooks, held at the Harry Ransom Center in Austin, Texas. 'Baile atha Cliath' is mentioned on page 5v of the first notebook (MS HRC SB Box 3, Folder 10, 5v); see Samuel Beckett, *L'Innommable / The Unnamable*: A Digital Genetic Edition (Series 'The Beckett Digital Manuscript Project', module 2), ed. Dirk Van Hulle, Shane Weller and Vincent Neyt (Brussels: University Press Antwerp (ASP/UPA), 2013), http://www.beckettarchive.org.
[36] O'Brien, *Third Policeman*, 64.
[37] Ibid., 58.

replacements or 'homuncules',[38] the Chinese boxes effect of narrators 'within' narrators touches upon a matter that is also suggested in *The Third Policeman*:

> A body with another body inside it in turn, thousands of such bodies within each other like the skins of an onion, receding to some unimaginable ultimatum? Was I in turn merely a link in a vast sequence of imponderable beings, the world I knew merely the interior of the being whose inner voice I myself was?[39]

This passage was most probably inspired by Dunne's *An Experiment with Time*:

> How would you define rationally a "*self-conscious*" observer . . . – he must be able to say: This is *my*-"self." And that means that he must be aware of *a "self" owning the "self" first considered*. Recognition of this second "self" involves, for similar reasons, knowledge of a third "self" – and so on *ad infinitum*.[40]

In *The Third Policeman*, this Chinese boxes effect is described very literally in terms of MacCruiskeen's chests within chests, which eventually become invisible.[41] Thierry Robin has aptly described these 'fractal-like hypodiegetic stories and objects' as illustrations of 'the *matryoshka* principle and the impossibility to delve into the essence and signification of things': 'The subject as a stable, reliable, autonomous concept is made impossible. As Keith Hopper says . . ., O'Brien uses anti-Cartesianism as a starting point in his novel.'[42] This 'anti-Cartesian' approach can be linked to what in cognitive sciences is called a 'post-Cartesian' paradigm, which works with the concept of the so-called 'extended' or 'extensive' mind. No matter how many or few of the annotations (discussed above) are O'Brien's, the marginalia show an intensive interplay with Joyce's text and thus illustrate the principle of the extensive mind at work. This form of enactive cognition – not necessarily the individual annotations separately but the marginalia in general, as traces of intelligent agents' interaction with a material and cultural environment – seems to have served as a model for the evocation of his characters' minds.

---

[38] *L'Innommable*, French manuscript, first notebook, MS HRC SB Box 3, Folder 10, 16v.
[39] O'Brien, *Third Policeman*, 118.
[40] Dunne, *Experiment*, 160.
[41] O'Brien, *Third Policeman*, 72–6.
[42] Thierry Robin, 'Representation as a Hollow Form, or the Paradoxical Magic of Idiocy and Skepticism in Flann O'Brien's Works', *Review of Contemporary Fiction* 31, 3 (2011): 37. Robin refers to Hopper, *Flann O'Brien*, 264.

Flann O'Brien is not the only late modernist with this anti-Cartesian or post-Cartesian perspective. It is also noticeable in Beckett's works.

Samuel Beckett's *L'Innommable*

In a letter to Georges Duthuit, Beckett wrote the following parenthesis on 2 March 1949, shortly before he started writing *L'Innommable*: '(odd how I always see things in terms of boxes)'.[43] The notion of seeing things in terms of boxes applies to the M-characters in Beckett's novels: the unnamed narrator in *L'Innommable / The Unnamable* creates the character Mahood and refers to the M-characters in Beckett's previous novels, 'All these Murphys, Molloys and Malones'.[44] One of the books from Beckett's library that played a role in the development of the inquiry into the human mind – which may be regarded as a core theme of *The Unnamable* – was Ernst Cassirer's Introduction to the complete works of Immanuel Kant.[45] From Cassirer's essay, Beckett excerpted the line 'De nobis ipsis silemus'.[46] On the inside of the first of two notebooks containing the manuscript of *L'Innommable*, Beckett noted the motto again, and he subsequently introduced it in the text (on page 44v of the same notebook).[47] The repeated act of excerpting this line emphasizes the apparent impossibility of its content, the impossibility to keep silent about ourselves. This expression of self-consciousness is given shape by means of the characters-within-characters' regression *ad infinitum*, concordant with Dunne's description of self-consciousness and MacCruiskeen's chests within chests in *The Third Policeman*.

This Chinese box-like regression seems to be the homunculus model[48] both O'Brien and Beckett are pushing to extremes in their works of the 1940s. In the

---

[43] Samuel Beckett, *The Letters of Samuel Beckett, vol. II, 1941–1956*, ed. George Craig, Martha Dow Fehsenfeld, Dan Gunn and Lois More Overbeck (Cambridge: Cambridge University Press, 2011), 129.
[44] Samuel Beckett, *The Unnamable*, ed. Steven Connor (London: Faber and Faber, 2010), 14.
[45] Immanuel Kant, *Immanuel Kants Werke*, ed. Ernst Cassirer, vol. 11 (Berlin: Bruno Cassirer, 1921–22).
[46] Marked in the margin and jotted down in the 'Whoroscope' Notebook; see Van Hulle and Nixon, *Samuel Beckett's Library*, 138.
[47] *L'Innommable/The Unnamable*, Beckett Digital Manuscript Project, module 2, www.beckettarchive.org.
[48] This homunculus model is what Daniel C. Dennett refers to as the 'Cartesian theatre', a metaphor of conscious experience that posits a homunculus, which interprets incoming sensory data in its theatre and which would therefore in its turn need a consciousness with another homunculus, whose consciousness would in its turn contain a smaller homunculus etc. See Daniel C. Dennett, *Consciousness Explained* (London: Penguin, 1991), 107.

manuscript of *L'Innommable*, there is actually a *matryoska*-doll-like doodle of a homunculus inside another head, suggesting a *matryoshka* model of the mind similar to MacCruiskeen's chests.[49] With these chests, MacCruiskeen introduces the first-person narrator to the ineluctable modality of the visible – as Joyce might call it – or, more precisely, the ineluctable modality of the almost invisible. The chapter of the boxes closes with a peculiar word that Flann O'Brien may have first encountered in *Ulysses*. Examining this word will bring us by a 'commodius vicus of recirculation'[50] back to *Ulysses* and to the conclusion of this essay.

Conclusion and coda: The parallax Joyce–Beckett–O'Brien

After the exhibition of his chests, MacCruiskeen demonstrates his 'personal musical instrument', whose tones are so high that the average human ear cannot hear its frequencies. 'Now what do you think of that?' he asks the first-person narrator, who answers: 'I think it is extremely acatalectic.'[51] There the chapter ends. In the opening paragraphs of the Proteus episode of *Ulysses*, shortly after Stephen has mentioned the ineluctable modality of the visible, he analyses the line 'Won't you come to Sandymount' as an 'acatalectic tetrameter of iambs'.[52] As Sam Slote notes, 'A catalectic line has an incomplete final foot'[53] – the '-mount' in Sandymount. The adjective 'acatalectic' is a double negative describing a line with a not-incomplete final foot. By telling MacCruiskeen that his tricks are 'extremely acatalectic', the first-person narrator thus seems to admire their infinitesimal quality, or the fact that they are 'not-incomplete' to the extreme.

But most probably the word 'acatalectic' in *Ulysses* is simply the result of a copying mistake.[54] That would make it quite suitable to characterize MacCruiskeen's tricks. In general, Flann O'Brien's use of the Joycean reference at the end of Chapter 5 in *The Third Policeman* is appropriate since it concerns

---

[49] Dirk Van Hulle and Shane Weller, *The Making of Samuel Beckett's* L'Innommable/The Unnamable (Brussels/London: University Press Antwerp/Bloomsbury, 2014), 160.
[50] Joyce, *Finnegans Wake*, 3.
[51] O'Brien, *Third Policeman*, 77.
[52] Joyce, *Ulysses* (ed. Gabler et al.), 31 (episode 3, lines 17–24).
[53] James Joyce, *Ulysses*, with annotations by Sam Slote (Richmond, Surrey: Alma Classics, 2012), 568.
[54] Not all editions have the reading 'Acatalectic'. The 2012 Alma Classics edition with annotations by Sam Slote, based on the 1939 Odyssey Press edition, reads 'A catalectic tetrameter', which seems to be what the Rosenbach fair copy and the manuscript read as well (second draft, Buffalo V.A.3, 1r).

the 'ineluctable modality' of the (in)audible music from MacCruiskeen's instrument. On the opening page of Chapter 6, MacCruiskeen is called 'a menace to the mind'.⁵⁵ Flann O'Brien seems to poke fun at the internalist model of the mind when he makes the Sergeant insist three times on the internal aspect of his mind, as he asks MacCruiskeen for the readings in order that he can 'make mental comparisons *inside* the *interior* of [his] *inner* head'.⁵⁶ Later on, the same Sergeant tells the narrator that one should 'widen out' the mind: '"It does a man no harm," the Sergeant remarked pleasantly, "to move around a bit and see things. It is a great thing for widening out the mind. A wide mind is a grand thing, it nearly always leads to farseeing inventions."'⁵⁷ This 'widening out' of the mind (typographically illustrated by the narrator's numerous extensive footnotes on De Selby) arguably prefigures the philosophical suggestion that the mind is extended or extensive.

So, in terms of the parallax Joyce–Beckett–O'Brien we have done what Sir Robert Ball advised us to do: to measure the distance of the star O'Brien, we placed on the window a thin strip of paper vertically in the middle of one of the panes; we put an eye patch over the left eye to look at O'Brien from a Joycean perspective. We then closed the right eye and again observed the position of the strip of paper, this time from a Beckettian perspective. And I think we can safely conclude that the distance to Flann O'Brien is much smaller than expected. However, I do have to add an important disclaimer – by way of a coda.

Part of this conclusion is based on Flann O'Brien's/Brian O'Nolan's copy of Joyce's *Ulysses*. Apart from their bibliographical value, the marginalia in this copy inevitably also constitute a constant reminder of O'Brien's (Myles na gCopaleen's) column in the *Irish Times*, notably his series of pieces that started as a reaction against 'Waama', the Irish Writers, Actors, Artists, Musicians Association. One of the pieces, 'Buchhandlung', is about 'a man of great wealth and vulgarity' who 'bought several book-cases and paid some rascally middleman to stuff them with all manner of new books'.⁵⁸ When the columnist noticed that they looked as if none of them had ever been opened, he came up with the idea of a book-handler. 'Why should a wealthy person . . . be put to the trouble of pretending to read at all? Why not a professional book-handler to go in and suitably maul his library for so-much per shelf?' Myles suggests four types of handling:

---

[55] O'Brien, *Third Policeman*, 78.
[56] Ibid., 106; emphasis added.
[57] Ibid., 134.
[58] Myles na Gopaleen, *The Best of Myles: A Selection from 'Cruiskeen Lawn'*, ed. Kevin O Nolan (London and Sydney: Picador/Pan Books, 1978), 17.

1. 'Popular Handling – Each volume to be well and truly handled, four leaves in each to be dog-eared, and a tram ticket, cloak-room docket or other comparable article inserted in each as a forgotten book-mark.'[59]
2. 'Premier Handling – Each volume to be thoroughly handled, eight leaves in each to be dog-eared, a suitable passage in not less than 25 volumes to be underlined in red pencil, and a leaflet in French on the works of Victor Hugo to be inserted as a forgotten book-mark in each.'[60]
3. 'De Luxe Handling – Each volume to be mauled savagely, the spines of the smaller volumes to be damaged in a manner that will give the impression that they have been carried around in pockets . . ., not less than 30 volumes to be treated with old coffee, tea, porter or whiskey stains, and not less than 5 volumes to be inscribed with forged signatures of the authors.'[61]

And finally,

4. 'Le Traitement Superbe', which implies that 'suitable passages in not less than 50 per cent of the books [are] to be underlined in good-quality red ink and an appropriate phrase . . . inserted in the margin', such as: 'Rubbish!', 'Yes, indeed!', 'How true, how true!', 'Nonsense, nonsense!', 'I remember poor Joyce saying the very same thing to me.'[62]

In conclusion, we cannot exclude the possibility that the empirical evidence for this research – preserved at Boston College – was faked or 'handled'. But even if that were the case, I think we must admit that faking marginalia in one's copy of *Ulysses* would be the work of a 'wide mind' and that the treatment that was given to *Ulysses* was 'Le Traitement Superbe'.

---

[59] *Best of Myles*, 19.
[60] Ibid.
[61] Ibid.
[62] Ibid., 20–1.

9

'Truth is an Odd Number':
Flann O'Brien and Infinite Imperfection

Baylee Brits

> *The Pooka MacPhellimey, a member of the devil class, sat in his hut in the middle of a firwood meditating on the nature of the numerals and segregating in his mind the odd ones from the even.*[1]

> *A number of miracles were wrought as one and together*[2]

This chapter looks at the curious preoccupation with numerology in Flann O'Brien's novel *At Swim-Two-Birds*, in particular, the numerical system of 'Good' and 'Evil' numerals that governs the lives of certain of the characters. At first the subversions of numeracy in O'Brien's work appear as mere anti-scientific hilarity, but when read more widely in terms of the persistent comminglings between antitheses in the novels, the numerical transgressions emerge as much more sophisticated recognitions of the speculative dimension that literature shares with science and mathematics. This idea of good or evil numbers comes from an assertion in the book made by the Pooka McPhellimey, who lives his life as 'a member of the devil class'[3] according to an unorthodox numerical system: 'Evil is even, truth is an odd number, and death is a full stop.'[4] The 'Pooka' or 'An Púca' is an ambiguous figure from Irish mythology. The term 'often designates a solitary bogey' who can shape shift[5] (Correll, 16) and who may help or hinder humans at whim. For the Pooka in O'Brien's novel, 'Number One' is the prime truth and fount of goodness and it is from Number One that the Pooka takes

---

[1] Flann O'Brien, *The Complete Novels* (New York: Alfred A. Knopf, 2007), 5.
[2] Ibid., 174.
[3] Ibid., 5.
[4] Ibid., 215.
[5] Timothy Correll, 'Believers, Sceptics, and Charlatans: Evidential Rhetoric, the Fairies, and Fairy Healers in Irish Oral Narrative and Belief', *Folklore* 116, 1 (2005): 16.

his orders, but he of course (being a Pooka) is 'Number Two'. As such, his life is lived in accordance with even and thus evil numbers, and he undertakes paired actions, making sure the number of shirt tails he wears are always even or that the pains he inflicts on the character Dermot Trellis are even in number ('A burst eyeball, a crushed ear and bone-breaks two in number . . .'[6]), so as to conform with this numerological principle. The numerical inflection upon the Pooka's evil nature is entirely a creation of O'Brien's, and exemplifies an idiosyncratic knitting together of quantitative and absolute value that contributes to the destabilizing humour of *At Swim-Two-Birds*. Here I will draw out the ways that this manipulation of numbers refracts the composition of the superstitious and the scientific in O'Brien's novels more broadly. I will argue that O'Brien's subversion of numeracy is no simple parody of mathematics or claims to empirical objectivity, but instead establishes a link between modes of fiction and scientific thought that I will describe as 'speculative'. Here I hope to bring this link into relief by isolating the speculative element that occurs in the mixing of incommensurable aspects of experience and knowledge in O'Brien's fiction, which I will characterize as a radicalization of quantification that causes it to lapse into what is supposedly antithetical to quantity: the qualitative. In other words, I hope to point to a shared problem across both metamathematics (as regards the numerical status of infinity, or ∞) and fiction, which will illuminate an alliance rather than incompatibility between O'Brien's work and the sciences. This alliance is concentrated in what I will here call a 'speculative moment' that emerges from both domains. This is a structural comparison between the mathematical infinite and O'Brien's good and evil numbers, which surprisingly reveals agreement where one expects to see antithesis.

O'Brien's work is distinctive for its irreverent engagement with twentieth century science, especially physics: his characters discuss and often disparage theories of time and space, while the narrative worlds patently refuse the hierarchies and metaphysics of the world we call real. O'Brien most famously created the rogue theorist and 'savant' de Selby, who appears first in the novel *The Third Policeman* whose narrator undertakes a lengthy process of indexing the works of de Selby, and then as a major character in *The Dalkey Archive*. De Selby is, as Keith Donohue notes in the introduction to *The Complete Novels*, 'thoroughly mad' and his theories take up twentieth century physics in a vigorous though utterly warped manner that is properly indicated by some of his concepts being homophonous with genuinely scientific ones (the 'mollycule' for instance), but departing

---

[6] O'Brien, *The Complete Novels* (New York: Alfred A. Knopf, 2007), 175.

lexically to indicate that something is fundamentally awry in his thought. De Selby is the arbiter par excellence of truths devoid of relevance or efficacy, tirades devoid of fact, and untrammelled logical fallacy. Theories and speculations regarding metaphysics abound within the conversations of the other characters too, while the form of the novels express their own, often fantastic, forms of temporality: most obviously in the circular form of *The Third Policeman*, and the stacked narratives in *At Swim-Two-Birds*. Twentieth century physics is distinct in the history of science for raising theories (notably special relativity) that defied what had been considered the pillars of the scientific endeavour: the possibility of a single objective viewpoint, with both quantum mechanics and special relativity defying the possibility of a stable account of an atomic event. The figure of de Selby devotes much energy to denigrating these subversive and unimaginable discoveries of physics, most especially the theory of special relativity, but O'Brien's narratives of circular time, and the formal defiance of authorship in his texts run against the grain of the intra-textual discussions of science that preoccupy the characters to affirm precisely the (meta)physical instability that these dialogues on physics often mock. There is a contradiction between form and rant, here, that is telling: it fosters a comfortable quotidian mix of the mad and the scientific that mingle until it becomes difficult to tell the one from the other.

O'Brien's preoccupations with and subversions of quantitative science emerge from two different and historically separated circumstances: superstition and the scientific imagination of early twentieth century physics which presumes to theorize and give account of the elements in the universe that contradict the human experience of time, space and causality (the Big Bang, for instance, being a prime example of a theory from physics that must, in terms of the strictures of phenomenology, be speculative). It is the knotting together of these elements that produces not only part of the comedy of O'Brien, but also a bold imaginative response to the warping of time and space that occurs in the realities that physics and mathematics describe. Here, I use the term 'speculative' in accordance with the definition used by Alfred North Whitehead (leaving aside, in this case, the vastly diverse body of 'speculative' endeavours that have emerged in philosophy over the last 15 years). Whitehead defines speculative thought in the opening to his magisterial *Process and Reality* in terms of a radical phenomenology: 'Speculative Philosophy is the endeavour to frame a coherent, logical, necessary system of general ideas in terms of which every element of our experience can be interpreted. By this notion of "interpretation" I mean that everything of which we are conscious, as enjoyed, perceived, willed, or thought, shall have the character of a particular instance of the general scheme.'[7] This is, admittedly, a systematic, epistemological term in Whitehead's rendering, but one that I feel has resonance for an aesthetics that brings together forms of experience and affect that would usually cleave from each other. Here I am interested in the construction of a narrative (or poetics) rather than a system of 'general ideas', where a narrative incorporates an 'idea' or 'thesis' that contradicts another element of experience. In this case, these 'antithetical elements' of experience are scientific knowledge and the supernatural or divine encounter or mythos, which, as I develop this, will be concentrated down into the quantitative and the qualitative. O'Brien has of course been associated with the literature of the fantastic[8] (O'Connell) as well as the pataphysical[9] (Adams), and in terms of his interest in mental objects and different worlds in fiction, he has been aligned with writers like Jorge Luis Borges and Lewis Carroll.[10] In O'Brien's case, this 'literature of the fantastic' seems to arise from the speculative condition that inheres both in the co-existing but mutually exclusive multiple worlds of Irish mythology and twentieth century science. Perhaps the most important example of this speculative modality in *At Swim-Two-Birds* is the coexistence of an absolute value (good or evil) combined with ordinary quantification – odd and even numerals – in the lives of the Pooka and the Good Fairy. O'Brien's work brings into relief a compossibility between the two of these: which is not to create a shared ground but rather a speculative literary world, where antithetical forms of experience exist side by side. The Pooka, for instance, is but one of many mythical creatures that populate O'Brien's novels. He is woken at the start of *At Swim* by the Good Fairy, who, as the antithesis of the Pooka, is obviously associated with odd numbers. The Good Fairy is invisible but, by virtue of its apparent ability to skate in the Pooka's frying pan, and be carried in the Pooka's pocket, seems to retain some element of grounding in the physical world. The Good Fairy also, despite being an embodiment of absolute value (it is Good in opposition to Evil), has quite a complicated series of hang ups, is characteristically over sensitive (much like

---

[7] Alfred North Whitehead, *Process and Reality* (New York: The Free Press, 1978), 3.
[8] See: Mark O'Connell, 'How to Handle Eternity: Infinity and the Theories of J. W. Dunne in the Fiction of Jorge Luis Borges and Flann O'Brien's The Third Policeman', *Irish Studies Review* 17, 2c (2009): 223–37.
[9] See: Anthony Adams, 'Butter-Spades, Footnotes, and Omnium: The Third Policeman as 'Pataphysical Fiction', *Review of Contemporary Fiction* 31, 3 (2011): 106–19.
[10] O'Connell associates O'Brien with 'literary fiction of the fantastic' and aligns him in this regard with Jorge Luis Borges, and a group of writers that came into contact with Dunne and valued the 'imaginative possibility' rather than scientific acuity of his theoretical work. See: O'Connell, 'How to handle eternity: infinity and the theories of J. W. Dunne in the fiction of Jorge Luis Borges and Flann O'Brien's The Third Policeman', *Irish Studies Review* 17, 2 (2009): 223–37.

the soul, 'Joe' of the narrator in *The Third Policeman*), and at one point even lies (placing a bet in a card game without having money) and must plead with the Pooka to cover for him or her. The disjunction between the status and actual character of the fairy is a source of much comedy, and indeed the novel is filled with such characters that occupy comic positions: flawed and boisterous characters in afflicted bodies. This same disjunction, between mythical or even transcendental figures and materiality, is taken up in the combination of the purely fantastic and convivial reasonableness. Take, for instance, the narrator's friends, whom he consults on his manuscript and who respond by weighing up the plausibility and ingenuity of his narrative: 'This explanation, I am glad to say, gave instant satisfaction and was represented as ingenious by at least one of the inquirers concerned.'[11] There is an equally vigorous (and lengthy) preoccupation with minor details and addenda, which, in the listings of minutiae – '*Minutiae*: No. of cigarettes smoked, average 8.3; glasses of stout or other comparable intoxicant, av. 1.2; times to stool, av. 2.65; hours of study, av. 1.4; spare time or recreative pursuits, 6.63 circulating'[12] – resemble obsessive logical procedures rather than evoking any sense of quotidian realism.

This form – attentive fact checking and reasonable weighting of positions combined with the fantastic – in fact echoes the social colloquy surrounding stories of encounters with fairies. Anthropological accounts characterize rural Irish narratives of encounters with fairies within a register of truth telling and validity, where the moral integrity of the narrator relating an encounter with the fairies would be at stake. These stories are not simply cases of superstition but relate experiences of the supernatural, and as such are weighted with the need for verisimilitude and realism so as to avoid questioning the moral integrity of the speaker (at risk of being a liar, or mad, or impressionable) and also to give credence to the experience. Timothy Correll's anthropological account of 'conjecture concerning the reality of fairies and those believed to derive magical powers from them' situates these narrative events as 'an integral feature of the fireside exchanges of local lore and fairy stories that occurred customarily at wakes, during night visiting at neighbours' houses, and other rural gatherings'[13] (Correll, 3). These stories become significant in terms of the balance between the fantastic and believable: '[these s]ocial occasions that involved the telling of supernatural tales were often forums for considering truth, or colloquies over the nature of reality, in

---

[11] O'Brien, *The Complete Novels* (New York: Alfred A. Knopf, 2007), 143.
[12] Ibid., 147.
[13] Timothy Correll, 'Believers, Sceptics, and Charlatans: Evidential Rhetoric, the Fairies, and Fairy Healers in Irish Oral Narrative and Belief', *Folklore* 116, 1 (2005): 3.

which the validity of fairy beliefs was assessed and debated'.[14] Correll's work affirms and extends Deasun Breatnach's anthropological work on the Púca conclusions, showing how traditional practices of storytelling and belief in fairies was scaffolded by a careful balancing of evidence and the assertions of reasonableness: 'It is not surprising, then, that the moral integrity, lack of superstition, or lucidity of individuals who had uncanny experiences were often presented as part of an evidential rhetoric by narrators who wished to convince their audiences of the veracity of stories they were passing on second- hand.'[15] These stories are fascinating locutionary exercises given that they involve two very significant but seemingly opposed stakes: the moral integrity of the speaker as well as the stability of the world or reality and the balance of this is an appeal to detail and fact; the metaphysical and the moral wrapped up together. This same negotiation is echoed in the mode of reasoned argumentation and the conveyance of facts that O'Brien's characters seem to enjoy and certainly engage in at length. Take, for instance, the extract from a newspaper article relaying the story of the appearance of John Furriskey, a character created by the preposterous process of 'aestho-autogamy', which is basically the creation of a fictional character literalized, so that the character walks, talks and influences the world of the writer, Dermot Trellis. Furriskey is 'Stated to be doing "very nicely," [and] the new arrival is about 5 feet 8 inches in height, well built, dark, and clean-shaven. The eyes are blue and the teeth well formed and good, though stained somewhat by tobacco; there are two fillings in the molars of the left upperside and a cavity threatened in the left canine.'[16] Without properly founding the science behind Furriskey's birth, this extract appeals to publicly accepted facts and figures, and provides a variety of details that establish Furriskey as a 'real' character. This is realism doubled over: the instance of verisimilitude insisted upon in a world that defies ontic and metaphysical norms. This is a recurring comic form in O'Brien, and later the same effect is produced when the Good Fairy and the Pooka engage in extensive and jovial reasoned argumentation even though much of it does not make sense: it is a perfect example of *senseless* reason, the assertion of a reasonableness despite radical ontic and metaphysical defiance of reason and realism. These rogue combinations of reasonableness and unreason echo those stories of encounters with fairies that are rendered by careful collation of facts and plait the senseless or the supernatural together. The final standoff between the Pooka and Trellis is perhaps the climax of this contradictory form: 'In addition to his person, his room was also the

---

[14] Ibid.
[15] Ibid., 5.
[16] O'Brien, *The Complete Novels* (New York: Alfred A. Knopf, 2007), 36.

subject of mutations unexplained by any purely physical hypothesis and not to be accounted for by mechanical devices relating to the manipulation of guy-ropes, pulley-blocks, or mechanical collapsible wallsteads of German manufacture, nor did the movements of the room conform to any known laws relating to the behaviour of projectiles as ascertained by a study of gravitation enforced by calculations based on the postulate of the science of ballistics.'[17] Here, the insistent polite and convivial language and excessive length of the sentence enforces the ridiculousness of the situation. The overarching tone of both these forms of rhetoric is one that connects such argumentation to the upstanding character of the speaker, affect overriding epistemology.

The existence of these fantastic or mythical creatures and their personal concern with verisimilitude or reasonableness in *At Swim-Two-Birds* appears in parallel with the fantastic conception of writers and their characters that undergirds the narrator's theories of literary practice. *At Swim-Two-Birds* revolves around one writer writing about another writer: the narrator is writing a novel about Dermot Trellis, who himself 'is writing a book on sin and the wages attaching thereto',[18] with the intention of creating a character so depraved as to jolt the audience into becoming upstanding moral subjects. As mentioned above, the writer (who is also a character) Dermot Trellis creates the central character for the book he is working on – a man named John Furriskey who is supposed to be the epitome of evil – through the process of aestho-autogamy, which is the (mysteriously low on detail) process of creating a live character who has no clear maternity, paternity or infancy, rather appearing as a fully grown adult, complete with somewhat outdated clothing and a smoking habit: 'There was nothing unusual in the appearance of Mr John Furriskey but actually he had one distinction that is rarely encountered – he was born at the age of 25 and entered the world with a memory but without a personal experience to account for it. His teeth were well-formed but stained by tobacco, with two molars filled and a cavity threatened in the left canine. His knowledge of physics was moderate and extended to Boyle's Law and the Parallelogram of Forces.'[19] The theory of fiction and literary history that accompanies this is quite quickly made explicit in one of the narrator's excerpts on his craft: 'Characters should be interchangeable as between one book and another. The entire corpus of existing literature should be regarded as a limbo from which discerning authors could draw their characters as required, creating only when they

---

[17] Ibid., 174.
[18] Ibid., 31.
[19] Ibid., 5.

failed to find a suitable existing puppet.'[20] The inclusion of such theorizing facilitates an unravelling of the tale in anticipation of the critic, and auto-theorizing of the form of the novel within the novel. The Pooka and the Good Fairy are thus placed on a continuum of the fantastic that includes both products of the imagination, however realistic, as well as human figures from Irish mythology (though often, in their actions, equally out of the ordinary). This does something curious to the practice of fiction writing: it places mental products and irreality on the same plane, associating novelistic narrative with the characters that ordinarily populate superstition.

What these forms emphasize is the sense of reason without reason proper, that is, the uncrossable divide between reason and 'reasonableness'. That is, the experience of something and its actual factual status. It is precisely this alliance of reasonableness with the fantastic that does not defy a genuine link with science, but rather fosters it. This form, against expectation, opens O'Brien's work to connections with and stakes in numerals on multiple different levels, most notably around the fraught concept of infinity. Like the Pooka's 'good and evil' numerals, historically the concept of infinity incorporates contradictory aspects of the quantitative and the qualitative, which warp together under the elusive character of the concept: infinity, by nature, recedes from knowledge; the concept, like a quantum particle, jumps away from its own definition. The historian of mathematics Morris Kline explained the distinction between mathematical signs and natural language signs in terms of mathematical abstraction and the mental existence of mathematical entities: 'One of the great Greek contributions to the very concept of mathematics was the conscious recognition and emphasis of the fact that mathematical entities are abstractions, ideas entertained by the mind and sharply distinguished from physical objects or pictures.'[21] It is in this specificity of the activity of mathematics that we start to see the defiance of numerals that will play out most acutely in the recesses of the numeral line. The problem of infinity rests in the disconnect between reason and experience; what is conceivable in our phenomenal world (what may be reasonable) and limits of thought (the points at which reason erodes). Infinity is by no means a neutral territory: it implies a certain philosophy. The stakes in the notion of the infinite are based around whether or not mathematics is a closed system: does the number line end, or does it not? And, moreover, is working with the concept of the infinite merely sophistry, given that humans are finite beings and can never properly arrive at or 'discover' the infinite

---

[20] Ibid., 21.
[21] Morris Kline quoted in: David Foster Wallace, *Everything and More* (New York: W.W. Norton and Company, 2003), 10.

in the way that other mathematical truths can be? By virtue of the fact that infinity is not a number that can itself be worked with, but must rather be commuted to a form called the 'transfinite', it is possible to oppose a theory of the infinite in mathematics and claim that mathematics is a finite system in a host of different ways. This possibility arose from the work of Georg Cantor, who, in 1874 produced 'infinity proofs', and effectively laid the foundations for modern metamathematics that uses transfinite numbers to measure different sizes of infinities. The usual intuitive proof of infinity is the simple 'plus one' thought experiment: for every potential 'last' number that exists, it is perfectly possible to apply the principle of adding one to it, thus generating a new, last number. Like pataphysics, theories of the transfinite and proofs of the infinite can be considered speculative solutions in the sense that they anticipate a fact about something that we can posit but never fully know.[22] Set theory, which Cantor has a significant role in developing, looks at the relation between objects and sets and whether objects are members of sets or subsets; it also provides a universal theory of mathematics (metamathematics) that encompasses all mathematical objects and procedures. In this sense set theory solves the problem of the consistency of mathematics, given that one can demarcate types of numbers, for instance, which behave differently under different laws or circumstances. The set of irrational numbers and the set of integers are separate, for instance, but are both encompassed in the larger set of real numbers. Cantor recognized that the set of integers is infinite, but that, by virtue of being contained in a larger infinite set of numbers – real numbers – it would thereby be a smaller infinity than the infinity of the latter set. As such, Cantor conceived of not one absolute infinite (which would have been perfectly acceptable to his contemporaries and precursors) but infinite infinities of variable sizes.

The idea of multiple infinities was – problematically in Cantor's day – a polytheistic one: to preserve the notion of a monotheistic God as infinity, or the infinite, or the absolute, one would have to posit the notion of an infinity of infinities (taking God up a transcendental notch) which is subject to all the same claims of Cantor's plural infinities. Nevertheless, Cantor was no secularist or polytheist and, with his *Grundlagen einer allgemeinen Mannigfaltigkeitslehre* produced a bizarre philosophy and theology to

---

[22] Adams quotes Alfred Jarry's definition of pataphysics to elaborate Flann O'Brien's own pataphysical form: 'Pataphysics is the science of imaginary solutions, which symbolically attributes the properties of objects, described by their virtuality, to their lineaments'. Alfred Jarry, *Selected Works*, ed. Roger Shattuck and Simon Watson Taylor (London: Eyre Methuen, 1965), 193, quoted in Adams, 'Butter-Spades, Footnotes, and Omnium: *The Third Policeman* as "Pataphysical Fiction"', *Review of Contemporary Fiction* 31, 3 (2011): 108.

accompany his mathematical proofs. For Cantor, his proofs were angelic anyhow: they were delivered to him by God and he was merely a vehicle through which God communicated certain symbolic figurations of the divine. Yet there were many religious objections to Cantor's work. This opposition is perhaps best represented through a historical distinction made by St Thomas Aquinas. According to St Thomas there is an irreconcilability between perfection and infinity, because infinity is always material. In St Thomas' view, the infinite and God could not ever be equated because (although this seems a jarring lapse within St Thomas' thought) the infinite is always a quantification. This is an objection that Cantor's proofs easily counter, quite surprisingly. Infinity is, indeed, the moment at which a quantificatory, analytic mathematics becomes something that necessarily defies quantification: becomes, by eluding the mathematician and by being that which leaks out of the net of mathematics, a qualitative sign that only blasphemously occupies the status of numeral.

It is here that we start to see an integration of the quantitative and the qualitative that is comparable to the subversive mixing of these two opposed senses in Flann O'Brien's work. For the Pooka, the number one fulfils a sort of God function: number one is truth and also goodness. The Pooka, being of the devil class, is hence associated with the number two. Number one, however, is not a supreme atomic truth that cannot be separated or broken, but rather its purview extends to all other odd numbers; it has a material instantiation in all the other points on the number line (or fantastic creatures) that are identified as odd (or perhaps that have allegiance, whether ontic or agential, to the good or evil). There are here at least two infinities: good and odd numbers, and evil and even numbers. Within the infinite set of real numbers, therefore, there are at least two value-inflected, binary opposed sets: good and evil numerals. More importantly, however, the absolute that is associated with the odd and even sets is that of good and bad, in the sense that is associated with heaven and hell or angels and devils. This absolute is an absolute of quality, not of quantity. Similarly, when we are confronted with the nuances of the mathematical infinite, we find ourselves arriving at a radicalization of the quantitative that becomes the qualitative.

In this sense it does not seem coincidental that another novel that deals with both mathematics and mythology – John Banville's *The Infinities* – deals with gods who have flawed and angular personalities who have materialized to visit a mathematician on his deathbed, who is also one of their kin. Much is made in Banville's novel of the semi-divine nature of the mathematics of infinity; the part-material, part-transcendental make-up of the gods that Banville creates, and the good or evil mythical creatures of O'Brien's novel, present beings adequate to a world modified by the existence of the lemniscate. Here we begin to see the fictional world as echoing the part-divinity part-materiality that is the imaginative task of infinite mathematics, of post-Cantorian transfinite set theory.

The other key objection to Cantor's transfinite proofs came in the form of a linguistic qualification, which is best represented in the refutation from the German mathematician Carl Friedrich Gauss, who contended that Cantor's proof was illegitimate given that the infinite was not a complete concept but a manner of speaking.[23] As far as Gauss is concerned, the infinite is only a manner of speaking, and hence should be removed from any status as a serious scientific concept. Here, the infinite is gestural, a mannerism, and nothing more. The infinite is in this sense a matter of conversation and not truth and taking the symbolic attribution too far is foolish. Gauss might have argued that we simply cannot prove infinity: we do not know whether we will eventually get to a number that we cannot theoretically add one to, and hence reaching a stopping point. We should not speak of what we do not know is there. Transfinite proofs do not work in a linear fashion: making the same case for every number successively, but set their stakes in both the infinite and the finite, positing 'sizes' of infinities by observing a type of correspondence between numbers known as a bijection. Here is how Cantor negotiates this: 'What I assert and believe to have demonstrated in this and earlier works is that following the finite there is a transfinite (which one could also call the supra-finite), that is an unbounded ascending ladder of definite modes, which by their nature are not finite but infinite, but which just like the finite can be determined by well-defined and distinguishable numbers.'[24] Yet, despite the definite modes of the transfinite, on one level, even these numbers cannot properly counter Gauss's objection. Cantor's theory of infinite sets is marred by the fact that knowledge of the infinite is arrived at using premises and proofs that were established to deal with finite sets and problems. One does not know, for instance, where the laws of continuity (with a linear implication) may break down: numbers may start to diminish or rot at certain levels or frequencies, causing a curve in the set and hence, eventually, disrupting the set's identity as infinite. Entropy in extraordinary numerical environments

---

[23] For a discussion of Gauss' objection, cf. Louis Narens, *Theories of Meaningfulness* (Mahwah, NJ: Laurence Erlbaum Associates Inc, 2002), 41.

[24] Georg Cantor, 'Über Unendliche, Lineare Punktmannichfaltigkeiten'. Cf. Cantor, *Gesammelte Abhandlugen mathematischen und philosophischen Inhalts* (1932), ed. Ernst Zermelo (Berlin: Springer, 1966), 174, quoted in Valerie Therrien, 'Wittgenstein and the Labyrinth of "Actual Infinity": The Critique of Transfinite Set Theory', *Ithaque* 10 (2012): 48.

cannot be fully ruled out. There is thus an unholy mixing at work, here: the use of finite means to prove the existence of the infinite, a sign of a fundamentally different order. This problem is equally the problem of the use of quantitative means to prove the qualitative: the logic turns back upon the process of counting to point to the qualitative aspect of what is supposedly an exclusively quantitative procedure. It is this moment that I want to identify as speculative: the moment that two antithetical forms of experience coincide, and in fact exist in a relation of impossible causality.

It is this speculative moment necessary to the assertion of infinity that resonates with the speculative mix of the quantitative and the qualitative in Flann O'Brien's work. And of course this resonance teaches us that there is a moment of compossibility between literature and mathematics where each takes a speculative turn. There is also a lesson here regarding the aesthetic inflexion of the speculative moments in the sciences. The transfinite proof is adequate to establish a knowledge of infinity in the sense that it works with exactly that which recedes from reasonableness to become reason, the quantitative lapse into the qualitative. The aesthetic correlate of this resides in unaccountable truth, the truth that emerges when the repetitive counting finally mutates into quality: good and bad numerals. This is not a divorce between counting and value, but rather the binding of one to the other.

What this comparison makes clear is the canniness of O'Brien's mixing of a supernatural and material world, and of qualitative and quantificatory realms. The humour here is striking because it arrives at the point at which the mathematical turns back on itself, radicalizing the quantitative into the qualitative, and opening up the place at the heart of the mathematical that is speculative, and requires a non-analytical (in the mathematical sense) production of truth. This is where the Pooka's formulations of good and bad numerals stop seeming patently absurd and we see the knotted truth of quantity and quality, the finite and the infinite, and reason and its sense that rings true with mathematics, rather than only staking out a parody of pretensions to reason, or to objectivity. There is also a lesson regarding the aesthetic link to that moment of speculative transformation, or radicalization, depending on how one looks at it. This affective rather than epistemic production of the destabilizing lapse from the quantitative to the qualitative is rooted in the comic combination of opposites that never quite gels together, and in the creation of fiction lives that occupy a quasi-materiality. This not in any simple defiance of science, or an 'anti-mathematics', but rather revels in the place between speculation and verisimilitude, the node at which the two arcs of the lemniscate meet, perhaps. The humour of the contradiction between the divine and perpetual counting is manifest precisely in these very material and banal infinities that we find in the Pooka, the Good Fairy, the cleric Ronan and the king Sweeney. The constant friction between the banal, the bodily, and the supernatural does not make a parody of mathematics, but rather constitutes a recognition of the unexpected links between the elements that have no place in enlightenment and the torsions of the limits of modern mathematics.

10

'An Astonishing Parade of Nullity':
Nihilism in *The Third Policeman*

Rónán McDonald

The values of Brian O'Nolan's work resist tabulation or neat identification. Like his own shifting name, and his puckish refusals of authority, his political and moral ideology seems mercurial, shape-changing, unfixed. O'Nolan's work seems to value the provisionality of value, as much as his famous manifesto on the democracy of character in *At Swim-Two-Birds*. Despite his voluminous prose and opinion pieces, mostly in Myles na Gopaleen's *Irish Times* column, his position or worldview is hard to fix into a clear position, and not only because his civil service job required a certain level of self-censorship. Myles mocks the censorious, insular climate of the Irish Free State, and also the liberal intellectuals and writers around the magazine *The Bell* that sought to critique it. His views and attitudes are shrouded in irony, ambiguity, linguistic play, ingenious obfuscation. There is abundant satire in his novels, as in his journalism, though the po-faced scholasticism of Flann contrasts with the populist posture of Myles. He lampoons patriotic Gaels in *An Béal Bocht*, the mythologies of the Irish revival in *At Swim-Two-Birds*, finicky academicians in *The Third Policeman*. There are certainly moments when O'Nolan/O'Brien/NaGopaleen's pen seems motivated by indignation and mockery – for cant, for pretension, for cabals. Yet, if he is a formal revolutionary in his novels, he is by no means a political one. There is arguably a conservative reflex to Myles's satirical impulse, a predilection to deride the pretentious, the high-falutin', the radical that might even appeal to the 'Plain People of Ireland'. Satire obtains its force from an implied norm and an incongruity, a centre and a deviation. For all the enlistment of O'Nolan into a tradition of Menippean satire, his popular appeal, especially in his journalism, partly rests on a comedy that is based on reassuring and familiar codes that lampoon the too ostentatious and eccentric as well as the too banal and clichéd.[1] In this

---

[1] Keith M. Booker, *Flann O'Brien, Bakhtin and Menippean Satire* (Syracuse: Syracuse University Press, 1995).

respect the formal audacity of Flann O'Brien's novels contrasts with the orthodox values of Myles NaGopaleen's journalism.

Yet there is another dimension to O'Brien in which the satire seems leached of normative value and detached from a moral target, playfully mocking without holding up an alternative. In such cases, satire shifts into the more ethically evacuated, ludic parody that we associate with postmodernism. Aside from parody for its own playful sake lies another sort of satire severed from moral positioning: one informed by nihilism. If nihilism (at least in one respect) is the belief that all values are groundless and meaning, at best, provisional and contingent, then in nihilistic comedy, errant morals and pieties are mocked but the implied norm or value is contingent and fragile. This essay seeks to probe the question of nihilism in relation to *The Third Policeman*, a novel which plays with subverts philosophical questions more than any of his other novels, and where the moral stance seems especially fragile and obscured even as the issue of morality – murder, law, sin, punishment – seems most foregrounded. But the topsy-turvy world of *The Third Policeman*, where famously the laws of physics operate with a deviant plausibility, also pertains to values, both moral and existential.

The various roots of nihilism, in political, philosophical and aesthetic soil, are intimately tied with those of modernism. Both emerge from the severance between fact and value brought about by the Enlightenment, perhaps most evident in the growth of nineteenth-century science and its destruction of traditional modes and rhythms of human value. The growth of secularization, rationalism, liberalism, capitalism, urbanization, the destruction of feudalism, the growth of democracy and technology led alternately to a heady sense of 'progress' and a traumatic severance from a sense of the sacred and providential. The sense of modernity as Weberian 'disenchantment' meant that from the various European avant-garde art movements, to Heidegger's ontology, to the rise of fascism, modernism was part of an inter-war attempt at re-sacralization. But at the same time, from Baudelaire in the mid-nineteenth century, through the Decadent movement to Kafka and Beckett and the absurdists, modernist writing has been seen as a manifestation of modern alienation. The concept of nihilism has been deployed both by advocates of modern art, such as Theodor Adorno, who see it as the due expression of a modernity contaminated by the dominating impulses of instrumental reason, and by detractors, such as Georg Lukács, who indict Kafka and Joyce for enacting the severance between the observer and the observed and thereby negating the fundamental social nature of human being: 'Man, for these writers, is by nature solitary, asocial, unable to enter into relationships with other beings,' an observation that could certainly be made of *The Third Policeman*.[2]

So modernist art is variously understood both as an expression of *and* a resistance to the depredations of modernity, a divide that does not simply align with those who would wish to indict and defend experimentalism or anti-realism in art. Even within the work of Nietzsche, the key philosophical interpreter of nihilism, aesthetic creation alternates between symptom and cure of the modern condition. Nietzsche also takes the origins of nihilism in what he perceives as the anti-aesthetic orientation of Christianity and Platonic philosophy, allying the moral with the nihilistic, both opposed to the invigorating 'transvaluation of values' afforded by art.[3] Nietzsche writes that

> A nihilist is a man who judges of the world as it *ought* not to be, and of the world as it ought to be that it does not exist. According to this view, our existence (action, suffering, willing, feeling) has no meaning: the pathos of the "in vain" is the nihilists' pathos – at the same time, as pathos, an inconsistency on the part of the nihilists.[4]

So the image of the world presented by nihilism has a potent 'ought not', articulated explicitly or not. But the familiar fatalistic or pessimistic overtures here exist, according to Nietzsche, because we are caught by the dead hand of morality. This 'passive' nihilism, still caught up with a moral interpretation of the world which the world flagrantly refuses, is countered by Nietzsche with an active, destructive nihilism that breaks out of inherited value systems and goes beyond good and evil, affirming a view of life as becoming and eternal recurrence. The notions of purification and creative destruction here would influence the deployments of nihilistic ideas by right-wing thinkers, like Ernst Jünger and Martin Heidegger; but the idea that there is an implicit 'ought' in the nihilistic outlook, that it stands against blithe optimism revealing the deep contamination of modern political structures, also influences radical thinkers like Adorno, who argues that:

> The true nihilists are the ones who oppose nihilism with their more and more faded positivities, the ones who are thus conspiring with the extant

---

[2] Georg Lukács, *The Meaning of Contemporary Realism*, trans. John Mander and Necke Mander (London: Merlin, 1963), 19–20.
[3] Nietzsche's most extensive reflections on 'nihilism' are contained in the posthumously published collection of his notes, *The Will to Power*, ed. Walter Kaufmann, trans. Walter Hoffmann and R. J. Hollingdale (New York: Vintage, 1968).
[4] Nietzsche, *The Will to Power*, 318.

malice, and eventually with the destructive principle itself. Thought honours itself by defending what is damned as nihilism.[5]

Within this passage one can see the word nihilism doing double-duty and enacting the contradictory implication between its connotations and denotations. In the first use, Adorno deploys the connotation of 'nihilists' as pejorative, in the second and third, he defends what he regards as the emancipatory power of 'nihilism'. One of the confusing aspects of the word and concept of nihilism, picked up here by Adorno, is its tendency to cleave to pejorative associations, so that rather than a neutral philosophical or aesthetical viewpoint, it becomes a red flag, signalling danger to be avoided or a disease to be cured.[6] Nihilism, then, is a concept which seeks to describe a sense of meaninglessness or the groundlessness of value but because it is so heavily invested in descriptions of value becomes itself an evaluative term.

Where within these debates might O'Brien's *The Third Policeman* fit? The question of nihilism in O'Brien is critically unresolved. Anthony Cronin refers to the 'innate nihilism of the comic vision' and Denis Donoghue has described O'Brien as a nihilist in his Preface to the *The Third Policeman*.[7] Other critics rush to 'defend' O'Brien against the 'charge' of nihilism, still often seen as a philosophical dead-end to be avoided. The effort to find something redemptive or transmuting in O'Brien (we find a similar tendency through the history of Beckett criticism), to rescue him from pessimism, is part of the project to ally him to a modernist project conceived as rebirth, an anti-decadent force aimed at the perceived spiritual sickness besetting modernity. What makes O'Brien a difficult figure for such reclamation is not just his own cunning refusal to be so enlisted, but also his besetting belatedness, emerging as he does at the end of revolutionary impulses both aesthetic and political. O'Brien, as many critics have pointed out, continually struggles with Joyce's legacy, with uneven success. He also lives and writes in a social context beset with counter-revolutionary stagnancy. The energies unleashed in Ireland in the first decades of the twentieth century had, following the war of independence and civil war in the 1920s, atrophied into the confessional, repressed, impoverished Free State of the 1930s, drained by isolationism, exhaustion and emigration. The defiant opening of *At Swim-Two-Birds*, with

---

[5] Theodor Adorno, *Negative Dialectics*, trans. E. B. Ashton (London: Routledge & Kegan Paul, 1973), 381.
[6] A recent attempt to counter this reflex that nihilism is something to be avoided or 'overcome' is Ray Brassier's, *Nihil Unbound: Enlightenment and Extinction* (Basingstoke: Palgrave Macmillan, 2007), which argues that philosophy must unflinchingly confront the lack of transcendent value and meaning and the inevitability of extinction.
[7] Anthony Cronin, *No Laughing Matter: The Life and Times of Flann O'Brien* (London: Grafton, 1989), 104.

the narrator declaring that '[t]he modern novel should be largely a work of reference', since virtually all characters have already been invented, attests to the sense of everything having happened already which powerfully feeds his creative agenda (21).[8]

If the project of renovation and renewal is one strand in the contradictory skein of modernism, another is the sense of pessimism and aporia that is revealed or rendered pressingly acute by uneven social or political conditions. Art that merits the label modernist recognizes the ineffability and alterity of the world, a pained awareness in the face of contradiction, contingency and arbitrariness of a world which has lost the sacred. The dignity of such art is in its recognition of this irreconcilable crisis, not giving in to false utopias or fabricated meaning. Since modernism fluctuates from an effort to salve this ache of modernity on the one hand, to confront it on the other, the history of modernism's relationship to nihilism can be figured as modernism *versus* nihilism on the one hand and modernism *as* nihilism on the other.[9]

Fredric Jameson describes the modernity stemming from eighteenth-century rationalism as a 'catastrophe' since it 'dashes traditional structures and lifeways to pieces, sweeps away the sacred, undermines immemorial habits and inherited languages, and leaves the world as a set of raw materials to be reconstructed rationally'.[10] The world of *The Third Policeman* is amongst other things a parody of the view of the world as a rational reconstruction of raw materials, as the reduction of all things to the mysterious 'omnium' attests.

However, there are crucial differences between O'Brien's social conditions and those of this instrumentalized modernity more generally. It is true that Irish literary culture of the twentieth century, including that of Joyce, is haunted by a series of upheavals of the traditional way of life, most notably the catastrophic Famine of the mid nineteenth-century, with its rapid depletion of the Irish rural population through starvation and emigration, and the resultant extirpation of the Irish language. Ireland in one respect was traumatically dragged into modernity in the nineteenth century and, for all his mockery of the pieties of the language movement, O'Brien was brought up speaking the language and his work registers its loss acutely. But the Irish culture from which O'Brien wrote was characterized not by the uneven distortions of the modern but rather by the stagnant and remaindered residues of the premodern. The Irish Free State in the 1930s was still a

---

[8] All references to O'Brien's novels to *The Complete Novels*, intro. Keith Donoghue (New York and London: Everyman Library, 2007).
[9] Shane Weller, *Modernism and Nihilism* (London: Palgrave, 2011), 2.
[10] Fredric Jameson, *The Seeds of Time* (New York: Columbia University Press, 1994), 84.

largely agricultural country, where imminent electrification was the most notable industrial advance. This unevenness between old and new was also reflected in the ideological and political terrain. The revolutionary fervour of an earlier generation had atrophied into a staid separatist ideology, which imposed an ideal of cultural and economic self-sufficiency, not globalization or mainstream capitalist development. But self-sufficiency was only achievable precisely through the leaching of novelty by emigration, depletion and repetition, rather than new population infusion or innovative social and economic thinking. In this respect any dialogue between O'Brien's work and the global forces of the marketplace should be tempered with a recognition that he emerges from an anomalous social context, shot through with postcolonial torpor and parochialism. The same is true for the intellectual formation of O'Brien, and the philosophical discourses upon which *The Third Policeman* rests. Here is a novel where the pull of the local continually conflicts with discourses of universalism. It is the impulse to enter a sphere of philosophical abstraction, represented by de Selby, that leads the narrator to murderous disavowal of community obligation and local life. But even in the 'after-life' he cannot escape the shapes, customs and idiolects of the 'parish', however bizarre and misshapen their reconstruction.

The pyrotechnics of his novels are at one level a counterpoint to the sclerosis of Irish social conditions and at another a reflection of the contradictions upon which Irish society rested: a post-revolutionary conservatism, a hierarchical ex-colony. If 'cowboy books' and popular culture jostle together with Gaelic sagas and Irish folklore, this reflects the anomalous elements of tradition and modernity within Irish society. For all the indebtedness of *The Third Policeman* to the new sciences, it is a novel profoundly attuned to the local and rural, the values of the parish, the farm and the pub. Its parodic treatment of bureaucracy and the brutalities of the system may derive from European urban alienation, but it also stems from O'Brien's day job working in the Department of Local Government of the Irish civil service. And I will argue here that O'Brien's engagement with European nihilism is self-consciously undone by the presence of the inexorable local, the *in situ* particularity of a stagnant social formation that is neither modern nor premodern, but incongruously hybrid.

Where does value, and its negation, reside in the depictions of an enervated culture and the disillusionment that impoverished, partially independent Ireland has brought? In *The Third Policeman* we find ethical and epistemological values skewed and fixated in ways that lead towards nullity and arrest. When the nameless narrator meets Old Mathers, whom he has murdered, the victim has made a decision to answer always in the negative: '"No" is, generally speaking, a better answer than "Yes,"' he declares, 'everything you do is in response to a request or a suggestion made to you by some other party either inside you or outside. Some of these suggestions are good and praiseworthy and some of them are undoubtedly delightful. But the majority of them are definitely bad and are pretty considerable sins as sins go' (243–4). Mathers finds that this instrumentalist strategy, arrived at through a cost-benefit analysis, brings him great peace and certainty. Joe (the narrator's soul who speaks in italics), claims that the old miser is a *'saintly man'* (245), his strenuous path of refusal mocks the *via negativa* in that like so much else in the novel it is programmatic, mechanistic and comic. It detaches from ends (refusal) because it gets caught up in the remorseless logic of means (renunciation), losing ontological connection through linguistic games. So, for instance, he records that his friends get him to accept whiskey by asking him if he will not refuse a glass, to which his answer is 'NO' (245).

There are many other presentations of nullity of various sorts here that skirt around a nihilist posture, even as they mock and refute nihilism, and all other philosophical postures or outlooks. In *The Spectre of the Absurd*, Donald A. Crosby suggests a taxonomy of nihilism, that includes five distinct types: political, moral, epistemological, cosmic and existential – each denying a specific aspect of human life or meaning:

> *Political nihilism* negates the political structures within which life is currently lived, as well as social and cultural outlooks that inform these structures. It has little or no vision of the constructive alternatives or of how to achieve them. *Moral nihilism* denies the sense of moral obligation, the objectivity of moral principles, or the moral viewpoint. *Epistemological nihilism* denies that there can be anything like truths or meanings not strictly confined within, or wholly relative to, a single individual group, or conceptual scheme. *Cosmic nihilism* disavows intelligibility or value in nature, seeing it as indifferent or hostile to fundamental human concerns. *Existential nihilism* denies the meaning of life.[11]

All these overlapping Olympian rings resonate in O'Brien's novel. The political structures are inscrutable, bizarre, beholden to wayward circuits of determination, but there is no asserted or implied alternative in place. There are blind spots, political and moral. The story begins with a casual account of a murder, and most characters are motivated by breezy self-interest. Sergeant Pluck likes to offer avuncular nuggets of life advice to the narrator. "'The first

---

[11] Donald A. Crosby, *The Spectre of the Absurd: Sources and Criticism of Modern Nihilism* (Albany, NY: Statue University of New York Press, 1988), 35.

beginnings of wisdom," he said, "is to ask questions and never to answer any,"' which combines hopeless epistemological opacity with a certain defensive cunning. The second is to turn 'everything you hear to your own advantage'. (272). The narrator needs no encouragement to live according to such a value system and nor do the others in the novel. His moral compass is subject to the same wayward gravity as the laws of physics, with his decision to murder Old Mathers the founding instance.

Furthermore, *The Third Policeman*, while liberally laced with eulogies to nature, an incongruous pastoral code that contrasts with the mechanical and artificial logic, also exposes a contingent, clunky and indifferent natural world. From this context, existence itself seems pointless, without meaning or – as comically framed in this novel – without 'use'. One of the most celebrated passages expresses a nihilistic view of life at the same time as lampooning utilitarian or instrumentalist reasoning:

> "Is it life?" he answered. "I would rather be without it," he said, "for there is a queer small utility in it. You cannot eat it or drink or smoke it in your pipe, it does not keep the rain out and it is a poor armful in the dark if you strip it and take it to bed with you after a night of porter when you are shivering with the red passion. It is a great mistake and thing better done without, like bed-jars and foreign bacon." (257)

This is Martin Finnucane, a '*slippery-looking customer,*' according to Joe, a pipe-smoking trickster by the roadside who straddles the plays of Synge and the philosophy of Sartre. If this is Weberian disenchantment, it is rinsed through a comically mundane utilitarianism. It also anticipates Marshall Berman's point that capitalist nihilism was diagnosed not by Nietzsche but by Marx, even if he does not use the word nihilism: 'All the anarchic, measureless, explosive drives that a later generation will baptize by the name of nihilism . . . are located by Marx in the seemingly banal everyday working of the market economy.'[12] Finnucane's only concept of value is that of exchange, but this is taken to comically ludicrous directions and given to a figure who for all his eccentricity also evokes the deep banality of Irish rural life. As such it creates a destabilizing anomaly that hollows out the possibility of profundity. It could be then that the existential nihilism is here presented irreverently, like the philosophical conundrums posed by de Selby. The comedy lies in pushing the conception of life in objective terms – 'Out

---

[12] Marshall Berman, *All That Is Solid Melts into Air: The Experience of Modernity* (London: Verso, 1983), 100.

out brief candle – life is but a waking shadow' – to ridiculous conclusions, rendering it as itself a material object, like bed-jars and foreign bacon. There is a category confusion here that nonetheless casts doubt on the idea that 'life' can be observed or judged from within 'life'. Samuel Beckett rejected the notion of the absurd on the grounds that this 'implies a judgement of value. It's not even possible to talk about truth. That's part of the anguish.'[13] O'Brien's comic juxtaposition explodes the idea of existential nihilism by, implicitly, running it against the epistemological variety. He undoes nihilism through scepticism. We cannot know whether life is worthless or without meaning because our knowledge of life is so opaque and circumscribed, so contingent on social circumstances. In this case, the social circumstances are so thoroughly shot through the abstract philosophizing that the latter becomes impossible. 'I am told there is a better brand of it in the cities than in the country parts and there is said to be a very superior brand of it to be had in certain parts of France' (258). The anomie of the roadside exchange and its self-conscious marginality expose the postcolonial torpor of its context (the allusion to France possibly a slight at contemporary continental philosophy). The Hiberno-English idiom used, so recognizably Mylesian – 'More power to yourself', 'then by Dad' – reinforces the rural Irish comic routines creating a comic incongruity that also turns a sceptical eye on the continental pretensions of the judgement.

The 'tricky' man's lack of respect for life also leads him like so many of the other characters into amorality, especially when it comes to murder, though also into self-contradiction: 'If I kill enough men there will be more life to go round and maybe then I will be able to live till I am a thousand and not have the old rattle in my neck when I am quite seventy' (259). So, in a motif that is repeated, abstract thought and contemplative wisdom end up being twisted to selfish ends. Finnucane asserts the valuelessness of life to justify being a robber and murderer but folds the ethical into the quantitative or measurable, and, treating life instrumentally, as a finite resource, contradictorily wants to enhance his own life through denying others theirs. It is an instance of the bizarre moral calculus in this strange afterlife.

It resonates also with Sergeant Pluck's later ruminations on how he can justify hanging the narrator, in which the bureaucratic and the existential are conflated in a comically incompetent version of Kafka. As he has no name, according to the genial Pluck, the narrator does not exist. Therefore this extra-judicial non-entity can be disposed of without obstacle. In Sergeant Pluck's eyes, he does not belong to the moral or even physical sphere. 'Anything you

---

[13] Charles Juliet, 'Meeting Beckett', *TriQuarterly* 77 (Winter 1989/90): 17.

do is a lie and nothing that happens to you is true . . . we can take you and hang the life out of you and you are not hanged at all and there is no entry to be made in the death papers.' This is a multiple negation, but based crucially on the eclipse of the real by the socially confined and authorized. The man who is not a man (because nameless) can be put to a death that is not a death. 'The particular death you die is not even a death (which is an inferior phenomenon at best) only an insanitary abstraction in the backyard, a piece of negative nullity neutralized and rendered void by asphyxiation and the fracture of the spinal string' (311). Again, the comic effect is released through category confusions. Without a name, the narrator has no legitimacy in terms of the polity, he is thus without 'worth' or substance in the eyes of the system and its functionaries – a 'negative nullity', that can be neutralized without process or consequence. The other nullity here, unspecified by the policeman, is the loss of any moral aspect outside the bureaucratese of his job which enables him to reify his prisoner to the brute facticity of his material body ('rendered void by asphyxiation and the fracture of the spinal string'). It is as if the policeman's sensibility is reduced to a confined, clockwork array of possibilities, like the specific, limited list of names that he can conceive for the narrator.

The narrator's response to his imminent execution is an assertion of conventional, humanist affect that seems comically unnerving precisely because of its anomalous force when placed against the bureaucratic nonsense of the policeman and the narrator's own erstwhile amorality:

> I felt so sad and entirely disappointed that tears came into my eyes and a lump of incommunicable poignancy swelled tragically in my throat. I began to feel intensely every fragment of my equal humanity. The life that was bubbling at the end of my fingers was real and nearly painful in intensity and so was the beauty of my warm face and the loose humanity of my limbs and the racy health of my red rich blood. To leave it all without good reason and to smash the little empire into small fragments was a thing too pitiful even to refuse to think about. (312)

The textual language here is paradoxically programmatic: even in its affective extremity, an adjectival looseness that seems both sincere and cheaply earned, or in a word 'sentimental'. It is also undermined by the atomistic and materialist view that underlies and destabilizes the conventional humanism. His 'little empire', for all its poignancy and beauty, is simply made up of fragments, inert objects, the raw materials of the human form that Pluck has described.

The same impression is often given in *The Third Policeman* where the natural world is concerned, where the pastoral earnestness seems incongruous in this two-dimensional, cartoonish world. Even though, as it turns out in the end, the narrator is in a sort of a hell, his experiences in this after-life are not all torture. He is often transported into a pastoral bliss, a surge of appreciation not just for his humanity but for the glories of nature. Yet at the same time, these encomiums are undermined by their cartoonish exaggeration. For the readers, the colours are too vivid, nature too commodified in its bucolic splendour, so that the impression is given of a two-dimensional scene, transformed to borrow Seamus Deane's distinction, from land to landscape.[14] Anthony Cronin observes that *The Third Policeman* is 'full of oddly generalized and amorphous description, that of landscape, which occupies such a large part of it, being composed in the most laborious way out of mere landscape elements, like a child's picture'.[15] This is one of the many tensions in the novel between a rural setting and a sensibility infused by aspects of the urban and industrial. The land is prettified because of the distance between the viewer and the viewed, the fact that the narrator's livelihood is separate from it. The whole is left with a virtual quality, a thin unreality strategically designed to reveal the mechanics behind it. There is a sense on many levels in the novel of something taking its course, operating according to a system of determinism. This becomes part of the plot of the novel, both by the revelation at the end that the narrator is partaking in a hellish cycle, that puns with the obsession with bicycles throughout, and the revelation that the whole experiential world is controlled by the policemen, from 'eternity', a place secreted in the forest that closely resembles a factory. The bucolic setting is dangerously unmasked: behind it is not the hand of God, but rather the machinations of an industrial complex.

There is a logic of mechanization throughout the novel, despite the rural context, which evokes modern nihilism with its erosion of human agency, its abandonment to blind process. And this ties into a deterministic system that challenges or erodes the grounds of value, that brings modern disenchantment and desacralization to the Irish parish. The human beings here are clockwork characters – that some have wooden legs and that they meld with bicycles is less a category shift than it might at first appear. All here move towards reification. The human is atomized, remorselessly material, fragmentary. This is doubled into the mechanization of literary form and voice. The translated

---

[14] Seamus Deane, *Strange Country* (Oxford: Clarendon Press, 1997), 148.
[15] Cronin, *No Laughing Matter*, Quoted by Hugh Kenner, 'The Fourth Policeman' in ed. Anne Clune and Tess Hurson, *Conjuring Complexities: Essays on Flann O'Brien* (Belfast: Institute of Irish Studies, 1997), 64.

quality of the prose, the calm courtesy of the policeman juxtaposed with their bureaucratic procedures, reinforces a programmatic narrative quality, where the human and humane qualities in the narrative voice are either exaggerated to caricature or leached altogether. The tone is calm and level-headed: even when describing intense emotion the narrator invests in the rational voice of the reliable witness.

This quietly reasonable voice sets up the most famous satirical gambit of the novel, that against academicians, embodied in the ludicrous philosophy of de Selby and his commentators. The narrator's obsession with De Selby is the occasion for his crime of murder. Though O'Brien critics often call De Selby a philosopher, he straddles and confuses disciplines and fields with, we are told, 'dignity and eminence as a physicist, ballistician, philosopher and psychologist' (373 n. 1). One of the cardinal motifs in de Selby's work is its idiosyncratic relationship with value, a motif that comes in the context of neutral scientific description. He comically violates the 'fact-value' distinction in outlandish modes. Thus, for instance, his disquisition on the history and materiality of roads espouses a 'good road' that will have 'character and certain air of destiny' (252), his association of happy state with as much water as possible, praising its 'circumambiency, equiponderance and equitableness' as opposed to 'the hated and "insanitary night"' (353-4).

Much of the comedy of de Selby, such as his run-ins with the law for water wastage, comes from twisting fact with value in eccentric ways. But when it comes to conventional values de Selby's system is comically inept. Chapter 7 details the consolations of philosophy and religion, as the narrator explains the salutary effect that his interest in de Selby has had on his life. 'They seem to lighten dark places and give strength to bear the unaccustomed load.' (302) But in pragmatic terms, de Selby's help seems markedly unsuited to bearing out the truth of this cliché. Since the *savant* held that 'the usual processes of living were illusory', he therefore 'did not pay much attention to life's adversities and he does not in fact offer much suggestion as to how they should be met' (302). So a lovelorn young man comes to him for advice, and de Selby responds by presenting him with 'some fifty imponderable propositions' that dwarf 'the conundrum of his lady to nothingness'. It does not seem that much of a consolation however: 'the young man who had come fearing the possibility of a bad thing left the house completely convinced of the worst and cheerfully contemplating suicide' (303). So again nihilism as a philosophical position is mocked by virtue of its comic self-inflation. De Selby does treat some of the big issues where philosophy may indeed provide 'some genuine moral sustenance'. His 'Layman's Atlas', we are told 'deals explicitly' with those areas of life and its extremities where value and meaning are most tested: 'bereavement, old age, love, sin, death and the other saliences of existence'. However, he 'allows them only some six lines but this is due to his devastating assertion that they are all "unnecessary"' (303).

So de Selby's philosophy of value would seem in the logic of the novel to cast doubt on the value of philosophy. His negation of what is worthwhile, important, necessary, together with his idiosyncratic, perhaps insane estimate of alternatives, would seem to be itself, negated. However, the novel for all its satire, is not really establishing an alternative to philosophy, it is not posing against de Selby a more humane and pragmatic viewpoint or against intellectualism a humanist common sense. Rather it is operating in a realm that negates and refuses assertion and attitudinizing of all sorts, that seeks to avoid the trap of fixity and complacency. In this respect, the figuring of Old Mathers's ethics of refusal, for all its absurdity, chimes with a key trope in the novel and is, perhaps, why we find repeated exchanges in the novel based upon an interlocutor answered by a repeated word 'No'. The 'no' of nihilism becomes here a 'no' to nihilism. The novel seems tempted by negation, and so cannot 'affirm' the nihilistic values and discourses with which it engages. The treatment of de Selby mocks philosophical declarations of worth or worthlessness, meaning or meaninglessness, just as it reveals the absurdity of Martin Finnucane's disquisition on the valuelessness of 'life' through the remorseless instrumentalism of his premises. *The Third Policeman* depicts a world much undone by the hyper-rationalized, procedural and deterministic forces of the modern. But if it draws back from the diagnosis of nihilism, in ontological terms, it also eschews any attempt to overcome the disenchantments of modernity that led other writers of the 1930s down a path towards fascism.

When explaining to Martin Finnucane the existence of his wooden leg, the narrator remarks: 'I think I got the disorder in Mullingar' (260). The mention of this nondescript town in the Irish midlands is one of the few signals of actual locale in the novel, which is both unmistakably Irish and also strategically distanced from any recognizable geography, if not idiolect. But despite this distantiation, such 'disorders' that are represented in a novel full of physical and moral malaise are grounded in circumstances rather than abstract notions of existence. In this respect, the novel's investment in the queer and uncanny, originating in the anomalies of independent Ireland, signal a postcolonial resistance to the absurd or to universal assertions about the value or meaninglessness of existence. In this respect, for all the investment in nihilistic discourses, the novel resists Nietzschean pronouncements of the transvaluation of value or Heideggerian concerns about the forgetting of Being. If we were to diagnose the sort of nihilism here it would be one of epistemology rather than ontology, scepticism rather than pessimism. This stems in part because its modernism is one of the periphery, a periphery which could never mistake its own situatedness for a universal condition. Ultimately the ludic spirals of this version of hell signal not the absurdity of 'life' but the opacity of a system that is never less or more than concrete and immanent, with the political, historical, economic and social registers that, though parodied, are always present.

11

Flann O'Brien and Modern Character

Julian Murphet

In the protracted rearrangement of aesthetic energies and laws associated with modernism, the question of literary character was a particularly vexed one. On the one hand, there can be no doubt that in the long series of bourgeois adjustments to the 'magical narratives' of the Middle Ages, the artistic conquest of representable persons ranks as a paramount achievement, to be measured against the *cogito* itself as a philosophical victory.[1] But, on the other, the accumulated weight of nineteenth-century fiction and stage melodrama would appear to have smothered the once-radical energies of a Quixote, a Crusoe or a Shandy in blankets of conformity and sentimental cliché. The growing sense of characters becoming people 'fixed in a mould' led Strindberg to make his well-known defence of a new approach: 'My souls (or characters) are agglomerations of past and present cultures, scraps from books and newspapers, fragments of humanity, torn shreds of once-fine clothing that has become rags, in just the way that a human soul is patched together.'[2] Novel here was the emphasis on a multiplicity of incommensurable scraps and fragments subtending the conventional domain of represented persons: no longer simple or singular, these characters are 'conglomerations' of an indeterminate plurality. In another place, I have argued for a consideration of the 'crisis' of literary character in modernism in terms of an abiding contestation between the residual unitary figure of the One (as the best way of stabilizing an imaginary self and suturing heterogeneity), and the aesthetic eruption of an irresistible multiplicity on the precincts of the One (under the sign of the infinite), such that the arbitrary 'patching together' of souls now begins to appear a necessary emergency procedure.[3] Alain Badiou's conception of an 'indifferent multiplicity . . . that secularizes

---

[1] See on the origins of this Elizabeth Fowler's *Literary Character: The Human Figure in Early English Writing* (Ithaca: Cornell University Press, 2003).

[2] August Strindberg, 'Author's Preface' to *Miss Julie*, in *Strindberg: The Plays, Vol. 1*, rev. edn, trans. Michael Meyer (London: Secker & Warburg, 1975), 103.

[3] See Julian Murphet, 'The Mole and the Multiple: A Chiasmus of Character', *New Literary History* 42, 2 (Spring 2011): 255–76.

and disperses the infinite, grasps us humans in terms of this dispersion, and advances the prospect of a world evacuated of every tutelary figure of the One,' summarizes the representational issues at stake.[4] To perforate the One such that the infinite begins to show through: such might stand as a condensed version of the aesthetic transvaluation at work on the ground of modernist characterization. In any event, there were few writers at greater pains to make this kind of transvaluation *count* than Flann O'Brien.[5]

The Third Policeman, written in the last year of the 1930s but not published until 1967, arranges the terms of its Menippean satire in the conventional *topos* of a personal afterlife, where, having himself been killed after murdering Old Mathers, our narrator is held in narrative suspension while abstract ideas and intellectual enthusiasms assume disproportionate density. His afterlife is a sort of theatre for the chiasmic transference of human characteristics to non-living agents, and of inorganic properties to fictional persons. In Marx's phrase, a 'definite social relation between men ... assumes here, for them, the fantastic form of a relation between things', and vice versa.[6] The 'sort of hell which he earned'[7] is a kind of phantasmagoria of industrial capitalism, where objects take on fetishistic vitality at the cost of a relative dehumanization of the persons who handle them. This tactical inversion is within the line of descent of the Menippean form, whose tendency is to deal 'less with people as such than with mental attitudes': 'The Menippean satire thus resembles the confession in its ability to handle abstract ideas and theories, and differs from the novel in its characterization, which is stylized rather than naturalistic, and presents people as mouthpieces of the ideas they represent.'[8] The specifically 'modernist' inflection of this is to amplify the effect such that the characters – here specifically the three policemen, MacCruiskeen, Fox and Sergeant Pluck, and the supernumeraries Finnucane, Gilhaney and O'Feersa – are in turn subordinated to the sinister 'omnium' of the object-world itself, of which they can be said to be simple functionaries and servo-mechanisms. Thus, these

---

[4] Alain Badiou, 'Philosophy and Mathematics', in *Theoretical Writings*, ed. and trans. Ray Brassier and Alberto Toscano (London: Continuum, 2004), 37.
[5] The *locus classicus* of O'Brien's metacommentary on the arbitrariness of literary characterization is, of course *At Swim-Two-Birds*–for which see Sascha Morrell's essay in this volume. The effort here is to extend this line of thinking into the more conventionally 'stabilized' characterology of his next novel.
[6] Karl Marx, *Capital, Vol. 1*, trans. Ben Fowkes (London: Penguin, 1990), 165.
[7] Letter from Brian O'Nolan to William Saroyan, 14 February 1940, quoted in the 'Publisher's Note' to Flann O'Brien, *The Third Policeman* (London: Flamingo/Harper Collins, 2001), 228.
[8] Northrop Frye, *Anatomy of Criticism* (Princeton, NJ: Princeton University Press, 1957), 309.

non-naturalistic characters are less 'mouthpieces of the ideas they represent' than they are manifestations of the capacity to be objectified by the ideas that are already objectified in things: bicycles, pumps, lamps, levers, lift shafts, gauges, wooden legs, sweets and so forth.

But this double transference could be said to have provided merely the stage for the central achievement of *The Third Policeman*, namely the series of formal decisions regarding the narrator himself, abandoned to a Menippean scenography and characterology as to a private inferno, but reacting to it in a suite of logically related ways. Dating his extraction from the world of the living from the unrepresentable moment in Old Mathers' house when the bomb planted there by his partner in crime hypothetically goes off (somewhere near the beginning of Chapter 2) – and yet allowing for the conceit that the entirety of this past-tense narration must be recounted posthumously – we can delineate a cluster of conditions for the protagonist's progressive disintegration as a locus of consistency, and thus his relative disposition towards the drift of the infinite in a mathematical register. These are:

1. Effective **de-nomination**: 'I did not know my name, did not remember who I was. I was not certain where I had come from or what my business was in that room. I found I was sure of nothing save my search for the black box.'[9]
2. The numinous **event**: 'some change which came upon me ... indescribably subtle, yet momentous, ineffable'. (20)
3. The apparition of the **Other** as a nested multiplicity of deceitful object-demons: '... the eyes were horrible. Looking at them I got the feeling that they were not genuine eyes at all but mechanical dummies animated by electricity or the like, with a tiny pinhole in the centre of the "pupil" through which the real eye gazed out secretively and with great coldness. Such a conception ... gave rise in my mind to interminable speculations ... as to whether, indeed, it was real at all or merely another dummy with its pinhole on the same plane as the first one so that the real eye, possibly behind thousands of these disguises, gazed out through a barrel of serried peep-holes.' (22)
4. The symptomatic splitting of the narrating instance into **Two**, namely 'me' and 'Joe', 'my soul', who *speaks in italics*.
5. The nominalistic infinity engendered by the **rejection of memory** as a structuring principle: 'to believe what my eyes were looking at rather than to place my trust in a memory'. (24)

---

[9] Flann O'Brien, *The Third Policeman* (London: Flamingo/Harper Collins, 2001), 30. All further references in text.

But it is specifically the numerical sublime accessed through the 'not genuine eyes' of the Other that opens up a door in narratological space for the protagonist to step through and undertake his unsentimental education in the consequences of the infinite for his own being. In what will become a recurrent trope, the figure of recursion introduces a conspicuous anxiety about the multiple residing inside the One – an apt illustration of the crisis of character in modernity, which we have posited in terms of an overwhelming of the singular by the multiple.

The tendency of a given unity to shade off, imperceptibly, into the infinite is constitutive of *The Third Policeman*'s concept of perdition. Constable MacCruiskeen is the fairy-tale 'donor' of a brace of magical objects that exemplify what is finally a problem of being. The problem at issue is that of number, and number's pull away from any phenomenological frame of reference towards a supersensible infra- or meta-reality that cannot be gathered into the coordinates of a world. This is what MacCruiskeen's tapering spear, and his nested chests, emblematize for the narrator: each object, appearing consistent and unitary within the perceptual horizon, turns out on closer inspection to extend indefinitely beyond it. The spear has two dimensions of 'sharpness', one sensible, and the other which 'could go into your hand and out in the other extremity externally and you would not feel a bit of it and you would see nothing and hear nothing. It is so thin that maybe it does not exist at all'. (73) It is this latter sharpness, 'to airy thinness beat', which confounds the coordinates of cognition itself, and explicitly threatens the idea of self-consistency: 'About an inch from the end it is so sharp that . . . you cannot think of it or try to make it the subject of a little idea because you will hurt your box with the excruciation of it.' (73) The presentation of the infinite *pains consciousness*; it is what exceeds cognition and representation, the 'little ideas' used to delineate a world.

It is the same with the series of ever-smaller chests tucked away one inside another, the least of which are not visible either: a series that can only be adequately construed mathematically. This recapitulation of the inaugural image of Old Mathers's recursive eyes underlines the degree to which the narration is haunted by a numerical sublime that it can only register through figures of recursion. The mathematical sublime, intuited in these figures, shatters the commonsensical screen of 'what my eyes were looking at' and extends the domain of the infinite in all directions beyond and within the bounds of the sensible. The fatal image of recursion is then, logically enough, applied to the dialectical Two into which the narrator has been sundered by the unrepresentable event. Joe himself, 'my soul' (23), is insulted by the implication that he has 'scaly' skin (in other words, that he is tainted by Original Sin); but his reaction triggers these suspicions in his alter ego:

> What if he *had* a body? A body with another body inside it in turn, thousands of such bodies within each other like the skins of an onion, receding to some unimaginable ultimum? Was I in turn merely a link in a vast sequence of imponderable beings, the world I knew merely the interior of the being whose inner voice I myself was? Who or what was the core and what monster in what world was the final uncontained colossus? God? Nothing? (132)

Thus the numerical sublime of infinite recursion – 'receding to some unimaginable ultimum' – usurps characterology. The narrator/protagonist now imagines himself as an endlessly nested series of matryoshka dolls, from the most 'scaly' and loathsome, to the divine, each one the 'inner voice' of the next being 'up' the scale. Literary character, modulated into a logic of self-similar patterning along an infinite scale, has become fractal.

To this fractal being, one can pose the question of a name; but the question will have become comically inexhaustible. 'All people have names of one kind or another. Some are arbitrary labels related to the appearance of the person, some represent merely genealogical associations but most of them afford some clue as to the parents of the person named and confer a certain advantage in the execution of legal documents.' (40) It is 'legal documents' that benefit from the stabilization of identity conferred by a name; ontologically, however, the name is a count-for-one that functions as pure fiction. The truth is a 'blank anonymity' (according to the a priori conditions of de-nomination and pure multiplicity), but rather than an occasion to retreat in dumb horror, this is initially an invitation to *over-nominate* the recursive being, 'with the genial interest of a good joke'. 'I light-heartedly gave a list of names which, for all I knew, I *might* hear':

> Hugh Murray.
> Constantin Petrie.
> Peter Small.
> Signor Beniamino Bari.
> The Honourable Alex O'Brannigan, Bart.
> Kurt Freund.
> Mr John P. de Salis, M. A.
> Dr Solway Garr.
> Bonaparte Gosworth.
> Legs O'Hagan. (41–2)

Around two of these, Joe then constructs semi-plausible fictions to stabilize the proper names among recurrent semiological sequences. Briefly, it is as Barthes observed: 'When identical semes traverse the same proper name several times and appear to settle upon it, a character is created. . . . The proper name acts as a magnetic field for the semes; referring in fact to a body, it draws the semic configuration into an evolving (biographical) tense.'[10] And yet, there are now too many names, all crowding around and potentially referring to the same body. Over-nominating is not a durable solution, given that none of these names can even fitfully be permitted to identify the narrator, and that the list is incomplete; being, in principle, infinite. So the next solution is to attract names in order that they be negated, as in the following interrogation, which partakes of the underlying conversational form of the novel: a sequence of plausible suggestions, all of them gainsaid.

> "Are you completely doubtless that you are nameless?" he asked.
> "Positively certain."
> "Would it be Mick Barry?"
> "No."
> "Charlemagne O'Keefe?"
> "No."
> "Sir Justin Spens?"
> "Not that."
> "Kimberley?"
> "No."
> "Bernard Fann?"
> "No."
> "Joseph Poe or Nolan?"
> "No."
> "One of the Garvins or the Moynihans?"
> "Not them."
> "Rozencrantz O'Dowd?"
> "No."
> "Would it be O'Benson?"
> "Not O'Benson."
> "The Quigleys, the Mulrooneys or the Hounimen?"
> "No."
> . . . (110–11)

---

[10] Roland Barthes, *S/Z*, trans. Richard Miller (Oxford: Basil Blackwell, 1990), 67–8.

The inquisition goes on for another page, an extraordinary insistence on the logic of de-nomination as generative of infinite negation. It is worth dwelling on the fact that the hell into which our narrator has been cast is a place populated by police and orchestrated by their ideological interpellations – the paradox of damnation to this inferno is that its denizens will not cease to interpellate what is no longer namable. One 'is' in this space in the condition of the 'not'; and that raises very significant questions about the status of the dead and the realm of the possible. Charles Sanders Peirce, who along with Georg Cantor and Richard Dedekind was among the first to argue on behalf of truly infinite collections, wrote in 1898 that:

> We start, then, with nothing, pure zero. But this is not the nothing of negation. For not means other than, and other is merely a synonym of the ordinal numeral second. As such it implies a first; while the present pure zero is prior to every first. The nothing of negation is the nothing of death, which comes second to, or after, everything. But this pure zero is the nothing of not having been born. There is no individual thing, no compulsion, outward nor inward, no law. It is the germinal nothing, in which the whole universe is involved or foreshadowed. As such, it is absolutely undefined and unlimited possibility – boundless possibility. There is no compulsion and no law. It is boundless freedom.[11]

Peirce stresses the discontinuity between the 'pure zero' and the 'nothing of negation' in terms of a logical sequence. The difference between not having been at all, and having ceased to be, is the stark difference between pure unborn possibility and possibility's quietus in death. The narrator of *The Third Policeman* first experiences his de-nomination as a mathematical rush that seems giddy with unborn possibility (all the 'names which, for all I knew, I *might* hear'), yet is swiftly delivered by the legal act of interpellation over to the death drive – a limitless negation, an incessant 'not that', which parries all nomination but cannot avoid the fact that it is simply an 'ordinal numeral second', implying a 'first' which it can no longer name.

It is this radical occupation of the space of the death drive that nevertheless allows for a distinctive mode of possibility that follows the 'ceasing to have been' of death – if you like, an *ordinal numeral third* in the pulse of the dialectic. In the first place, sleep is eulogized as an unstitching of the ground

---

[11] Charles Sanders Peirce, 'Logic of Events' (c.1898), para. 217, *Collected Papers*, vol. 6, Scientific Metaphysics, ed. C. Hartshorne and P. Weiss (Cambridge, MA: Harvard University Press, 1934), 148.

of being and embodiment. This is a metaphor for death that redistributes its valences, and reclaims it for possibility (*pace* Peirce):

> My knees opened up like rosebuds in rich sunlight, pushing my shins two inches further to the bottom of the bed. Every joint became loose and foolish and devoid of true utility. . . . United with the bed I became momentous and planetary. . . . Robbing me of the reassurance of my eyesight, [the night] was disintegrating my bodily personality into a flux of colour, smell, recollection, desire – all the strange uncounted essences of terrestrial and spiritual existence. I was deprived of definition, position and magnitude and my significance was considerably diminished. (129–30)

This is the first phase of the character's open disposition towards the drift of the infinite: sleep as the disintegration of all coordinates of integrity and coherence. The diminishment of significance in this 'momentous' becoming-planetary is the echo of that inaugural event of death itself – 'some change which came upon me . . . indescribably subtle, yet momentous, ineffable' (20). It is now as if Peirce's 'nothing of negation . . . the nothing of death, which comes second to, or after, everything', is itself reprioritized in a dialectical sublation of its own secondariness. The fact of succeeding 'having-been' is irradiated by the infinite, something that for the 'pure zero' must remain only virtual, 'possible'. Death is a subsumption of the infinite within the 'not' (it is an infinity of 'not thats', a serial negation of every name), and that is consequential for being. Specifically, it elicits the second phase of this disposition towards the drift of the infinite, within the key of becoming: namely, reincarnation. Only, this concept is now rid of the theological overtones of its origins, and made available for a productive nihilism.

So it is that the grandest statement of *The Third Policeman* is offered in the accents of a properly Nietzschean affirmation, where the always-already extinct 'I' (the inconsequential 'thinking animal'[12]) wills its own overcoming in the unstable potentiality of molecular redistribution.

> Down into the earth where dead men go I would go soon and maybe come out of it again in some healthy way, free and innocent of all human perplexity. I would perhaps be the chill of an April wind, an essential part of some indomitable river or be personally concerned in the ageless perfection of some rank mountain bearing down upon the mind by occupying forever a position in the blue easy distance. Or perhaps a

---

[12] Friedrich Nietzsche, 'On Truth and Lie in an Extra-Moral Sense', in *Writings from the Early Notebooks*, ed. Raymond Geuss and Alexander Nehamas (Cambridge: Cambridge University Press, 2009), 253.

smaller thing like movement in the grass on an unbearable breathless yellow day, some hidden creature going about its business – I might well be responsible for that or for some important part of it. Or even those unaccountable distinctions that make an evening recognisable from its own morning, the smells and sounds and sights of the perfected and matured essences of the day, these might not be innocent of my meddling and my abiding presence. (179)

The immortal that is *in us more than us* is here framed in terms of a successive yet accretive rhetoric of mutually non-exclusive alternative subjunctive clauses. This is the affirmative answer to the consistent rhetoric of negation that underpins the conversations of this book; what we have here is a potentially infinite series of optative phrases where 'my abiding presence' is joyously construed in the dimension of an object-oriented ontology. What is more, the momentum of these phrases carries this exultant language towards the numerical sublime that has been its innermost impulse from the very start. The final rapprochement with the infinite takes place such that the individual character in death is rendered 'dividual' to such an extent that it can literally become again that 'absolutely undefined and unlimited possibility' ascribed by Peirce to the 'pure zero'.

> There are in the great world whirls of fluid and vaporous existences obtaining in their own unpassing time, unwatched and uninterpreted, valid only in their essential un-understandable mystery, justified only in their eyeless and mindless immeasurability, unassailable in their actual abstraction; of the inner quality of such a thing I might well in my own time be the true quintessential pith. (180)

The rhetoric of negation now inheres in the prefixes and suffixes that imbue the modifiers and substantives to which they are affixed with a sense of their innermost void; and that has the effect of opening up the intuited infinity of being to a temporality of immortal becoming. As Badiou declares, the edge of the void of any situation is its evental site:

> I will term *evental site* an entirely abnormal multiple; that is, a multiple such that none of its elements are presented in the situation. The site, itself, is presented, but "beneath" it nothing from which it is composed is presented. As such, the site is not a part of the situation. I will also say of such a multiple that it is *on the edge of the void*, or *foundational*.[13]

---

[13] Alain Badiou, *Being and Event*, trans. Oliver Feltham (London and New York: Continuum, 2005), 175.

What is this great image of the 'whirls of fluid and vaporous existences', if it is not a multiple 'such that none of its elements are presented in the situation'? All that can be said of it is that it is 'un-'/'-less', so far does it outstrip the capacity of a merely human imagination to present it. This is indeed the uppermost limit of that nested matryoshka-doll incoherence of the narrator's own nameless multiplicity – the immeasurable nebular swirls and galactic abysses that finally, on this inhuman scale, resolve themselves into 'things' of which 'I' may eventually become the 'true quintessential pith'. Here, then, the 'I' is fatefully transposed into the mode of a speculative event inhering in the unstable multiplicity of an unrepresentable totality. This *foundational reincarnation* discovers within the resources of nihilism the potential for an affirmative post-humanism – a characterological dismantlement that endorses extinction as a ticket to the infinite.

In scalar terms, we are a long way from that risible 'Atomic Theory' that Sergeant Pluck uses to explain the dissolution of human bodies through their ongoing contact with various means of motility – bicycles and roads, predominantly. Recall that the Sergeant, in his role as pedagogue, declares the following:

> Everything is composed of small particles of itself and they are flying around in concentric circles and arcs and segments and innumerable other geometrical figures too numerous to mention collectively, never standing still or resting but spinning away and darting hither and thither and back again, all the time on the go. These diminutive gentlemen are called atoms. (91)

Despite the scalar antithesis, we are back among figures of swirls and arcs and segmentary ellipses; firmly within the numerical sublime. Mathematics being the only effective line of approach to these atomic mysteries, the good Sergeant first offers a word of warning on the work involved: 'proving a bit of it with rulers and cosines and similar other instruments and then at the wind-up not believe what you had proved at all. If that happened you would have to go back over it till you got a place where you could believe your own facts and figures as delineated from Hall and Knight's Algebra and then go on again from that particular place till you had the whole thing properly believed and not have bits of it half-believed or a doubt in your head hurting you like when you lose the stud of your shirt in bed.' (92) Mathematics, once again, *hurts the head* – it frustrates the spontaneous humanisms of phenomenology, and replaces them (we are advised) with a cold, logical access to 'proper belief'. However, when this belief comes, it is the opposite of mathematical truth:

> "The gross and net result of it is that people who spend most of their natural lives riding iron bicycles over the rocky roadsteads of this parish get their personalities mixed up with the personalities of their bicycle as a result of the interchanging of the atoms of each of them and you would be surprised at the number of people in these parts who nearly are half people and half bicycles."
>
> I let go a gasp of astonishment that made a sound in the air like a bad puncture.
>
> "And you would be flabbergasted at the number of bicycles that are half-human almost half-man, half-partaking of humanity." (93)

This figural concretion of the text's human/inhuman chiasmus is the comic counterpoint to the sublime affirmation of its subjective 'pith' among the cosmic dust. And we can precisely specify the nature of this inversion, and so the inadequacy of the Sergeant's 'proper belief'. At the outer limits, where the human imagination is obliged to cede its authority to the object-totality of interstellar 'swirls', there is no question of any kind of immortality that is not conceived in the light of Nietzsche's chill laughter: 'There were eternities in which [the human intellect] did not exist; and when it is gone nothing will have happened.'[14] In so vast a perspective, grasping the 'essential un-understandable mystery' means overcoming the human intellect's narcissistic self-projections, and putting an end to character as a means of organizing information in narrative terms. Here the 'I' floats free of characterological prescriptions, and approaches the very edge of the totality's void – a speculative evental flicker within the background radiation of the Big Bang. However, at the molecular level, where backside meets bicycle seat and foot nestles against pedal, things are set on a radically different footing. Here, at the crowded interface between body and commodity, we are being hectored by a policeman with one species of materialism, where another would be infinitely preferable. His cavalier atomic disaggregation of 'molar' beings into molecular orbits and trajectories which can transpose the properties of one body into another, and vice versa, is a crudely Lucretian materialism for which there can be no thought of the *social* mechanisms

---

[14] Friedrich Nietzsche, 'On Truth and Lie in an Extra-Moral Sense', in *Writings from the Early Notebooks*, ed. Raymond Geuss and Alexander Nehamas (Cambridge: Cambridge University Press, 2009), 253.

that actually do displace human properties onto inanimate objects, and then return the favour.

For rather than a fatuous 'object-oriented ontology' at this scale of things, what is desperately needed is a *political economy of objects*, such that the tautologous inherency of 'omnium' – 'Omnium is the essential inherent interior essence which is hidden inside the root of the kernel of everything and it is always the same' (121) – can stand revealed as the mystery of value itself. But that, of course, is not forthcoming here. In this private hell, value (the 'Great Whatsit' lurking within the black box that had originally eclipsed the narrator's name: 'I was sure of nothing save my search for the black box,' 30) can never be unravelled. Instead, given that value is precisely the alienated property of human labour, it hands the universe, bound and gagged, over to the narrow acquisitive imagination from which it threatened to liberate itself in the Nietzschean affirmative paradise of reincarnating 'pith'. Hell, instead, is the recursion of worldly omnipotence within the echo-chamber of value:

> Formless speculations crowded in upon me, fantastic fears and hopes, inexpressible fancies, intoxicating foreshadowing of creations, annihilations and god-like interferences. Sitting at home with my box of omnium I could do anything, see anything and know anything with no limit to my powers save that of my own imagination. Perhaps I could use it to extend my imagination. I could destroy, alter and improve the universe at will. (214–25)

Such fantastic omnipotence is, of course, nothing but infernal servitude and repetition, a fatal recalibration of the figure of recursion. Damnation has glimpsed its exit velocity, in the nebular annihilation of all human 'little ideas', but cannot attain it. The object world of commodities reclaims that inhuman sublimity for a puerile, infantile narcissism, for which the universe is the sport of our 'god-like' intoxication at the bar of value.

The Third Policeman positions literary character between two powerful figures of the infinite, and allegorically demonstrates the incapacity of that traditional narrative function to withstand the competing pulls. On the one hand, there is a genuine tarrying with the infinite as such – a mathematical concept related to death, and perilous to any humanistic hub of integrity and cohesion, such as character, in that its tendency is to erode consistency with the constant wash of an irregular multiple. On the other, there is the 'Atomic Theory' that masks commodity fetishism, and serves as its alibi. The tidal pull of omnium (or, value) is so powerful because it counteracts the characterological dissolutions of the numerical infinite as such: recurring to a figure of the absolutely powerful 'I', animated by fantasies of its own infinite reach, albeit in the domain of a repetitious inferno. Onmium is the spurious infinity of exchange value as such, a neutral network of market equivalences, in which everything is finally the same, but only because it is secretly what Marx figured as the '*Gallerte*': metaphorically the 'undifferentiated mess of glue-yielding . . . animal substances industrially boiled down into condiments',[15] or, literally, the atomized 'human brains, muscles, nerves, hands, etc.' of which value is comprised in the alienated labour process.[16] People become bicycles, and bicycles people, thanks to this disgusting *mélange* of an infinite number of concrete, material practices boiled down into one 'general' equivalent.

Literary character, forced into orbit around this double sun (of the mathematical sublime, and of its negation within the money form), founders on its internal contradictions. There where it most feels itself to be One, amid the flattering fantasies of infinite purchasing power, it surrenders its own essence abjectly to the general equivalent of omnium. And where it feels most essential – where it momentarily grasps its own immortal 'pith' – it is nothing other than a dispersal of innumerable molecules among the infinity of an inhuman universe. Has any author so 'stretched' the concept of character into the antinomian reaches of its own death drive?

---

[15] Keston Sutherland, *Stupefaction: A Radical Anatomy of Phantoms* (London: Seagull, 2011), 41–2.
[16] Marx, *Capital*, 134.

12

'No Unauthorized Boozing': Flann O'Brien and the Thirsty Muse

Sam Dickson

For there to be art, for there to be any kind of aesthetic doing and seeing, one physiological precondition is indispensable: intoxication.
– Friedrich Nietzsche, *Twilight of the Idols*[1]

The idea of a productive relationship between alcohol and the arts is not a new one but it has emerged as a popular myth for readers of modern literature. Tom Dardis, in his study of four key modernist writers and their drinking habits, argues against this romanticized notion that 'drinking writers [are], in effect, good writers'.[2] 'The Thirsty Muse: Alcohol and the American Writer' outlines critical biographies of William Faulkner, F. Scott Fitzgerald, Ernest Hemingway and Eugene O'Neill, contending that excessive consumption over their lives in fact led to a progressive decline in the literary merit of their work. It upends the common conviction held between them that they had 'benefited richly from their early pact with alcohol' and 'that it had been a necessary ingredient in the brief yet golden period of their youth'.[3] Also central to this conception of alcohol as a destructive muse 'deaf to the pleas of . . . writers as they age' is its national character. Dardis claims that 'in the twentieth century the idea of the writer as drinker seems to be a particularly American one: no such line of thinking prevailed among European or English writers, suggesting that on the subject of alcohol we are a nation apart'.[4]

---

[1] Friedrich Nietzsche, *Twilight of the Idols*, trans. Duncan Large (Oxford: Oxford University Press, 1998), 46–7.
[2] Tom Dardis, *The Thirsty Muse: Alcohol and the American Writer* (New York: Ticknor & Fields, 1989), 5.
[3] Ibid.
[4] Dardis, *The Thirsty Muse: Alcohol and the American Writer*, 4. This claim is supported by another recent study, Olivia Laing, *The Trip to Echo Spring: On Writers and Drinking* (Edinburgh: Canongate, 2013). Laing's study widens the field to include Tennessee Williams, John Berryman, John Cheever and Raymond Chandler; all still American writers.

There is, of course, no shortage of heavy drinking among modern Irish writers. Taking the oeuvre of two of Ireland's modernist giants, Samuel Beckett and James Joyce, there is little to suggest that the model of the 'thirsty muse', a career trajectory marked by declining quality caused by excessive alcohol consumption, is common in Irish writing. Beckett's literary accomplishments were consistent throughout his oeuvre, a talent seemingly unimpaired by stories of his habitual evening drinking. In the fiction itself, mentions of drinking and alcoholism are sparse. The many figures of physical infirmity in his novels are necessary extensions of Beckett's experimental form rather than any obvious cultural and national determinant. It is fitting, then, that one of the few instances of heavy drinking is found in the youthful experiences of Belacqua in his earliest novel, *Dream of Fair to Middling Women*, an apprentice work that still exhibits a stylistic debt to Joyce.[5] The reputation of James Joyce himself as a heavy drinker is not reflected in diminished literary returns; *Finnegan's Wake* was published 2 years before his death. Unlike Beckett, however, the ubiquity of alcoholism and alcoholics in Joyce is symptomatic of a cultural degeneracy specific to its Irish context, a critical view that opposes the American myth of the successful 'writer-drinker'.

The correlation between alcoholism and squandered talent is all too evident in the case of Flann O'Brien, whose career as a novelist flailed after his second novel, *The Third Policeman*, failed to find a publisher. A tendency towards heavy drinking only exacerbated the problem of pursuing a career as a novelist. Anthony Cronin, in his biography of O'Brien, identifies the connection as late as 1954, noting that 'he was still certainly ambitious to write novels and he was quite aware that drink was one of his problems'.[6] Rather than simply reiterating the tragic consequences of Brian O'Nolan's real-life alcoholism, it is worth reflecting on how this biographical fact can inform a critical understanding of his actual literary achievements. A considerable amount of his fiction and journalism features excessive drinking, but it does so in a more explicitly comic mode than is evident in the depiction of drunkenness as a cultural trait in such texts as Joyce's *Dubliners*. Collectively, O'Brien's fiction and journalism offer a fittingly self-reflexive set of ideas regarding the relation between author and text, particularly the discursive notion of the writer-as-drinker that so many modern American writers perpetuated at the time.

---

[5] Beckett wrote *Dream of Fair to Middling Women* in 1932 but it remained unpublished until 1992, 3 years after his death.
[6] Anthony Cronin, *No Laughing Matter: The Life and Times of Flann O'Brien* (London: Grafton Books, 1989), 197.

This chapter will explore some of the ways in which O'Brien's depiction of drinking and intoxication is implicated in a particular mode of spatio-temporal evasion. An analysis of the spatial relation between the young protagonist's drinking and literary composition in *At Swim-Two-Birds* supports the notion of alcohol as a productive literary agent. This reading will be complicated by a consideration of various journalism pieces and short fictions published under the Myles na gCopaleen pseudonym, where the influence of American mass culture is depicted as a new form of cultural imperialism which further imperils an Irish tradition already caught in old English imperial forms. His attitude to the 'productivity' of drink is ambivalent, at once offering a fecund source of inspiration, particularly in its invocation of the non-rational, and also recognizing that such advantages are fleeting. The spatiotemporal warping of intoxication inevitably yields to a sobering return into the inescapable limitations of material conditions.

This portrayal of drinking as a perceptual escape is emblematically rendered in O'Brien's short critique of Joyce, 'A Bash in the Tunnel' (1951), which relates the story of an interloper drinking in a stationary train. The intended timespan of the 'bash' ('I always try to see, for the good of me health, that a bash doesn't last more than a day and night'), which is usually indicated by the appearance of daylight through the carriage windows, is disrupted by its stationary parking spot in a tunnel, leaving the storyteller to consume well past his allotted drinking time: 'I was three quarters into the jigs when they pulled me out of the tunnel. . . . I was in bed for a week.'[7] This depiction of an alcoholic bender as a comic disruption of all temporal coordinates returns in one of his short pieces, 'Drink and Time in Dublin' (1946). It presents a conversation between two unnamed voices, one a storyteller, who relates to an interlocutor his confusion during and after an alcoholic binge in which time and space became a series of fleeting reference points. Told in long stretches of dialogue, the short sentences move swiftly through locations and times that seem to continually elude the narrator:

> There's lights showing in the houses. That means it's night-time and not early in the morning. Then I see a bus. That means it's not yet half-nine, because they stopped at half-nine that time. Then I see a clock. It's twenty past nine! But I still don't know what day it is and it's too late to buy an evening paper. There's only one thing – into a pub and get a look at one. So I march into the nearest, very quiet and correct and say a bottle of stout please.[8]

---

[7] Flann O'Brien, 'A Bash in the Tunnel', in *Stories and Plays*, intro. Keith Donohue (London: Hart-Davis, MacGibbon, 1973), 205.
[8] Myles na gCopaleen, 'Drink and Time in Dublin', *Irish Writing* 1 (1946): 75.

Both of these stories display a comic quality that relies upon the exaggeration of perceptual impairment brought on by excessive drinking, but undercut this with an ironic return to the stable world conditions that the drinker seeks to avoid or ignore through intoxication. In 'A Bash in the Tunnel', the story serves as a personal criticism of Joyce on the grounds of his anti-Irish sentiments, and also presents a vague yet grim allegorical figure of an Irish artist whose 'bash' is still always held in the environs of the colonizer:

> But surely there you have the Irish artist? Sitting fully dressed, innerly locked in the toilet of a locked coach where he has no right to be, resentfully drinking somebody else's whiskey, being whisked hither and thither by anonymous shunters, keeping fastidiously the while on the outer face of his door the simple word, ENGAGED? I think the image fits Joyce: but particularly in his manifestation of a most Irish characteristic – the transgressor's resentment with the nongressor.[9]

Similarly, 'Time and Drink in Dublin' ends with its storyteller's dignity undercut in a punchline where his interlocutor suggests that the temporal confusion of his drinking escapades could have been quickly solved with a quick glance at the date on his sleeping pill prescription. This long argument is precipitated by a pointed reference to Billy Wilder's 1946 film *The Lost Weekend*. The character describes the film as 'tripe', one of many disparaging sentiments directed at Hollywood and, by extension, at US cultural imperialism. The film must have been of particular interest to O'Brien, as he wrote about it for a 'Cruiskeen Lawn' column in 1946. The column not only mocks the film for its earnest, negative portrayal of alcoholism but also takes the Don Birnam character as a starting point for mocking the very idea of the American 'writer-as-drinker' myth by offering an absurd application of that myth to the Irish literary scene:

> ... it is by no means Mr. Jackson's novel ... his perceptive document merely recorded certain phenomena, leaving it to the individual conscience to make an adjudication thereon. The cine people ... rather misquote the book, make it appear that a man who is enjoying himself is thereby in peril of death, and thereupon proceed to the monstrous thesis that heavy drinking is bad! (!) Indeed, substituting "reform" for Mr. Jackson's farewell hint that things are only beginning to happen to his bibulous hero, they wind up with a homily, shocking in its banality, warning all and sundry to keep away from the bottle ...

[9] O'Brien, *Stories and Plays*, 206.

"The Law's Weak End" – the film, not the book – also interested me in my capacity as official observer of the Irish scene. The film offers drunkards an immediate and rather startling remedy for their malady. Wouldst be cured of dipsomania? Well, they argue that all you have to do is write a book. It's as simple as that: all you need is a typewriter (portable), gigantic hangover – and there you are. You write a book and never drink again.

Now let's apply all the foregoing to Ireland. You have here your reverend Irish Academy of Letters, composed of persons who have written books. Search these books for the trace of a solitary motive for their composition: find you will none. But does not this ingenious suggestion that book-writing is a by-product of alcoholic excess at least explain the impulse that has deluged decent London publishers with unique literary curiosities packed with wee gaelic indecencies, mostly about girls – of all people? I think so. Your authors, then, are just ex-drunks? Fine![10]

The 'monstrous thesis' and sententious message of Wilder's film is similar to that of the Dardis project. This mode of anxious critical address must derive in part as a corollary to the very self-styled mythology of the American writer as drinker. Each instance of alcoholic bravado from the likes of Hemingway fuels a responsive tragic narrative of the 'author'. Myles's comic recuperation of the thirsty muse proceeds from pushing this hysterical drama of the alcoholic writer from its anxious mode into farce.

Seeking to find simple correspondences between the instances of drinking in Brian O'Nolan's writing and his personal life risks a basic critical error that is particularly egregious when applied to a writer whose use of multiple nom-de-plumes explicitly undermines a naïve conflation of author and text. However, it is difficult to read the protagonist of *At Swim-Two-Birds*, a young writer, without imagining some degree of biographical influence, given that the novel is the work of a young writer. In 'A Bash in the Tunnel', O'Brien excoriates Joyce for producing what was clearly a version of himself in his own literature: 'Joyce spent a lifetime establishing himself as a character in fiction. Joyce created, in narcissus fascination, the ageless Stephen. Beginning with importing real characters into his books, he achieves the magnificent inversion of making them legendary and fictional. It is quite preposterous.'[11] O'Brien is critical here of the self-mythologizing connection between author and character, a feature we can also identify in the authorial personas

---

[10] Myles na gCopaleen, 'The Cruiskeen Lawn', *The Irish Times*, 23 March 1946.
[11] O'Brien, *Stories and Plays*, 206.

developed by his American counterparts, especially Fitzgerald. The principle of 'aestho-autogamy' described in *At Swim-Two-Birds* might well be seen as a further expression of O'Brien's desire to complicate, if not erase entirely, a coherent link between the writer and the written word. However, to pursue the analogy somewhat, O'Brien composed much of *At Swim-Two-Birds* in his bedroom, much like that novel's protagonist.[12] Accordingly, while we should hesitate to conflate the young Brian O'Nolan with the young protagonist of *At Swim-Two-Birds*, it seems appropriate – given O'Brien's dedication to a metafictional approach – that traces of O'Nolan's alcohol consumption and literary practice are taken up as self-conscious content in the penned works of O'Brien and Myles.

Early in *At Swim-Two-Birds*, the student explains to Brinsley that Mr Trellis intends for his invented characters to live with him in the Red Swan Hotel, 'so that he can keep an eye on them and see that there is no boozing'. He subsequently explains, however, that Mr Trellis' moralizing work would be littered with indecent assaults, drenched in whiskey and porter.

> I thought there was to be no boozing, Brinsley said.
> No unauthorized boozing, I answered.

The protagonist's authorization of drinking doubles the tacit consent of O'Brien, whose first novel might well be a text written piecemeal over a few years under the influence of heavy drinking, chronicling a youth undertaking the very same labour. In this case, the flow of booze would appropriately permeate through the textual layers through to its decentred authorial source and beyond, functioning less as the fateful, destructive muse than the fuel for the chaotic production of fiction.

The Don Birnam character in Wilder's film considers himself two people, one a writer and the other a drunk, the two of which can never coincide. O'Brien's *At Swim-Two-Birds* is, among other things, the story of an undergraduate's developing drinking and writing habits. However, its metafictional layering traverses the trapped Moebius-strip structure of Birnam's hell where writing and drinking are mutually exclusive, partitioning a private retreat for its protagonist's reverie-fuelled fiction. David Cohen suggests that the elliptical, episodic form of *At Swim-Two-Birds* may be attributed to its scattershot construction, in contrast with the polished product of a 'Daedalean workshop'. Rather than a 'predetermined, structured work', it is best thought of as a compilation, with O'Brien 'integrating it into his daily life and giving over the details of his own experiences to

---

[12] Anthony Cronin, *No Laughing Matter*, 30–1.

the narrator'.[13] The unnamed narrator is above all an accretion of everyday experiences, dispassionately detailed in biographical reminiscences. He frequently characterizes himself as an object, describing his bodily functions in the empirical mode of mechanism or chemical reaction. His head is an empty space for his mind, fronted by the 'apertures'[14] of his eyes, while his guts are an empty tract for the circulation – and often rejection – of stout. The narrator's dispassionate descriptions of himself are consistent with O'Brien's admiration of Charles Jackson's writing, which 'merely recorded certain phenomena'.[15]

His experiences with alcohol are recorded as effects by this body sensorium dominated by the eyes and stomach. In his first biographical reminiscence he tells us that he had his 'first experience of intoxicating beverages and their strange intestinal chemistry' a few months before beginning composition on his stories. The reproduced Christian Brothers reader warns against alcohol as a 'double poison', at once a degenerate intoxicant to excite the brain and a narcotic that blunts the nervous system, 'a muscular depression followed by complete paralysis of the body'. The first time he suffers 'painful and blinding fits of vomiting' he recalls it as puking till the eyes nearly left his head and leaving his stomach on the floor. The writer is however more intrigued by the recital of strange adventures from his drinking peers: he reasons that 'the mind may be impaired by alcohol . . . but withal it may be pleasantly impaired'.[16] These sentiments are confirmed later when he and some drinking friends are 'occupied in putting glasses of stout into the interior of our bodies and expressing by fine disputation the resulting sense of physical and mental well-being. . . . The stout was of superior quality, soft against the tongue but sharp upon the orifice of the throat, softly efficient in its magical circulation through the conduits of the body'.[17]

While drinking is registered in its circulation through the body and its offence to the senses, the basis of literary creation takes place in a withdrawn imaginary activity of the mind unaffected by the body's sensorium. At the opening of the book the author tells us: 'Having placed in my mouth sufficient bread for three minutes' chewing, I withdrew my powers of sensual perception and retired into the privacy of my mind . . .'[18] After providing three narrative openings, the author is brought back to his senses, a hurt tooth recalling him to the perception of his surroundings. The mind takes on a private spatial

---

[13] David Cohen, 'An Atomy of the Novel: Flann O'Brien's "At Swim-Two-Birds"', *Twentieth Century Literature* 39, 2 (Summer 1993): 208.
[14] Flann O'Brien, *At Swim-Two-Birds* (Penguin: London, 2000), 34.
[15] Myles na gCopaleen, 'The Cruiskeen Lawn', *The Irish Times*, 23 March 1946.
[16] O'Brien, *At Swim-Two-Birds*, 22–3.
[17] Ibid., 38.
[18] Ibid., 9.

quality inside the head: 'I went to the tender trestle of my bed. . . . I closed my eyes, hurting slightly my right stye, and retired into the kingdom of my mind. For a time there was complete darkness and an absence of movement on the part of the cerebral mechanism.' In this mental 'kingdom' the Finn MacCool character 'comes out from the shadow'.[19] The next time the writer withdraws to the bedroom for extended repose, he is shaking off his first hangover, during which the Dermot Trellis narrative emerges. Rather than presenting the young writer struggling to write under the influence, the sensuous shock of drinking is passed into the mental activity of the sleeping drunkard. The thread between narrative frames is suggested by their sequential proximity on the page but is cemented further by the narrative involution between private spaces. The bedroom telescopes into the privacy of the mind and into another bedroom with the next sleeping writer, Dermot Trellis. This recursive movement ceases only with the self-destructive advent of aestho-autogamy, where the next level of fictional production instead turns on its sleeping master.

If the dormant Trellis is left to incur and sleep off the undergraduate's hangover, then the Pooka and Sweeney narratives might be thought of as the literary output of alcoholic hallucinosis. The connection between such fantastical characters and the student's alcohol consumption is foreshadowed at his inaugural drink, where the young author subjects himself to an 'inward interrogation', spirits lifted by the potent possibilities of Bacchic revelry: 'Who are my future cronies, where our mad carousals? What neat repast shall feast us light and choice of Attic taste with wine . . .? What mad pursuit? What pipes and timbrels? What wild ecstasy?'[20] That the future cronies and mad pursuits are found in the student's alcohol-influenced stories rather than daily life is a comic irony that is revisited by Myles in the aforementioned 'Lost Weekend' column. He notes:

> The point is made, and very properly, that the man who drinks to X. Hess, never sees pink elephants or other gigantic mammalian – only very small creatures such as tiny turkeys wearing straw hats, mice, beetles and little men. . . . The fairies and the "little people" are part of the charm, part of the traditional national resources of this country. We have seen above that these are alcoholic figments.[21]

To follow Myles's comic logic, the preponderance of imagined creatures, large and small, in the student's fiction would seem to be borrowed from

[19] Ibid., 13.
[20] Ibid., 22.
[21] Myles na gCopaleen, 'The Cruiskeen Lawn', *The Irish Times*, 23 March 1946.

a collective hallucinosis, the treasury of 'national resources' an effect of alcoholic figments. Underlying the imaginative play assisted by intoxication, however, is the economic support for the youth that is felt most directly from the interrupting harangues from his uncle but which is also present in the space of the bedroom itself.

In the bedroom of the narrator, next to the books by Joyce and Huxley, is a mirror symbolically frosted with the commercial trace of a local brewery: 'The mirror at which I shaved every second day was of the type supplied gratis by Messrs Watkins, Jameson and Pim and bore brief letterpress in reference to a proprietary brand of ale between the words of which I had acquired considerable skill in inserting the reflection of my countenance.'[22] This reflected portrait of the unnamed artist comes tagged with the commercial trace of beer. Its token placement connects the mental topography of the bedroom to the pub setting and its discursive proliferation of 'pub-talk'. It is doubled within the Trellis fictional space, the bedroom located in the Red Swan Hotel that provides the locus for the eventual collision of the multiple threads of parodied styles and voices. It also slots into the minor relation the student's bedroom has to the rest of the house. His uncle, and guardian, is fittingly employed as a clerk by Guinness, the larger brewery whose market-share dominated that of Watkins, Jameson and Pim. The vulnerable student's bedroom writing is comparable to the 'bash' in the carriage bathroom, at the mercy of external shunting.

The public house appears elsewhere in O'Nolan's writing as a metonym for a disappearing Irish culture in the face of mass culture. The incursion of American mass culture is explicitly decried in a newspaper piece from 1940 called 'The Trade in Dublin', where a new 'cinema-going' clientele and transformed space signify some diminishing 'national' character:

> The white-coated server who has ousted the curate in some pubs may be taken as a sign of the decline of faith. The Irish brand of humanity, expansive and voluble, is hardening and contracting under the hammer-blows of international mammon, dealt through the radio, press and cinema. Among the stupider section of the younger generation a shabby and rather comic "smartness" may be discerned, even in the simple task of dealing with a bottle of brown stout. Their cinema-going has taught them the great truth that William Powell does not walk up to a counter, bellow for a schooner or a scoop and ask Mick whether the brother is expected up for the match on Sunday. William is modern and drinks out

---

[22] O'Brien, *At Swim-Two-Birds*, 11.

of glasses with long stems in a cushioned corner with his doxy. His many imitators (what could be more flimsy than an imitation of a flat two-dimensional picture-house ghost?) have insisted on something similar, since they, too, have to go out with Myrna Loy. The Select Lounge has been the handsome answer of the trade in Dublin. . . . The other [less good] places afford a pathetic insight into the meaning attached to the word "modern" by many publicans. They think that it means just tubes – tubular chairs, repellent alike to eye and seat, tubular lighting, tubular effects in decoration. Those who have been to prison immediately recognise the lamentable simplicity of the decor and the severity of the furnishings. The ugliness of such a tavern cannot be completely offset by the fact that most of the customers appear to be film-stars or that the man who serves you is a bell-hop from New York.[23]

The space of the pub also appears early in *The Third Policeman*, where Divney, the profligate and scheming acquaintance of the protagonist, squanders his inheritance under the auspices of maintaining a public house, but notes that it is a 'very serious thing to surrender a licence'.[24] One of O'Brien's plays, 'Thirst' (1942), features a publican who trades outside of licensed hours and is interrupted by a policeman. His skilful and detailed descriptions of a dehydrating march in the desert induce such a thirst in the policeman that he is convinced to join the three drinkers. Ann Clissman notes the alignment here of the storytelling publican with the artist: 'O'Brien had already said that the writer was on the same economic level as the labourer who was excluded from the heaven of the lounge bar. It is clear then, that he associated drink and creativity. The publican in *Thirst* is a master of language in his own way. The artist, like the drinker, is a degenerate. The glow of creativity is like the glow gained from alcohol which transforms the world. . . . Yes this sense of wellbeing is, like everything associated with enjoyment in Ireland, accompanied by a sense of sin.'[25] The association between drink and creativity is evident across a variety of the literary forms and authorial personas employed by Brian O'Nolan, but more than a sense of mere sin undercuts their attendant 'glow'. The transformation of the world that appears before the intoxicated artist is lovingly portrayed as a distension of time that interrupts the logical proceeding of rational modern time ('I never carry a

---

[23] Flann O'Brien, 'The Trade In Dublin', *The Bell* 1, 2 (November 1940): 7–8.
[24] Flann O'Brien, 'The Third Policeman', in *The Complete Novels*, intro. Claud Cockburn (New York: Everyman's Library, 2007), 228.
[24] Anne Clissman, *Flann O'Brien: A Critical Introduction to His Writings* (Dublin: Gill & Macmillan, 1975), 233.

watch,' says the man having a 'bash'[26]), but the transient nature of intoxication is underscored by the suffocating spaces in which writing and drinking can occur. Whether it is the bedroom, remodelled public house or a toilet in a stationery train carriage, the material conditions of creativity in O'Brien's work remain fatalistically immovable beneath the imaginary flights of the drunken artist.

---

[26] O'Brien, *Stories and Plays*, 205.

13

Soft Drink, Hard Drink and Literary (Re)production in Flann O'Brien and Frank Moorhouse

Sascha Morrell

This essay compares how Flann O'Brien's *At Swim-Two-Birds* (1939) and Australian author Frank Moorhouse's *The Electrical Experience: A Discontinuous Narrative* (1974) use beer and soft drink manufacture, respectively, as conceits both for literary production and for the production of 'character'. In so doing, these texts offer challenging representations of authorial power, class relations and the intersections between literature and commodity culture. The Irish and the Australian authors were born a generation apart, and Moorhouse (b.1938) has never claimed O'Brien as a literary influence,[1] but the two authors' comic visions have certain affinities, most evident in how they draw imaginatively on the beverage industry to explore whether human life itself might be considered a mass product like Guinness or Coca-Cola.

Both O'Brien and Moorhouse are known for producing disconnected narratives. *At Swim-Two-Birds* presents an elaborate tissue of interpenetrating diegetic layers. The outmost frame tale features a Dublin college student with a penchant for porter who is writing a novel about a publican, Dermot Trellis, who himself is writing a novel featuring characters 'hired' from other novels and from Irish legend; Trellis then 'violat[es] frame-tale ontology' (to use Kim McMullen's phrase)[2] by raping and impregnating one of his characters, begetting a 'quasi-illusory' son,[3] Orlick, who leads Trellis' characters in a

---

[1] In a 1991 interview with Ray Willbanks, Moorhouse nominated Sherwood Anderson and J. D. Salinger as major influences: see Ray Willbanks and Frank Moorhouse, 'Frank Moorhouse', in ed. Ray Willbanks, *Speaking Volumes: Australian Writers and their Work* (Ringwood: Penguin, 1991), 158–70 (162).
[2] Kim McMullen, 'Culture as Colloquy: Flann O'Brien's Postmodern Dialogue with Irish Tradition', *NOVEL: A Forum on Fiction* 27, 1 (Autumn 1993): 62–84 (68).
[3] Flann O'Brien, *At Swim-Two-Birds* (London: Penguin, 1967), 145. Subsequent references are to this edition and cited parenthetically.

porter-fuelled narrative revolt against their author, constructing a story with Trellis as a character and subjecting him to elaborate punishments. *The Electrical Experience,* like Moorhouse's other 'discontinuous narratives', is a series of interrelated stories with recurring characters, presented out of chronological order. Spanning the 1920s to the 1950s, the stories exhibit various points in the life of George McDowell, the teetotalling founder of a soft-drink factory on New South Wales's south coast. Like O'Brien, Moorhouse disrupts the narrative with interpolated textual fragments and 'found documents' (both authentic and imaginary), numerous of which are fictionally authored by the protagonist. The text offers self-conscious commentary on its own construction, although its complexities do not rival those of *At Swim-Two-Birds,* with its paradoxical job-sharing between fictional authors and characters.

Whereas O'Brien tends to apply the language of labour relations to the production of literary art, Moorhouse generally does the opposite, with McDowell conceiving of his business as a kind of artistry. Nonetheless, the connections they create between these fields serve to undermine myths of artistic autonomy and myths of capitalist self-making in similar ways.

'You and your book and your porter'

That O'Brien 'associated drink and creativity' is well known.[4] The connection is established early on in *At Swim-Two-Birds,* through excerpts the frame narrator provides from his manuscript about the legendary Finn MacCool. MacCool offers extempore poetic recitals in nightly bouts of drinking with his followers, and his very body is stained with mead as he speaks verse (19). It then emerges that the frame narrator's account of Finn MacCool was itself inspired by drink: '*Biographical reminiscence, part the first:* It was only a few months before composing the foregoing that I had my first experience of intoxicating beverages' (20). He learnt, from that first experience, that alcohol loosens tongues: 'under the influence of alcohol' his friends surprised him with 'recital of their strange adventures', modern equivalents for MacCool's nights of poetic carousal (22).

'You can't beat a good pint,' the frame narrator tells his drinking companion Kelly, who replies, 'A pint of plain is your only man' (22). This will, of course, be taken up as the refrain of Jem Casey, the fictional working-class poet in Dermot

---

[4] Anne Clissman, *Flann O'Brien: A Critical Introduction to His Writings* (Dublin: Gill & Macmillan, 1975), 233. On the mythology of the 'thirsty muse', see Sam Dickson's essay in this volume.

Trellis' fictional novel. The equation of pint and man in that refrain – pint 'is' man – becomes significant in terms of *At Swim-Two-Birds'* broader concern with drink and creation. The narrator tells his friend Brinsley how, returning home after this drinking session, he 'puked' as he 'felt something inside me like a man trying to get out of my stomach', and that he relates this 'on the evening of the third day' links drink to Genesis (23). Within a few pages, he introduces Trellis who, as a publican, is responsible for the pulling of pints as well as the writing of books, and it is surely no coincidence that Trellis' semi-fictional son Orlick will first enter the novel as a 'stout form' (145).[5] O'Brien was by no means alone in associating drink with human origins: in Joyce's *Finnegans Wake*, for example, the publican HCE is described as having a whiskey barrel at his feet and a barrel of 'guenesis' at his head, a portmanteau word combining 'Guinness' and 'genesis'.[6] But O'Brien pursues the connection furthest in relation to fictional production.

Listening to the frame narrator in *At Swim-Two-Birds*, Brinsley chuckles at (as he explains) 'You and your book and your porter' (23), and it is evident that the three things are in mutually determining relation. As much as that of his uncle, who is thrice described as 'holder of Guinness clerkship the third class' (10, 30, 92), the frame narrator's very selfhood is implied to be bound up with booze in its commercial or 'proprietary' aspect:

> The mirror at which I shaved every second day was of the type supplied gratis by Messrs Watkins, Jameson and Pim and bore brief letterpress in reference to a proprietary brand of ale between the words of which I had acquired considerable skill in inserting the reflection of my countenance. (11)

---

[5] A recognized precursor for *At Swim-Two-Birds*, O'Brien's 1934 short story 'Scenes from a Novel', also features characters who revolt against their author, and whose creation is associated with drink: the protagonist was (the writer says) 'created one night when I swallowed nine stouts and was feeling vaguely blasphemous': Keith Hopper, *Flann O'Brien: A Portrait of the Artist as a Young Post-modernist* (Cork: Cork University Press, 1995), 41–2. The 'stout form' of humanity is evoked again in O'Brien's *The Third Policeman* (written 1939–40), in which Mathers' ghost describes his 'birth colour' darkening over his lifetime to 'that very dark sort of brownness one associates usually with stout': (Normal, IL: Dalkey Archive Press, 1999), 34; subsequent references are to this edition and cited parenthetically.

[6] James Joyce, *Finnegans Wake* (New York: Penguin Books, 1999), 6.27 cited in Cat Gubernatis Dannen, '"Genghis is ghoon for you": Guinness, Capitalism, and Nationalism in *Finnegans Wake*' *Hypermedia Joyce Studies (Special Prague Symposium Issue)* (2010–11). http://hjs.ff.cuni.cz/archives/v11_1/main/essays.php?essay=dannen. The brewery's famed slogan 'Guinness is good for you', first used in advertising campaigns in Scotland and England in 1928–29, itself associates Guinness with life-giving qualities: on the slogan see Bill Yenne, *Guinness: The 250 Year Quest for the Perfect Pint* (Hoboken, NJ: Wiley, 2007), 93.

Personal identity is mirrored within the brewer's corporate identity. The narrator's literary ambitions are also implicated, for the mirror is introduced immediately after the narrator describes his books: 'works ranging from those of Mr Joyce to . . . Mr A. Huxley' which are 'generally recognized as indispensable to all who aspire to an appreciation of the nature of contemporary literature' (11).

In *Ulysses* (1922), Leopold Bloom reflects that the 'best place for an ad to catch a woman's eye [is] on a mirror',[7] but O'Brien's readers were likely to recall that more famous Joycean mirror, the 'cracked lookingglass of a servant' that Stephen dubs a 'symbol of Irish art' (*Ulysses*, 7). Replacing the crack with the proprietary letterpress of a brewery, O'Brien hints at a close relationship between creative writing and alcohol consumption, while also suggesting the commodification of Irish art. Irish writers from Wilde and Yeats to Joyce had all stood in ambivalent relation to market forces[8]; in particular, Celtic Revival literature had become a major Irish export, hence Shanahan's description of Sweeney's poetry 'about the green hills and the bloody swords' as 'the real old stuff of the native land . . . stuff that brought scholars to our shore' (75).[9] Nor was O'Brien's own work exempt. As Harriman notes, no reprinting of *At Swim-Two-Birds* has appeared 'without including the blurb from Joyce: "That's a real writer, with the true comic spirit. A really funny book."'[10] The quote effectively works as a product endorsement from an established name in the business.

In *At Swim-Two-Birds,* the student writer's literary ambitions are bound up with proprietary ale in a more basic sense: he is dependent on the support of his uncle who, as a 'holder of Guinness clerkship', receives his pay from the titanic brewer, so that Guinness ultimately underwrites the youth's 'spare-time literary activities' (even as the mirror aligns him with one of

---

[7] James Joyce, *Ulysses* (New York: Oxford University Press, 1993), 355.
[8] See Declan Kiberd, 'W.B. Yeats – Building Amid Ruins', *Irish Classics* (London: Granta, 2000), 440–62, especially 442–3.
[9] Non-fiction writings show the same concerns. Writing in the *Irish Times* as Myles na Gopaleen, O'Brien complained of the 'exhibitionism' of Irish writers courting London publishers by 'putting up the witty celtic act' or 'pretending to be morose': see Myles na Gopaleen, *The Best of Myles*, ed. Kevin O'Nolan (London: MacGibbon & Kee, 1960), 234. Writing to Ethel Mannin in 1939, O'Brien described *At Swim-Two-Birds* as 'a sneer at all the slush' exported from Ireland to England, although the English 'manufacture[d] enough of their own odious slush to make the import unnecessary': cited in Joshua D. Esty, 'Flann O'Brien's *At Swim-Two-Birds* and the Post-Post Debate', *ARIEL* 26, 4 (October 1995): 23–46, 29.
[10] The quote was attributed by Niall Sheridan. See Lucas Harriman, 'Flann O'Brien's Creative Betrayal of Joyce', *New Hibernia Review* 14, 4 (Winter 2010): 90–109. On O'Brien's ambivalence about Joyce's praise, see Stephen Abblitt's essay in this volume.

Guinness' ill-fated competitors, a point I will return to). With this fact at bottom, questions of literary labour and economic dependency are examined at various levels throughout *At Swim-Two-Birds*, with the language of class relations applied to both intoxication and literary production.

'The author class'

The frame narrator quotes from a temperance pamphlet that describes alcohol as 'a merciless master', under the influence of which 'all will-power is gone' (22).[11] Authorship, too, is a form of mastery. As 'a member of the author class' (99), Dermot Trellis 'compel[s] all his characters to live with him in the Red Swan Hotel so that he can keep an eye on them and see that there is no [unauthorized] boozing' (35). It emerges that one form of mastery can influence the other. The narrator borrows his *'description of Trellis's person'* from a description of 'Dr Beattie' in *A Conspectus of the Arts and Natural Sciences* (a fictional intertext), which includes *'reference to a failing'*, namely, the 'too frequent use of wine' without which Beattie – and therefore Trellis – cannot sleep (30–1, italics original). Since Trellis can only sleep when he is drunk, the statement that 'Trellis's dominion over his characters . . . is impaired by his addiction to sleep' (99) becomes a covert reference to alcohol addiction. The 'merciless master' booze (here the grape rather than grain) overrides the author's mastery. This does not, however, mean an end to creativity. Rather, it is apparent that the controlling form of authorship Trellis practices in wakeful sobriety obstructs a freer creativity that is unleashed when he drinks and sleeps, when his characters themselves become creative, even putting 'sleeping-draughts in Trellis's porter' to extend their freedom (100).

Analogies between author-character relations and class relations prove unstable, for authors cannot simply be understood as masters. When telling Brinsley about his drinking session with Kelly, the frame narrator puts on 'the accent of the lower or working classes', then pokes his navel with a pencil (24). Somehow, the aspiring author's assumption of a working-class character prompts a form of navel-gazing that is linked by the pencil to writing.[12] With this curious connection established, the narrator advances

---

[11] For a valuable discussion of will-power in O'Brien, see Sean Pryor's essay in this volume.

[12] For further discussion of this image, see David Kelly's essay in this volume. Later, we read that Trellis' 'knowledge [. . . of] the origin of man was acquired from servants and public-house acquaintances', again associating genesis with drink and the working classes (99).

his oft-quoted theory of novelistic character, initially conceived in terms of workers' rights:

> It was undemocratic to compel characters to be uniformly good or bad or poor or rich. Each should be allowed a private life, self-determination and a decent standard of living.... Characters should be interchangeable as between one book and another. (24)

In this context, the conclusion that the modern novel should be largely 'a work of reference' from which 'authors could draw their characters as required' (32–3) suggests something less like an encyclopaedia and more like a business directory, with author-employers looking up characters like tradesmen. This impression is affirmed in the subsequent references to characters being 'hired' by Trellis (61).

But the narrator's class sympathies seem confused. Notwithstanding his egalitarian concern with characters' 'living standards', the idea of characters as 'interchangeable' raises the spectre of alienated labour – of human energies commodified, reduced to their exchange value – and the democratic impulse has certainly vanished when the narrator notes approvingly that reusing characters would require readers to be familiar with 'a wealth of references to existing texts' and so would 'preclude . . . persons of inferior education from an understanding of contemporary literature' (24–5). Further confusion results from the narrator's interest in saving authorial labour: reusing characters would 'obviate tiresome explanations', and authors would be tasked with 'creating' a character 'only when they failed to find a suitable existing puppet' (25). Authors are here conceived as workers, in which case the 'exchangeable' characters they produce should logically be conceived as commodities. This is certainly apparent after the court scene, when Furriskey reflects that 'he [Trellis] can't complain.... He got a fair trial and a jury of his own manufacture' (208).

The idea of character as commodity clearly applies to Trellis' house servant or 'slavey', Teresa, who is 'divided at the centre by the terminal ridge of a corset of inferior design'. Suggesting a seam from factory moulding, as Brinsley points out, this is 'the ineluctable badge of mass-production'. 'Slaveys,' he muses, 'were the Ford cars of humanity . . . created to a standard pattern by the hundred thousand' (43). Brinsley subsequently remarks the indistinguishability of Furriskey, Lamont and Shanahan, prompting the narrator to offer a cynical catalogue assigning them different features as one might distinguish different lines of a given product ('Configuration of nose: roman; snub; mastoid', 230).[13]

---

[13] Compare Orlick's flattering yet essentially interchangeable depictions of Shanahan, Lamont and Furriskey (187–91).

A tension thus arises between characters as workers (bearers of commodified labour power) and character as manufactured product (a commodity produced by authorial labour). Are writers employers, workers or both? And how does booze figure in all this?

Writer as worker

In line with its representations of literary characters as mass products, *At Swim-Two-Birds* repeatedly presents literary labour in terms of industrial wage labour, most explicitly in Shanahan's account of 'Jem Casey, Poet of the Pick'. By contrast with the aristocratic poets MacCool and Sweeney, Casey is emphatically 'a labouring man' who (Shanahan boasts) would 'be up at the [five o'clock] whistle with a pome a yard long' to put his social betters to shame. Shanahan's emphasis on quantity not quality ('a yard long') renders his working-class pride comical, but there is also a qualitative concern: Sweeney's poetry is 'good stuff, it's bloody nice', but 'you can get too much of that stuff', whereas Casey's poetry is 'stuff you'd never tire of' (75).

The very word 'stuff' puts poetry in the realm of the commodity, and the title of Casey's poem about porter, 'The Workman's Friend', sounds decidedly like a slogan, as does Shanahan's appraisal of the poem ('By God you can't beat it'). The verses themselves sound as much like an advertising jingle as the famous Plumtree's Potted Meat ditty in Joyce's *Ulysses*, although Casey names no particular brand:

> When things go wrong and will not come right,
> Though you do the best you can,
> When life looks black as the hour of night –
> A PINT OF PLAIN IS YOUR ONLY MAN

But whereas advertising language would typically be ephemeral, Lamont praises Casey's 'pome' for its 'permanence', and the composition is hailed as a timeless masterpiece (77–8).

When the venerable Finn MacCool is asked to appraise Casey's work, his only answer is to resume his own recital of the travails of Sweeney. Given the running parallel between porter and literary production this is particularly revealing. As Shanahan seems to have endless pints of Casey's verse about the dark brew available on tap, so 'droning dark-voiced Finn' seems capable of ceaselessly spouting the story of Sweeney, whose own 'melodious staves' stream continuously, 'his mouth never halting from [their] recital' (126). The consistency of these poetic fluids suggests that they are no more exempt from commodity culture than the porter celebrated by the worker-poet Casey (and here we might recall Orlick entering his publican father's novel as a 'stout form'). The continuity is underlined when Shanahan fuses Sweeney's style with Casey's in a verse of his own: 'When stags appear on the mountain high, with flanks the colour of bran, when a badger bold can say good-bye, A PINT OF PLAIN IS YOUR ONLY MAN!' (113).

But Sweeney's poetry is based on 'watercress and water' (95), while Casey's is a stronger brew: 'None of your soft stuff for Mr Casey,' Willard retorts when the Good Fairy asks if Casey likes poems about flowers (120).[14] By this point, Casey has entered the text as a character, and he strengthens the poetry-porter connection when he begins a recital by making 'a demonstration with his arm' then speaks in a 'hard brassy voice' that is 'free from all inflexion'. This unmistakably suggests the pulling of a pint: the motion of the arm, the brass tap, the flow of a refined fluid.[15] But Casey now has a different refrain, crying 'here's the slogan for you and me –/ THE GIFT OF GOD IS A WORKIN' MAN' (121). The advertising language of 'the slogan' becomes explicit as the 'workin' man' replaces the pint of plain, so that even as Casey is expressing his working-class pride, he is indicating how capitalism commodifies the worker as a quantity of abstract labour-power. Indeed, the 'hardness' of Casey's poetry might partially consist in its political overtones. Bearing in mind that the fictional poet has now joined the ranks as a character, and given that the Good Fairy has just charged Casey with 'Bolshevism', Casey's 'demonstration with his arm' can be read as a revolutionary gesture. We are, after all, about to witness the revolt of the literary characters – as workers – against their author-employer.

The character as worker

The character Shanahan was 'hired' by Trellis from his fellow novelist William Tracy, an 'eminent [American] writer of Western romances' (61, 56). Accordingly, when Shanahan entertains his fellow characters with tales of his experiences 'cow-punch[ing] in the Ringsend district of Dublin city', he speaks of Tracy as his former boss: 'Tracy sent for me and gave me my orders and said it was one of his cowboy books' (53). What better source from which to draw a fictional proletariat than the United States, where the mass-market

---

[14] For a discussion of O'Brien and the pastoral tradition, see Joseph Brooker's essay in this volume.
[15] When Casey and Sweeney meet 'poet on poet', Casey is described as 'pouring' words into Sweeney's ear (126).

industrialization of literary production was furthest advanced?[16] Yet *At Swim-Two-Birds'* representation of American influence is not decidedly negative, for Tracy appears to have been a model employer. The 'little negro maids' he employed had no complaints about their 'conditions of service' (45), and Shanahan's fellow cowboy Willard attests that 'it was a pleasure to work for Mr Tracy', who was generous with his porter (117).[17]

The conceit of character as employee generates comic contradiction in the climactic scene of Trellis' trial:

> State your name and occupation, [the judge] said to Mr. Willard.
> Willard Slug, said Mr. Willard. I am a cattleman and a cowpuncher, a gentleman farmer in the western tradition.
> Have you ever been employed by the accused?
> Yes.
> In what capacity?
> As tram-conductor.
> Give in your own words a brief statement of the remuneration and conditions of service attaching to the position.
> My pay was fifteen shillings per week of seventy-two hours ...
> Under what circumstances were your services utilized?
> I was instructed to meet and accept his fare from Mr. Furriskey ...
> In what manner were you compelled to address Mr. Furriskey?
> In guttersnipe dialect, at all times repugnant to the instincts of a gentleman. (285)

Recognizable class categories are hopelessly ravelled in this scene. The characters bearing witness speak a genteel language and object to being rendered lowly in class terms (a 'guttersnipe dialect'), yet they are conceived as workers asserting their rights against the exploitative author-master. The scene's dramatic dialogue form recalls the narrator's reference to plays being 'consumed ... by large masses in places of public resort' (25), but while the

---

[16] It is even conceivable that the competition Irish writers increasingly faced from imported American paperback genre fiction might have inspired O'Brien's idea of authors 'hiring' preexisting characters as an efficiency measure. On the extraordinary growth of U.S. pulp fiction production in the 1920s and its relationship to 'high culture' modernism, see Susan Hegeman, 'U.S. Modernism', in *A Companion to Twentieth-Century United States Fiction*, ed. David Seed (Oxford: Blackwell, 2010), 11–23 (13–14).

[17] McMullen proposes that O'Brien is recognizing the creative potential of Irish-American cultural exchange: McMullen, 71. The Dublin cowpunching sequence has an energy and brio which seems attractive in contrast with the sterile parochialism of the uncle's Gaelic League friends, who reject U.S. and wider European influences alike: 'leave the waltz to the jazz-boys', Corcoran scoffs (133). Elsewhere, O'Brien was more critical of U.S. cultural imperialism, as noted by Sam Dickson in this volume.

court resembles a pub, it curiously compounds 'high-brow' and 'low-brow' elements: the bench looks like 'the counter of a *high-class* public house', the judges drink 'brown porter' from 'elegant' glasses, and their 'gowns' are 'inexpensive . . . manufactured from jute fibre' (194, emphasis added). Most importantly, the characters have now taken control of the narrative, forcing Trellis into service as a character – at once their co-worker and their puppet. Slug may object to 'inadequate pay', and Shanahan may protest that 'his food was bad and insufficient' (202), but they and their fellow witnesses gleefully subject Trellis to far worse treatment.

They are led in their rebellion by Trellis' 'quasi-illusory' son Orlick, who has been tutored in 'revolt and non-serviam' by the Pooka McPhellimey (145, 150). Yet the class confusion continues, for while the Pooka professes to 'admire the working man immensely' (120), Orlick is a decidedly haughty and condescending figure. He has been working on 'a high-class story' full of 'the names of painters and French wines' (164) when he is enlisted to 'compose a story on the subject of Trellis' by Furriskey, Shanahan and Lamont (164). These working-class listeners continually interrupt Orlick's narration, protesting that it is (in Shanahan's phrase) 'too high-up for us', demanding less of 'the fancy stuff' (166–9).[18] His listeners want a pint of plain, not Château Margaux, and when Orlick's telling does prove more satisfying, Shanahan says 'The same again, please,' as if ordering another round. Orlick's champagne socialism could conceivably be read as the elitism of a party vanguard, but it is actually consistent with other contradictions in the text, including the oddity that the working-class characters enact their revolt precisely by behaving like models of middle-class respectability: a 'social evening' at Furriskey's is a scene of 'marital bliss' where 'tea was stirred and bread was buttered swiftly and trisected' (151).

William Tracy's testimony against Trellis creates additional complexities. Acquainted 'professionally' with his fellow novelist, Tracy relates how Trellis approached him seeking 'the services of a female character of the slavey class'. When the girl returned pregnant from Trellis' employ, Tracy was obliged to 'creat[e] an otherwise unnecessary person' to marry her in his own novel *Jake's Last Throw*; this, he complains, 'added considerably to my labours' (199). Given the confusion here between author as labourer and author as employer, it seems rather perverse that O'Brien chooses this moment to invoke the quintessential scene of Marxist analysis, as Tracy explains that he found the slavey's child 'honest if unremunerative employment . . . [in] the cotton-milling industry' (199–200). The mills of

---

[18] We might recall Bloom's views on the sacrament in *Ulysses*: 'Wine. Makes it more aristocratic than for example if he drank what they are used to Guinness's porter' (78).

fictional creation will not submit to Marxist analysis as would the cotton mills of Lancashire; the relations of production between novelists and characters are far too unstable.

In the '*Conclusion of the book, penultimate*', Trellis' servant Teresa burns scattered papers which are identified as 'pages . . . of *the master's* novel, the pages which *made and sustained* the existence of Furriskey and his true friends' (215–16, emphases added). The idea of 'master' as 'maker' presents a final short-circuiting of the Marxian-Hegelian logic in which the position of the labour-master is sustained by the extraction of surplus value from the worker – logic already hopelessly tangled in this text. With porter as its emblem, the dialectic of literary production in O'Brien's novel is characterized by paradoxical conflations of producer and product, employer and employee, employee and commodity. Its complexity must confound any effort at schematization in Marxist terms or otherwise.

Frank Moorhouse and the 'Business-Man Artist'

Asked in a 1998 interview whether he had ever felt his characters 'running away with the book or taking control', Frank Moorhouse affirmed, 'the fiction does have a life of its own . . . you are amazed at what happens during that working spell or trance'.[19] This is the idea literalized in *At Swim-Two-Birds* as the characters rebel against their author, even using sleeping-draughts to keep him in his trance.

Moorhouse's work has not featured a fictional author who 'hires' unruly characters from existing texts. However, Moorhouse himself has frequently reused characters from his own fiction, even lifting whole stories and chapters for redeployment in subsequent books.[20] For Janice Shaw, this practice is representative of the 'somewhat elitist' Australian literary scene of the 1960s and 1970s, with writers tending to court 'the initiated and knowledgeable reader' through self-reflexivity and intertextual references.[21] We may recall

---

[19] Jennifer McDonell and Frank Moorhouse, 'Transgression, Diplomacy and the Art of Writing Fiction', *Meanjin* 57, 4 (1998): 713–27 (723).
[20] The story 'The St Louis Rotary Convention 1923, Recalled', for example, appears in both *The Americans, Baby* and *The Electrical Experience*. The characters Becker, George McDowell and Terri McDowell appear in both texts. A minor character in *Forty-seventeen* (1988) reappears as the heroine of *Grand Days* (1993). O'Brien also recycled figures in his fiction, such as the pedantic scholar De Selby who features in both *The Third Policeman* and *The Dalkey Archive*.
[21] Janice Shaw, 'Moorhouse and The Angry Decade', *Antipodes* 27, 1 (June 2013): 31–6 (35–6).

O'Brien's frame narrator proposing that the reuse of existing characters would exclude 'inferior' persons from literary understanding.

Like O'Brien, Moorhouse has had a close relationship with alcohol throughout his writing career; in a 1991 interview, Moorhouse admitted 'I am not an alcoholic but I have an alcohol dependency.'[22] Like O'Brien's, his work associates drinking with creativity, and frequently makes analogies between drink and human being. Such links are especially prominent in the suggestively-titled *Martini: A Memoir* (2005), the jacket of which features the rather twee tagline, 'How to live a martini and mix a life.' While providing a metaphor for human vitality throughout, liquor is also presented in literary terms: 'the martini cocktail . . . is one of the great narratives of modern folklore'.[23] The book abounds in references to various writers and their drinking habits, even proposing that 'the martini represents the modernist consciousness' (169).

Moorhouse's earlier fictional works *The Americans, Baby* (1972) and *The Electrical Experience* (1974) focus on non-alcoholic drinks, and here the connection with human being and literary creation is more problematic. In *The Americans*, numerous stories feature Becker, a U.S. Coca-Cola representative visiting Australia, who describes himself as 'the Coca-Cola kid . . . here from the parent company' (200).[24] The genealogical metaphor presents a soft-drink equivalent for the Joycean idea of 'Guenesis', equating Becker's very being with the brand. But soft drink tends to be dissociated from literature in this text, especially in contrast with alcohol. While drinking whiskey with an English teacher, Becker joins in an impromptu recital of John Masefield's poetry (125–6), and a bourbon with ice brings Robert Frost's poem 'Fire and Ice' to his mind (148), but Coke is decidedly more prosaic. When challenged by the English teacher, the best Becker can boast is that 'Coca-Cola is an everyday word in every language – it's in the dictionaries' (129).[25] Speaking as an 'evangelist' for Coke in an earlier tale, Becker stressed his own 'everydayness' in words that might echo O'Brien's Jem Casey: 'I think of myself as everybody's plain man' (109). As a drinker, Becker is 'not adverse to poetry or to jazz music', but as a soft-drink representative, he embraces economic rationalism and celebrates

---

[22] Willbanks and Moorhouse, 166.
[23] (Sydney: Random House, 2005), 113. Subsequent references are to this edition and cited parenthetically.
[24] (Sydney: Angus and Robertson, 1972), 200. Subsequent references are to this edition and cited parenthetically.
[25] When a secretary in the office sketches Becker's portrait, he asks her, 'is Coca-Cola subsidizing art now – or don't we give you enough to do?' (133).

'the joy of standardization' (148–9).[26] We might compare *At Swim-Two-Birds*, in which the frame narrator's creative colloquies with his drinking companions contrast with his 'perfunctory' exchanges with his uncle over tea (212); then again, we should not forget that, with his diet of watercress and water, the consummate poet Sweeney is also the ultimate teetotaller.

Becker reappears in *The Electrical Experience*, but the focus of the latter text is George McDowell and his independent Australian soft-drink factory. McDowell is an enthusiastic imbiber of American business culture, but he proudly asserts the value of 'distinctive local products' against the global economic conquest of Coca-Cola and other '[p]roprietary lines'.[27] McDowell identifies with his product still more profoundly than Becker, and in this small-business context Moorhouse allows a much stronger connection between soft drink and artistic creation. The resulting ironies afford instructive parallels with *At Swim-Two-Birds*, although McDowell is not an aspiring author like O'Brien's narrator. Rather, as his more literary friend (transparently named Scribner) puts it, he is a 'Business-man Artist' (110). McDowell considers 'the making of foodstuffs [to be] the most sacred of all crafts. Even if it was only soft drinks' (123).

An extended exchange between McDowell and Scribner in the story 'THE ANNUAL CONFERENCE OF 1930 AND SOUTH COAST DADA' frames the soft factory as a literary wellspring. A 'poet of sorts' (3), Scribner has written numerous advertisements and devised product names for McDowell's company, including 'Green River' for a lime drink. When McDowell suggests that Scribner 'could have done more with [his] talents', the poet replies, 'What more could I offer life, Mr McDowell? Why I have written a number of immortal labels for your aerated waters!' (108–9). Claiming immortality for drink labels seems still more absurd than Shanahan claiming 'permanence' for Jem Casey's porter jingles, but McDowell perceives no irony, musing 'It was true that Scribner could always find a new word for "refreshing"' and noting, as if it were a mark of literary merit, that 'all Scribner's names for new lines had gained [trademark] registration' (108).

Like Bloom in Joyce's *Ulysses*, Scribner appreciates 'the infinite possibilities hitherto unexploited of the modern art of advertisement' (*Ulysses*, 636). By the 1950s or 1960s, Scribner predicts, 'the label, the advertisement, will be

---

[26] On the standardization of Coca-Cola from the 1920s, see Mark Weiner, 'Consumer Culture and Participatory Democracy: The Story of Coca-Cola During World War II', in *Food in the USA: A Reader*, ed. Carole M. Counihan (London: Routledge, 2002), 123.

[27] (Sydney: Angus and Robertson, 1974), 165. Subsequent references are to this edition and cited parenthetically.

considered works of art... the Art of Our Times' (109). And, as Moorhouse's readers could recognize in hindsight, Scribner is not wrong: he anticipates the postmodern pop art aesthetic. *The Electrical Experience* itself demonstrates that aesthetic, with Moorhouse using varying layouts and typefaces, graphics and textual snippets (presented in white type on black) to mimic magazine design.[28] Numerous story titles appear in capitals like newspaper headlines or advertising tags: 'GEORGE MACDOWELL DOES THE JOB' and 'BUSINESS NO PICNIC' are two examples.

But if Scribner is looking forward, he is also looking back from 1930 to earlier twentieth-century artistic movements that incorporated mass-media materials, particularly Dada (hence the story's title) and Futurism. When McDowell asks Scribner whether he considers advertising 'the poetry of commerce', he answers like a true Futurist, 'Indeed I do. And the machines we use – the sculptures of industry' (108). In *At Swim-Two-Birds*, mass production furnished metaphors for artistic creation; here, the concrete means of production are themselves conceived as art. Scribner thus sidesteps a problem that, in 1930, Walter Benjamin had not yet articulated: 'the work of art in the age of mechanical reproduction' is precisely, for Scribner, mechanical reproduction.[29] Consistent with this idea, numerous photographs of early-twentieth century bottling machines and other factory equipment are interspersed throughout *The Electrical Experience*. At the same time, Scribner invites McDowell to see the mass-produced commodity in literary terms. Applying one of his slogans for McDowell's soft drinks to linguistic utterance itself, Scribner implies an equivalence between the two: '[w]ords are the "Sparkling Juices from the Fountain of Delight"', he tells McDowell (108).

He may admire Scribner, but McDowell's literary sensibility is repeatedly shown to be limited. In one story, asked what books have influenced him, the young McDowell can only recall 'manuals about cordials and their manufacture', despite 'consider[ing] himself a Reader' (85). We might compare the philistine uncle in *At Swim-Two-Birds,* whose interest in books does not extend beyond their price (a book must be great to 'cost five shillings') and policing his student nephew's work ethic ('tell me this, do you ever open a book at all?': *At Swim-Two-Birds*, 10, 44). Nonetheless, McDowell enjoys the idea of himself as an author. Encouraged by Scribner, he professes 'his

---

[28] Stephen Torre, 'The Short Story Since 1950', in *The Cambridge History of Australian Literature*, ed. Peter Pierce (Port Melbourne: Cambridge University Press, 2009), 419–51 (437).

[29] Walter Benjamin theorizes the distinction between the mechanically-reproduced artwork and the authentic original in his famous essay 'The Work of Art in the Age of Mechanical Reproduction' (1936) in *Illuminations*, trans. Harry Zohn (New York: Schocken Books, 1969), 217–51.

own belief in the "speech" and the "business letter" as the practical arts of commerce', leading the poet to remark, 'Why, you're a Futurist yourself' (109). Besides speeches and letters, McDowell composes numerous aphorisms and articles of faith, including a list of 'RULES AND PRACTICES FOR THE OVERCOMING OF SHYNESS' (65). He writes up handy hints for the local paper, and even drafts a creed for country schools which would require students to affirm: 'I believe that every piece of goods I help to manufacture or grow represents part of myself when it goes out into the world' (152–3). Meanwhile, McDowell's business generates a kind of literary archive, which he sees as the expression of himself:

> Business Card.
>   Letterhead.
>   Printed Invoice.
>   Painted Sign.
>   Printed Label.
>   Advertisements.
>   All bearing my name. A person becomes a business entity...
> A letterhead. (170)

The work of this 'Business-Man Artist' always has a materialist emphasis. In the opening tale, an ageing McDowell tells Becker, 'I do not care for words in top hats. *I believe in shirt-sleeve words.* I believe in getting the job done' (9, emphasis original). The pronouncement distinctly recalls Shanahan's proposal in *At Swim-Two-Birds* to 'take the bloody black hats off' persons of high social station and challenge them to write a poem with a pick in their hands (75). The irony in McDowell's case is that, while he may 'mov[e] a paperweight ... as if it were a driving-lever' (*Electrical*, 51), his position is far from blue-collar.

Self-authorship and mass production

As an employer of wage labour, George McDowell is continually misrecognizing himself as a worker who sweats and toils:

> The people who could take the raw, unshapen material from the earth and organize it into something of value were a special kind of person. He had always been proud to be that kind of person. (6)

Contra Marxian theory, McDowell understands the commodity (soft drink) not as the product of alienated labour but as a part of himself, the business owner, who is in direct relationship with the consumer: 'what you made with your hands and offered to people was . . . the presentation of yourself' (123). Meanwhile, McDowell's workers are conspicuous by their absence in this text's free indirect narration, skewed as it is to McDowell's perspective. We do, however, see him assist in putting down a strike in a friend's guesthouse business, and his class prejudices emerge strongly as he rails against the 'puny spirit' of 'the working people' (39) and clashes with a union representative who says he has heard of McDowell's 'goddam soft drink factory down the coast', though McDowell cannot fathom why (41). This is a fairly straightforward satire of bourgeois false consciousness when compared with *At Swim-Two-Birds,* for whereas O'Brien used wage-labour relations metaphorically in representing literary creation, Moorhouse is directly concerned with wage-labour relations as such. Nevertheless, insofar as McDowell understands himself as a 'practical art[ist]' engaged in a sacred 'craft' (109, 123), his erasure of his employees' labour can be seen to parallel the myth of artistic autonomy.

The magnum opus of this 'Business-man Artist' is ostensibly his own person. Since he equates himself with his soft drinks, and sees himself as their maker, McDowell considers himself 'a self-made man' (16). He is, however, a work in progress, and is ever bent on self-improvement: 'Daily he made himself think thoughts he had not thought before. . . . He fed his mind with maxims and precepts – the how-to-do-it manual of the mind' (55). McDowell is continually reformulating his self-characterizations, as when he reflects in the opening story, 'He was a modern man. . . . He was, well, put him down as one who served his fellow man, a business man, and a Rotarian' (16). His conscious 'rewriting' of himself is most literal in the story 'GEORGE MCDOWELL CHANGES NAMES'. The change in question is minimal – he decides to go by 'T. George McDowell' instead of 'George McDowell' and has a new letterhead printed accordingly (29) – but to McDowell it is important: with his business established, he has assumed the character of the 'person-about-town' (17) and the new name marks this development. Authoring an ideal self also involves extensive self-censorship, as we see when McDowell recalls his efforts to resist a married woman's advances:

> The flesh, the passions have no special rights or claims on the behaviour.
> Take the leverless fountain pen. (55)

Seeking an analogy for his controlled being, McDowell chooses a writing implement, although he is predictably more interested in the pen as a piece of technology ('he had no doubts that it would be superseded') than in its creative possibilities.

Reflecting the temperance movement's historical association with the work ethic of industrial capitalism, McDowell's excessive self-discipline is linked to his preference for 'temperance beverages' (107). Sometimes, we read, 'his spirit cried out . . . to be, just for one day, indolent. To say, drink alcohol, like some of the others' (43). Drinking represents 'a way of "getting outside oneself"' (66) and, by removing inhibitions, alcohol would enable the release, or the production, of another self: an 'unofficial self' McDowell consciously represses (21). We might compare how Trellis' characters in *At Swim-Two-Birds* are released from performing their preconceived roles when their author drinks and sleeps. Indeed, like the revolt of Trellis's characters against their author's 'mastery', McDowell's occasional rebellion against 'the yoke' (43) of his self-discipline has political overtones: immediately after his clash with the union representative, for example, he feels his 'body turning on itself' (44), suggesting the surfacing of energies at odds with his conscious political convictions.

A crucial irony arises in that, even as McDowell purports to shape his character, he conceives of himself in commodified terms which brand his being as mass-produced. In the opening tale, his thoughts segue directly from 'the ice-making business' to the production of human being: 'The South Coast produced a better sort of person' (8). He views human reproduction in the same terms that he understands his business: 'family plan[ing]' requires 'a Blueprint' along with 'initiative and capital' (15). The next story, 'GEORGE MCDOWELL DOES THE JOB,' opens with the words 'He assessed himself as "up to the date"' (16), with McDowell framing himself as the latest model of mankind – an idea that recalls Brinsley on 'the Ford cars of humanity' in *At Swim-Two-Birds*. Like McDowell's equation of himself with his soft drinks, these links associate McDowell's supposed 'self-ma[king]' with the factory floor, and thus with his suppressed dependence on his workers.

The joy of standardization

In 1924, the young George McDowell explains to a doctor friend how he distinguishes himself as a 'self-mover' from 'those who need to be supervised and led'. When the doctor suggests, 'maybe we don't arrange things properly so that everyone can be a Self-mover', McDowell's response reveals a political contrast that is associated with the men's choice of drinks:

> "No – " on this George was firm – "no, there are those who are individual and energized and those who simply follow. Everywhere I look in life, and everything I see, confirms this."

> They sat in silence then. The doctor still sipped rum.
> George sipped tea. (84–5)

The political associations of soft drink and alcohol are not neatly divided, however. Creative control, class exploitation and the mass-production of human being are all linked to alcohol in 'FILMING THE HATTED AUSTRALIAN', the penultimate story in *The Electrical Experience*. Set in the 1970s, after McDowell's death, it features a group of university-educated filmmakers who (as their snobbish director puts it) 'are looking for an Australian, vintage 1910 or thereabouts'. The viticultural reference is repeated when they find a man who they feel represents 'the self-contained Australian of this vintage: *The Australian of the First Half of the Century*' (184). The definite articles suggest a consistent, standardized product, and the filmmakers clearly conceive of working-class Australian character as mass-produced: they are thrilled with the 'stock response[s]' of their subject, who uses phrases like 'come again, mate' as if 'on cue'. When they take him for 'bellyful of booze', the man drunkenly sings 'Waltzing Matilda' (200), a song as iconically Australian as 'Tipperary' and 'Nellie Dean' (both referenced in *At Swim-Two-Birds*) are iconically Irish. The soft drink connection still persists, for it emerges that the man is a former employee of McDowell's – the first and only of his workers to have a voice in the text.

Through this marginalized figure, Moorhouse (like O'Brien) represents creative exploitation in terms of class difference. Having found a 'suitable existing puppet' (*At Swim-Two-Birds*, 25) to fulfil a preconceived role in their documentary, the filmmakers arrange to pay him, thus literalizing the idea of the 'hired' character. In *At Swim-Two-Birds*, Trellis' characters must 'simulate the immoral actions' their author 'demands of them', and in Moorhouse the coercive control of authors (or 'auteurs') over their human resources is also evident when, unsatisfied with some footage, one of the documentary-makers remarks, 'We have to fight with reality to get what we want' (189). The moment recalls an earlier fragment titled 'Aerated Waters – Some Technical Considerations', presumably authored by McDowell, which specified that 'natural juices and squashes do not produce a natural and convincing colour' and that tinting is necessary because 'people suspect the quality if the colour varies' (116).

Recalling Becker's remarks on 'the joy of standardization', this returns us to McDowell's own mass-produced character. George McDowell is a manufactured commodity not only in that his livelihood depends on his factory-worker's labour, but also in that the ideas and values that define him have been programmed by the ideology of free-market industrial capitalism, particularly as associated with the United States. In particular, although

McDowell considers himself 'an Individualist' (31), his very individualism bears the impress of an American mould. The American influence on McDowell's self-authorship is glaringly apparent on his 1928 trip to the USA, where McDowell meets Zane Grey, a fictional American novelist who 'wr[ites] of the wild west and self-reliant men' (95). Affirming his own belief in 'self-reliance', McDowell tells the writer 'I endure because I get off my backside and I bust my gut' (98). When McDowell changes names, he is pleased to be told that 'T. George McDowell' sounds 'Americanized' (109).

Learning that '[Zane Grey] was, like himself, a teetotaler,' the Australian presents the American with 'a sample range of his aerated waters' (95). But as Moorhouse knew well, both soft drink and cultural influence overwhelmingly ran the other way. After the union representative slams his 'rot-gut lolly water', McDowell heads 'to the California Café' and orders 'a soda with plenty of chipped ice' while espousing the value of free enterprise (42). The freedom McDowell values most is 'the freedom to buy and sell' (4), and when he laments to Becker that there were 'independent cordial-makers in every country town' before the invasion of global giants like Coca-Cola and Schweppes (165), he fails to realize that, in his embrace of modernization and American values, he himself has been complicit in the logic enabling Coke's conquest.

Like O'Brien, Moorhouse worked as a civil servant and journalist in establishing his literary career, immersing himself in debates over national identity in a postcolonial context. In the story 'The American Poet's Visit', Moorhouse's first-person narrator remarks, 'We [Australians] are culturally incapacitated and dependent. . . . A composite mimic culture' (*Americans*, 58). Comparably, O'Brien's celebrated essay 'A Bash in the Tunnel' (1951) remarks a composite mimic quality in Irish culture, epitomized in the symbol of the Irish artist 'resentfully drinking someone else's whiskey'.[30] The self-styled 'town cowboy' Becker (*Americans*, 145) might further be compared with O'Brien's 'Ringsend cowboys' as a symbol of the United States' global cultural dominance. Defending his company on charges of American imperialism, Becker insists that Coke is 'a simple goddam soft drink . . . it's not a damn political system' (*Americans*, 171). The 'Coca-Cola kid' doth protest too much. As Guinness became synonymous with Ireland, so Coca-Cola has served as a symbol of the 'American Way of Life',[31] and the conquest of American soft drink and the cultural influence of the American Western are inextricably associated.

---

[30] Flann O'Brien, 'A Bash in the Tunnel', in ed. Claud Cockburn, *Stories and Plays* (New York: Viking Press, 1973), 206.
[31] Weiner, 123.

Here it is worth recalling the brewer's mirror in O'Brien's *At Swim-Two-Birds*, connecting the narrator's literary ambitions with one of Guinness' failing competitors, Watkins, Jameson and Pim. The firm was forced to close in 1939, the very year of *At Swim-Two-Birds*' publication, and within a few years Guinness had completely annihilated Dublin's independent brewing industry.[32] Guinness did not come as a foreign conqueror, like Coca-Cola. But as part of the Anglo-Irish aristocracy, the Guinness family was Protestant, conservative, and had long opposed Irish home rule. Joyce alludes to Guinness' enduring association with Ireland's former colonizer in *Finnegans Wake*, dubbing Arthur Guinness 'All for Guineas' and linking 'Guinness' and 'Ghengis'.[33] Even as O'Brien associates the flow of porter with literary creation, Guinness looms in the background as the ambiguous emblem of a compromised national identity.[34]

To borrow the terms in which Marx described the commodity, fictional character in O'Brien is 'a very complicated thing, full of metaphysical subtlety'.[35] Moorhouse's vision is considerably less complex, but affords instructive parallels. Soft drink and hard drink provide O'Brien and Moorhouse with metaphorical resources for exploring the complexities of class relations, imaginative labour and the shaping of human personality. In *At Swim-Two-Birds* and *The Electrical Experience*, these things are bound up with various stages in the production and supply chain of the beverage industry, from class-conflict on the factory floor through to consumption. Although creativity and freedom tend to be associated with alcohol rather than soft drink, which tends to evoke restraint and conformity, such distinctions prove unstable, as all art and all drink become implicated in commodity culture and exploitative power relations. Whatever lines we draw in these texts are as liable to dissipate as if they were traced with a finger through spilled foam.

---

[32] See Thomas Halpin, 'History of the Irish Brewing Industry', *Journal of the Brewery History Society* 91 (Spring 1998): 2–12 and Mary Daly, *Dublin, the Deposed Capital: 1860-1914* (Cork: Cork University Press, 1984), 23–5. On the disappearance of brewing as a 'localized craft', see Stanley Dennison and Oliver MacDonagh, *Guinness 1886-1939: From Incorporation to the Second World War* (Cork: Cork University Press, 1998), xiii, 11.

[33] See Dannen for an extended discussion of Guinness' association with British imperialism in Joyce's *Finnegans Wake*.

[34] Dennison and MacDonagh, xiii.

[35] Marx's discussion of how, in commodity culture as in religion, 'the products of the human brain appear as autonomous figures endowed with a life of their own', possessed of 'free will' and the ability to form ideas, might well be applied to the creative autonomy of fictional characters in *At Swim-Two-Birds*: see 'The Fetishism of the Commodity and its Secret', in *Capital: Volume 1*, ed. Karl Marx, trans. Ben Fowkes (London: Penguin, 1990), 163–77 (164–5).

14

Flann O'Brien's Aestho-Autogamy

Mark Steven

'Women I have no interest in at all,' I said smiling.
'A fiddle is a better thing for diversion.'
— Flann O'Brien, *The Third Policeman*

Modernism, solitude, masturbation

In 1928, Virginia Woolf identified two requirements for the composition of modern literature: money, and a room of one's own. 'It is necessary,' she says, 'to have five hundred a year and a room with a lock on the door if you are to write fiction or poetry.'[1] If it is true that artistic creation demands pecuniary support as well as social distance, then modernism in literature will have come to occupy a curious dialectic in relation to its material conditions. Modernism is paradoxically dependent upon the very field from which it seeks autonomy. It requires a compositional space exempt from the historical moment within which it articulates, but that space appears to be reserved only for a league of writers protected by accumulated wealth. For those less fortunate, Woolf suggests, social reality will supervene and militate against the production of art. 'Everything is against the likelihood that it will come from the writer's mind whole and entire. Generally material circumstances are against it. Dogs will bark; people will interrupt; money must be made; health will break down.'[2] Woolf's bourgeois materialism finds an exceptionally weird and working-class echo, 33 years later, in Flann O'Brien's allegorical figure of the Irish modernist. 'I needn't tell you that crowd is a crowd of bastards,' explains a tactile inebriate, having cornered O'Brien in the Scotch

---

[1] Virginia Woolf, *A Room of One's Own* (Ontario: Broadview Press, 2001), 123.
[2] Woolf, *A Room of One's Own*, 62.

House, before launching into his legendary anecdote about taking a 'bash' in the unused dining cars of the Irish Railway:

> When the urge for a "bash" came upon him his routine was simple. Using his secret key, he secretly got into a parked and laden car very early in the morning, penetrated to the pantry, grabbed a jug of water, a glass and a bottle of whiskey and, with this assortment of material and utensil, locked himself in the lavatory.
> Reflect on that locking. So far as the whole world was concerned, the car was utterly empty. It was locked with special, unprecedented locks. Yet this man locked himself securely within those locks.[3]

To drunkenly occupy the locked bathroom of an already locked carriage is, for O'Brien, the definitive gesture of Irish modernism, for it involves the double negation of an external world and singularly manifests 'the transgressor's resentment with the nongressor',[4] epitomizing the modernist's strained relationship with the social as such, here figured in the 'crowd of bastards'.

Woolf's economically insulated room and the locus of O'Brien's booze-fuelled bash are united in two respects: both comprise the tactical reclamation of a momentarily inalienable sovereignty and both have been conceived of, either materially or allegorically, as exemplary sites of modernist composition. From these points of intersection, we might begin to extend David Trotter's argument that, at least in relation to the novel, 'modernist theory and practice might be thought of, by analogy with Nietzsche's will-to-power and will-to-life, as a will-to-literature'.[5] According to Woolf and O'Brien, modernism should also be thought of as a will-to-solitude. Building upon this premise, I want to discern something like a symptomatic tropology of solitude as it manifests itself in the practice of masturbation, a formal and narrative act that, I will soon demonstrate, allows for modernist literature to think through its own economic, political and aesthetic conditions of production. My goal is not to produce a catalogue of modernist masturbation. Rather, it is to use this thematic as a means of gauging some of the peculiarities in modernist literature and, specifically, to reveal how O'Brien's unique aesthetic is impacted by and reacts to its political and economic circumstances.

---

[3] Flann O'Brien, *Stories and Plays* (London: Hart-Davis, MacGibbon, 1973), 206.
[4] O'Brien, *Stories and Plays*, 206.
[5] David Trotter, 'The Modernist Novel', in *The Cambridge Companion to Modernism*, ed. Michael Levenson (Cambridge: Cambridge University Press, 1999), 74.

'I work in my bedroom,' announces the unnamed narrator of *At Swim-Two-Birds*. 'Whether in or out, I always kept the door locked.'[6] Given the principal virtue of the narrator's library – 'generally recognized as indispensable to all who aspire to an appreciation of the nature of contemporary literature'[7] – and what its defining contemporaneity could mean for his status as a student and for his disposition as a writer, we can safely conjecture that the solitary 'work' comprises, at least on some level, an engagement with literary modernism. What might or might not also take place within the locked bedroom should therefore collocate with an appreciation for, and the production of, modern art. 'A contemplative life has always been suitable to my disposition,' we are told, 'I was accustomed to stretch myself for many hours upon my bed . . . .'[8] It would probably be overreaching to read a sexual connotation into the transitive verb, 'stretch', and to thereby interpret its pronominal object, 'myself', as a euphemism for genitalia, but an accusation subsequently levelled by the narrator's uncle will mark these terms as suspect in just that way. 'I know the studying you do in your bedroom,' sounds the charge. 'Damn the studying you do in your bedroom.'[9] Implied here is that the narrator has followed an inauspicious passage from the solitary pleasures of literature to the solitary vice of onanism. If we think about exchanges like this as narrative events materialized by prose, what takes place here also registers a kind of elision whereby the implicit masturbation is only made semi-discernible in its abstention from narrative inclusion. Masturbation might therefore generate a literature of solitude, but only from within a space sequestered from solitude's usually intimate precincts. Disagreement between the narrative and its narration, between disclosure and reticence, redoubles the will-to-solitude and by doing so allows for the autoerotic act to emanate suspiciously from somewhere behind not one locked door but two.

If solitude can be linked to masturbation in O'Brien's writing, and if the two constellate together as a literary modernism, then O'Brien is in fine company, taking his place alongside the numerous other modernists in whose work masturbation is similarly (but more explicitly) troped. Proust, Joyce and Beckett are striking examples. The first volume of Marcel Proust's *In Search of Lost Time* includes an episode in which the narrator describes a youthful moment of solitary self-realization, giving powerful expression to a dynamic that will, as he matures, effloresce into the book's economy of desire.

---

[6] Flann O'Brien, *The Complete Novels* (New York: Alfred A Knopf, 2007), 6.
[7] O'Brien, *Complete Novels*, 7.
[8] Ibid., 6.
[9] Ibid., 7.

'I had peered out and seen nothing but the tower,' he recalls, 'framed in the square of the half-opened window', before disclosing that

> with the heroic scruples of a traveler setting forth for unknown climes, or of a desperate wretch hesitating on the verge of self-destruction, faint with emotion, I explored, across the bounds of my own experience, an untrodden path, which, I believed, might lead me to my death, even – until passion spent itself and left me shuddering among the sprays of flowering currant which, creeping in through the window, tumbled about my body.[10]

These lines have (somewhat facetiously) been described as 'one of the greatest artistic triumphs of modern literature',[11] and the assessment could even be accurate, but only if we take it on the premise that, in this episode, Proust is portraying his novel as a text singularly committed to exploring the extraordinarily inward and invariably sexual truths of the narrator.

A comparable structure obtains within James Joyce's *Ulysses*, in Leopold Bloom's infamous exposure to Gerty MacDowell, from an episode written with the sentiment and expression of a third-rate romance. 'The eyes that were fastened upon her set her pulses tingling,' we read. 'She looked at him a moment, meeting his glance, and a light broke in upon her. Whitehot passion was in that face, passion silent as the grave, and it had made her his.'[12] In this episode, erotic energies fuel the production of a tremendously tawdry style, straining towards a climax which yields a description that seems applicable to the prose itself: 'it gushed out of it a stream of rain gold hair threads and they shed and ah! they were all greeny dewy stars falling with golden, O so lovely, O, soft, sweet, soft!'[13]

Then there is Samuel Beckett, who serially employs masturbation as a means of worsening his characters, focalizing their social attenuation and denying them any sort of narrative closure. In *Molloy*, when Moran's bedroom reverie is disturbed by his son, he thinks to himself: 'I might just happen to be masturbating, before my cheval-glass. Father with yawning fly and starting eyes, toiling to scatter on the ground his joyless seed, that was no sight for a small boy.'[14] In Beckett, solitude becomes filial code for masturbation, but its

---

[10] Marcel Proust, *Remembrance of Things Past*, vol. 1, trans. Scott Moncrieff (Hertfordshire: Wordsworth Editions, 2006), 164.
[11] Stephen Greenblatt, 'Me, Myself, and I', *The New York Review of Books* (8 April 2004).
[12] James Joyce, *Ulysses* (Oxford and New York: Oxford University Press, 1993), 349.
[13] Joyce, *Ulysses*, 350.
[14] Samuel Beckett, *Three Novels: Molloy, Malone Dies, The Unnamable* (New York: Grove Press, 1991), 97.

comically miserable actuality is only a product of the characters' collective disaggregation. 'I took advantage of being alone at last,' Moran later reveals, 'with no other witness than God, to masturbate. My son must have had the same idea, he must have stopped on the way to masturbate. I hope he enjoyed it more than I did.'[15]

To open a parenthesis, it is tempting to interpret the prevalence of masturbation in the modernist novel as a result of modernism's epistemic negation of more prudish values, configuring modernist representations of sexuality and eroticism negatively, as so many responses to an established tradition that condemned such impulses. In Enlightenment philosophy, both Kant and Rousseau were determinedly opposed to masturbation: the former claimed it breached moral law; the latter called it a 'dangerous supplement which deceives nature'.[16] With the advent of psychoanalysis, it continued to be construed as an incurably neurasthenic 'primal addiction' that would only predispose the subject to multiple other vices.[17] Countering these approaches, Michel Foucault has been the strongest exponent of a relationship between autoerotic transgression and progressive politics, historicizing sexuality and its repression as the corollary to capitalism – the same economic referent through which the modernist novel generates most of its dialectical tensions. 'By placing the advent of the age of repression in the seventeenth century,' he says, 'after hundreds of years of open spaces and free expression, one adjusts it to coincide with the development of capitalism: it becomes an integral part of the bourgeois order'.[18] And, like the modernist artwork, sexual experience (including masturbation) is, Foucault contends, profoundly utopian: 'the essential thing is not this economic factor', he claims, 'but rather the existence in our era of a discourse in which sex, the revelation of truth, the overturning of global laws, the proclamation of a new day to come, and the promise of a certain felicity are linked together'.[19]

However interesting and influential these materials are, and while they might assist in the construction of an allegorical relationship between modernism and masturbation, we should close the parenthesis by insisting that to focus too broadly on discursive or cultural history would be to neglect

---

[15] Beckett, *Three Novels*, 139.
[16] Immanuel Kant, *The Metaphysics of Morals*, ed. and trans. Mary Gregor (Cambridge: Cambridge University Press, 1996), 179; Rousseau in Jean Stengers and Anne Van Neck, *Masturbation: The History of a Great Terror*, trans. Kathryn Hoffmann (New York: Palgrave, 2001).
[17] Sigmund Freud, *The Complete Psychological Works of Sigmund Freud*, vol. I, ed. and trans. James Strachey (London: The Hogarth Press, 1953), 272.
[18] Michel Foucault, *The History of Sexuality*, vol. I, trans. Robert Hurley (New York: Pantheon Books, 1978), 5.
[19] Foucault, *The History of Sexuality*, 7.

a strong convention of deploying the autoerotic act as a figure for certain kinds of intellectual and aesthetic labour. In particular, it would overlook the way that, as with Joyce and Beckett, modernism's radical ambivalence towards masturbation manifests in the trope's deployment as a narrative and stylistic avatar for the pointlessness of writing. In English, this conception has held currency ever since Lord Byron accused John Keats of 'a sort of mental masturbation', of 'frigging his Imagination'.[20] In German letters, in similar vein, Karl Marx and Friedrich Engels would attack Max Stirner, arguing that 'the predominant pursuit of a single passion, e.g., that of writing books' is politically deficient because of its supposedly tenuous grip on material reality. 'Philosophy and the study of the actual world,' they claim, 'have the same relation to one another as onanism and sexual love.'[21] Much later, and from within a different context, Eve Kosofsky Sedgwick would redeem masturbation as an object of serious literary analysis, maintaining that to employ masturbation as a rhetorical device (as do Byron, Marx and Engels) 'is actually to refer to a much vaster, indeed foundational, open secret about how hard it is to circumscribe the vibrations of the highly relational but, in practical terms, solitary pleasure and adventure of writing itself'.[22] Sedgwick's argument explores masturbation through Jane Austen's fiction, but whereas Sedgwick is largely concerned with its implications for sexual identity, I want to set that kind of reading aside and pursue the connection between masturbation and literary production. Modernist literature uses masturbation as a metonym for its own creation, and this is precisely what happens in the masturbatory episodes in Proust, Joyce, Beckett and, as we shall see, O'Brien: they all thematize the novel's formal production and simultaneously give impetus to that production's stylistic registration at the level of the prose, wherein the amatory interactions between hands and genitals repeat the artwork's architectonic structures and compositional 'vibrations' in miniature. Masturbation is not just a practice to be represented by literature; it is one of the privileged tropes through which literature represents itself.

O'Brien was the one modernist who so committed himself to an aesthetic of masturbation that he not only elevated it to the central position within an ordnance of narrative effects but also developed it into an almost utopian directive towards a lyrically generative solitude. In *At Swim-Two-Birds*,

---

[20] John Barnard, *John Keats* (Cambridge: Cambridge University Press, 1987), 48.
[21] Karl Marx and Friedrich Engels, *Collected Works*, vol. 5 (London: Lawrence & Wishart, 1975), 236.
[22] Eve Kosofsky Sedgwick, 'Jane Austen and the Masturbating Girl', *Critical Inquiry* 17, 4 (Summer 1991): 820.

Dermot Trellis accounts for a 'theory of aestho-autogamy', the ambition for which is encapsulated by the 'dream of producing a living mammal from an operation involving neither fertilization nor conception'.[23] Whereas modernist creation has been understood in aesthetic theory as analogous to procreative childbirth (according to Adorno, for instance, the artist 'severs the umbilical cord of tradition'[24]), the artistically productive gesture of aestho-autogamy can only be the artwork's masturbatory debasement. In its labyrinthine doublings and nested narratives, O'Brien's novel consciously approaches something like aestho-autogamy, a masturbatory writing which, it seems to explain, can only take shape amidst 'the general chaos which would result if all authors were disposed to seduce their female characters and bring into being, as a result, offspring of the quasi-illusory type'.[25] The point here is that literary production and its finished product, namely literature, develop an affinity with masturbation, which might also rely upon the creation or seduction of a fictional partner. While masturbation is not an aesthetic activity unto itself, or at least not in any straightforward way, its description in literary prose necessarily is, and to represent masturbation within a novel whose production is coded as masturbatory will therefore be to join the tradition of deploying that trope for aesthetic metonymy.

Haptic palm of the invisible hand

Surely the aestho-autogamous conjuncture of modernism, solitude and masturbation will have something to do with a shared historical context. Given, too, that solitude has already been presented as the dialectically compromised antipode to capital, it will be to the mode of production that we should look for historical explanations. The critical task will therefore be to determine why abstract economic forces materialize, through a kind of prosopopeia, in bodily forms and sexual practices together invested with psychical energy. O'Brien – writing as Myles na Gopaleen, in the voice of Chapman – refers to this very task as the blindspot for dialectical materialism, allegedly overlooked by Marx and Engels, whose untapped critical potential was, he suggests, to be found in its explanations of how 'economic and sociological planning could be demonstrated to condition

---

[23] O'Brien, *Complete Novels*, 37.
[24] Theodor Adorno, *Aesthetic Theory*, trans. Robert Hullot-Kentor (London and New York: Continuum, 1997), 43.
[25] O'Brien, *Complete Novels*, 37.

eugenics, birth-rates and anthropology'.[26] While the author (or at least one of his masks) seems to legislate in favour of materialist analyses wedded to biological and organic phenomenon, here we will examine O'Brien's prose in relation to one of the rhetorical predilections of economic writing. The objective for this will be to theorize the masturbatory trope's political and economic coordination as regards O'Brien's thought more generally and from within his national context before engaging the peculiarity of its novelized presentation.

Since the eighteenth century, when Adam Smith penned his inquiries into capitalist economics, one of the privileged figures with which classical economists have mystifyingly grasped at the apparently intangible dynamics of the market has been the 'invisible hand'. Smith's theory was that the capitalist class will, 'in spite of their natural selfishness and rapacity', unknowingly 'divide with the poor the produce of all their improvements', and thereby justify the massive schism opened up between themselves and the working- and under-classes.[27] The expression appears three times in his oeuvre, but its clearest formulation is this, from *The Theory of Moral Sentiments*:

> They are led by an invisible hand to make nearly the same distribution of the necessaries of life, which would have been made, had the earth been divided into equal portions among all its inhabitants, and thus without intending it, without knowing it, advance the interest of the society, and afford means to the multiplication of the species.[28]

A mandatory parallax shift should help to visualize Smith's apparently invisible hand and provide it with a name. Any 'distribution of the necessaries of life' is, within the context of capital, only going to be the management of 'the multiplication of the species', whose division into classes necessitates, for the sustained wealth of the rich, a right to subsistence for the poor. It is through this kind of management – primarily administered through families, institutionalized education, welfare, medicine, religion and work itself – that the market keeps its labouring classes productive while strengthening the ranks of what Marx famously called its 'industrial reserve army'.[29] Smith's figure of the hand, the primary organ of purposeful work, is

---

[26] O'Brien (Myles na Gopaleen), *The Best of Myles* (Illinois: Dalkey Archive Press, 1968), 195.

[27] Adam Smith, *Theory of Moral Sentiments*, ed. Knud Haakonssen (Cambridge: Cambridge University Press, 2002), 215.

[28] Smith, *Moral Sentiments*, 215.

[29] Karl Marx, *Capital: A Critique of Political Economy*, vol. 1, trans. Ben Fowkes (London: Penguin, 1990), 781.

an apposite manifestation of the market's irreducible necessity for human bodies, and of the market's intrusion into individual and collective life via its purchase on biopower, that well-documented 'explosion of numerous and diverse techniques for achieving the subjugations of bodies and the control of populations'.[30] But if capitalist production and its surplus values are thereby 'stimulated' (an increasingly popular neoliberal expression) by this kind of self-management, it might also be said that the theoretical inauguration of an invisible hand marks the world-historical moment at which the market's apologists first became conscious of an analogously masturbatory mechanism. Perhaps, then, the figure of masturbation will encode the incursions of the market into everyday life through biopower, for it is neither visible nor invisible but appropriately furtive.

To ascertain why O'Brien should be aesthetically responsive to biopower we should align these thoughts with Fredric Jameson, for whom modernist Ireland exemplifies the dialectic of capitalist imperialism wherein social space agglomerates the experience of both the colonized and the colonizers, the enforcers of biopower and its resultantly superintended citizens, giving shape to a remarkably isolated and sclerotic experience of capitalism. '[A]t least one such peculiar space exists,' he claims, 'in the historical contingency of our global system: it is Ireland, and the uniqueness of the Irish situation....'[31] The impact of an 'Irish situation' is, for Jameson, readily apprehensible in the lexical components of the national idiolect. The language, he says, is 'a result of imperialism, which condemns Ireland to an older rhetorical past and to the survivals of oratory (in the absence of action), and which freezes Dublin into an underdeveloped village in which gossip and rumor still reign supreme'.[32] Within the uneven and combined developments of global capitalism, Ireland experiences two homologous calcifications, of its economic production and of its linguistic expression, both of which sediment into the national literature. O'Brien's published reaction to this very phenomenon, the literary deformations symptomatic of imperialism, attaches itself to the sheer physicality of language, to its phonetic materiality, the national vocation of which had already been circumscribed by capital. He insists that the market corrupts Irish prose when its writers succumb to the twee expression and exotic images of Irishness expected of them. 'We in this country had a bad time through the centuries when England did not like us,' he writes. 'But words choke in the pen when one comes to describe what happened to us when the English discovered that we were rawther

---

[30] Foucault, *History of Sexuality*, 140.
[31] Fredric Jameson, *The Modernist Papers* (London: Verso, 2007), 164.
[32] Jameson, *Modernist Papers*, 164.

interesting peepul ek'tully. . . .'[33] The resulting literature is, for O'Brien, 'the pale froth of literary epilepsy', designed specifically for 'the snake-like eye of London publishers', and it is precisely the visceral quality of these images – the choking pen; the frothing prose; and the single, snake-like eye – that will be important to us.[34] If Irish novelists had responded favourably to English imperialism by embracing its literary market, and if O'Brien is so forcefully opposed to their aesthetic obsequiousness, it should be understood that his reaction makes recourse to the body, to that organic referent of the invisible hand, and that it does so in terms we could easily read as shadowed though probably unintentional metaphors for masturbation. Though O'Brien rarely expressed any serious anti-capitalist sentiment, his employment as a civil servant and as a newspaper columnist meant that he was constantly exposed to issues pertaining to the national character, and more importantly the traces of biopower are readily apparent all throughout his writing.

Elsewhere, and particularly in the novels, the mobilization of capital through biopower will be apprehended as a predominately physical incursion. Take, for example, the college presented in *At Swim-Two-Birds*. 'The hallway inside,' we are told, 'is composed of large black and white squares arranged in the orthodox chessboard pattern, and the surrounding walls, done in an unpretentious cream wash, bear three rough smudges caused by the heels, buttocks and shoulders of the students.'[35] Here the chessboard characterizes students and their lecturers as inhabitants of inflexible subject positions, but the accompanying description grounds this abstract symbol back in the realm of organic material: these are actual squares, marked by the indexical impress of bodies in space, by their heels, buttocks and shoulders, all of which somehow contain enough transferrable substance to have smeared physical traces down the hall. It is not that these smudges contain an implicit critique of biopower. Rather, and either consciously or not, the representation of the college as an obstructed chessboard suggests an awareness of that critique's social object, and the smudges only confirm the absolute physicality of its impact on numerous subjects. Irrespective of whether the students are lazily inactive, loitering and lingering against the walls, their status remains determined by the institute that must have at least momentarily commanded their physical obedience. Details like this suggest an authorial understanding that capitalism is mediated into everyday life via the management of bodies in space. The mode of production is embodied in those narrative quarters where the ideological apparatus intrudes through biological forms and into social life.

[33] O'Brien, *The Best of Myles*, 234.
[34] Ibid.
[35] O'Brien, *Complete Novels*, 30.

We have posited that capitalism enters organic life under the sign of biopower, that its theorization in orthodox economics might be encoded by the figure of masturbation, and that 'the Irish situation' predisposes O'Brien to a formal engagement with capitalism, biopower and organic figuration. To square this theoretical circle and inaugurate a political aesthetic of modernist masturbation, let us turn to Slavoj Žižek, who is the keenest philosopher (with the possible exceptions of Georges Bataille and Wilhelm Reich) to have mapped the ideological nexus of capitalism and biopower onto masturbation. 'What kind of sexuality fits this universe?', Žižek asks of life under capitalism. His answer is singularly novel in its reconfiguration of political identity: the sexuality appropriate to capitalist biopower is not just masturbation but the 'masturbathon', a de-collectivized orgy without physical interaction, during which multiple participants masturbate together and at once. This, for Žižek, epitomizes the social condition of capitalism in its barest form – a condition that is, he says,

> marked by a conflict between its form and content: it builds a collective out of individuals who are ready to *share* with others the solipsistic egotism of their stupid pleasure. This contradiction, however, is more apparent than real: Freud already knew about the link between narcissism and immersion in a crowd, best rendered precisely by the California phrase "to share an experience." This coincidence of the opposed features is grounded in the exclusion that they share: one not only can be, one *is* "alone in a crowd." Both an individual's isolation and his immersion in a crowd exclude intersubjectivity proper, the encounter with an Other.[36]

The point here is that this kind of sociality is, ultimately, the sexual expression of post-political atomization, a reification of the sublimely intersubjective energies of sexual passion into the vacuity of capitalist individualism. It is a delineation that can be readily apprehended through comparison between the eventually non-sexual though immortally affirmative relationship of Leopold and Molly Bloom to either the non-encounter between Leopold and Gerty or to the purely hedonistic tryst between Molly and Blazes Boylan. Masturbation cannot hope to instantiate the utopian mobilizations once championed by Foucault; rather, it subsumes sexual energy and recasts it as pure bourgeois culture. In this light we might even come to appreciate the social truth of Žižek's assessment that, without love, sexual intercourse will only attain to the phenomenological status of 'masturbation with a

---

[36] Slavoj Žižek, *Violence* (New York: Picador, 2008), 30–1.

real partner', in which 'I use the flesh-and-blood partner as a masturbatory prop for enacting my fantasies.'[37] Our previous examples of modernist masturbation, from Proust, Joyce and Beckett all exemplify this tendency to project a fantastical partner – which is, of course, a narcissistic projection of the self. But in each of those examples, the masturbatory act also operates as a formal metonym for the artwork as a whole. Perhaps, then, these moments in narrative should be understood as formal manifestations of both political and aesthetic discomfort, as surcharge to the fact that, when circumscribed by capital, literature might only be the artistic residue left behind once the author is spent from too much tarrying in the 'solipsistic egotism of their stupid pleasure', or the product of what na Gopaleen refers to using another bodily metaphor as the 'vast yeasty eructation of egotism'.[38] Here, then, is the function of aestho-autogamy in modernist writing: to make literature aware of its embarrassing actualizations through biopower, and to thereby produce moments of humiliating self-awareness comparable to that which (citing Žižek one last time) threatens every sexual experience, when the mind acquires self-awareness and 'all of a sudden one feels stupid' – 'My God, what am I doing here, doing these stupid repetitive movements?'[39] If literary masturbation manifests in moments of aesthetic self-awareness, ramifying literature's sense of its own compromise to biopower, then our final task will be to bring this foray more forcefully back to O'Brien, determining how his prose reacts to its conditions of production.

Lonerism to onanism

While the opening chapters of *The Third Policeman* are preoccupied with a will-to-solitude, almost all of the subsequent narrative takes place within the psychical interior of its narrator as he journeys through a kind of post-life purgatory that includes figures who dominated his pre-death existence, but are now warped out of shape and turned back against the mind they are fated to occupy. This narrative space, which performs the dialectic of modernist solitude, disposes the book as an exceptionally good artefact with which to explore the incursion of a massive historical situation into the particularized psyche and its accompanying body. That it climaxes with a fantastical episode of autoeroticism also suggests that the articulation of this very impulse might be aware of its aesthetic relation

---

[37] Žižek, *The Parallax View* (Cambridge, MA: MIT Press, 2006), 191.
[38] O'Brien, *The Best of Myles*, 237.
[39] Žižek, *The Pervert's Guide to Cinema*, dir. Sophie Fiennes (P Guide Ltd., 2006), DVD.

to the circumambience of that articulating situation. Suturing these hypotheses to our thoughts on economic imperialism and its recourse to biopower, there is an argument to be made as to why the narrative's internal landscape is estranged from and alien to its foremost inhabitant. Hugh Kenner provides the right connections here. 'If we are in Ireland it is a peculiar Ireland indeed,' he says. 'For eleven consecutive chapters – clear to the end of the book – there is no wind, no chill, and (save for a surly downpour on Execution Morning) no mention of rain falling.'[40] But the peculiarity is to be found in more than just meteorological pressures that have been made uncanny. To be sure, the world in which the story takes place only becomes accessible when its narrator, having been motivated by avarice to murder old Phillip Mathers, is trapped by a more enterprising thief, John Divney, who kills him with an unidentifiable explosive device. The initially inexplicable detonation – 'something happened', we read, 'I cannot hope to describe what it was . . .'[41] – delivers him to a new reality and simultaneously installs the peculiar style sustained throughout the novel. 'Words are not generating matter by their promiscuities,' writes Kenner: 'no, a man who has seen something outside the pale of anyone's experience is taking lengthy pains to find the words for it. He is in a place as queer as Ireland, and undergoing an assault from its queerness.'[42] What the book amounts to stylistically is a syntactical and lexical preoccupation with an absent cause, with representation of the moment at which invisible forces seize hold of the individual, and yet representational solidity coheres with the agents of biopower, concretizing the otherwise invisible into perceptible though indeterminate forms.

There can be no figure more recognizable as the very personification of biopower than a baton-wielding member of the police. 'The evolution of Western societies reveals *a contrario* that the policeman is one element in a social mechanism linking medicine, welfare, and culture,' writes Jacques Rancière. 'The police is thus first an order of bodies that defines the allocation of ways of doing, ways of being, and ways of saying, and sees that those bodies are assigned by name to a particular place and task. . . .'[43] It should therefore be no mystery why the novel's policemen are all, in their own ways, grotesquely physical. It is as though their impossibly excessive

---

[40] Hugh Kenner, *Historical Fictions* (Athens, Georgia: University of Georgia Press, 1990), 99.
[41] O'Brien, *Complete Novels*, 238.
[42] Kenner, *Historical Fictions*, 97.
[43] Jacques Rancière, *Disagreement: Politics and Philosophy*, trans. Julie Rose (Minnesota: University of Minnesota Press, 1999), 29.

embodiment ensures the materiality and so the representability of the forces for which they stand:

> ... standing with his back to me, [was] an enormous police-man. His back appearance was unusual. He was standing behind a little counter in a neat whitewashed day-room; his mouth was open and he was looking into a mirror which hung upon the wall. Again, I find it difficult to convey the precise reason why my eyes found his shape unprecedented and unfamiliar. He was very big and fat and the hair which strayed abundantly about the back of his bulging neck was a pale straw-colour; all that was striking but not unheard of. My glance ran over his great back, the thick arms and legs encased in the rough blue uniform. Ordinary enough as each part of him looked by itself, they all seemed to create together, by some undetectable discrepancy in association or proportion, a very disquieting impression of unnaturalness, amounting almost to what was horrible and monstrous. His hands were red, swollen and enormous and he appeared to have one of them half-way into his mouth as he gazed into the mirror.[44]

Our parallax view on the not-so-invisible hand is certainly at work in these lines. The policeman is presented through a series of contradictions, the efficacy of which barely resolves the otherwise innocuous vision of an overweight man, 'striking but not unheard of', into a 'horrible and monstrous' embodiment of the law. The schismatic forms that attend to his description are scarcely legible to the narrator; they are only made apparent 'by some undetectable discrepancy in association or proportion'. This is capitalist biopower projected through imperialism's house of mirrors, magnifying into the abject vision of an economic administrator consuming the very tool of labour, a now semi-visible hand, which appears to have grown 'red, swollen and enormous'. When the novel's queer rhetoric articulates through exemplary passages such as this, we should interpret its meticulously conflicted descriptions as a means of grappling with the world of biopower which, we shall now see, is deliberately formalized as the management of human bodies by and for capital.

One occupation for the novel's policemen is to steal bicycles from the citizens of their parish. This is, I will suggest, their way of managing an interaction between humans and capital so as to ensure the perpetuation of the species. The book's Atomic Theory of particle exchange, with which the theft of bicycles is defensible, is, of course, analogous to Marx's chiasmic

[44] O'Brien, *Complete Novels*, 266–7.

formulation of capitalist modernity. According to Marx, all social relations under capitalism reify into a 'thing-like' unintelligibility; 'they do not', he writes, 'appear as direct social relations between persons in their work, but rather as material relations between persons and social relations between things'.[45] This process resembles what takes place when riding O'Brien's bicycles. We are told that humans 'get their personalities mixed up with the personalities of their bicycle as a result of the interchanging of the atoms of each of them', and that 'you would be flabbergasted at the number of bicycles that are half-human almost half-man, half-partaking of humanity'.[46] The structural homology between ideological reification under capitalism, as managed by police, and the theory of particle exchange, also managed by police, can be extended into a consciously pronounced allegory for biopolitical administration if we situate it within O'Brien's sociological interpretation of the bicycle. 'The cyclist,' he claims, again writing as Myles na Gopaleen, 'is independent of public transport because he has succeeded in becoming a capitalist in a small way; his contribution to a rate-sustained transport system would be individually small but his numbers being great the aggregate would be considerable.'[47] In this view, the cyclist is analogous to Woolf and O'Brien's visions of a solitary modernism, the room and the tunnel, in that all three are removed from the economic situation by which they are dialectically compromised.

The book's masturbatory climax is motivated by an encounter with a bicycle that has been presented as the capitalist 'thing' *par excellence*. Sergeant Pluck's bicycle is an ostensibly inanimate object that has been invested with so much energy as to have acquired sociality: 'The bicycle itself seemed to have some peculiar quality of shape or personality which gave it distinction and importance far beyond that usually possessed by such machines.'[48] The indeterminate verb 'seem' abounds all throughout this episode, and tempers back the actuality of the bicycle's personality, suggesting that its real metamorphosis from thing to human only occupies the realm of fantasy; it is a 'masturbatory prop', encased by the psychical dimension of ideology. 'I passed my hand,' the narrator continues, 'with unintended tenderness – sensuously, indeed – across the saddle. Inexplicably it reminded me of a human face, not by any simple resemblance of shape or feature but by some association of textures, some incomprehensible familiarity at the fingertips.'[49]

---

[45] Marx, *Capital*, 165.
[46] O'Brien, *Complete Novels*, 296.
[47] O'Brien, *The Best of Myles*, 370.
[48] O'Brien, *Complete Novels*, 378.
[49] Ibid.

Indeterminacy charges the inanimate thing with human sensuality, elevating it through the ideological chiasmus and extending it towards human experience, just as metonymy begins to stir from beneath narrative, in the very grain of its prose:

> I knew that I liked this bicycle more than I had ever liked any other bicycle, better even than I had liked some people with two legs. I liked her unassuming competence, her docility, the simple dignity of her quiet way. She now seemed to rest beneath my friendly eyes like a tame fowl which will crouch submissively, awaiting with out-hunched wings the caressing hand. Her saddle seemed to spread invitingly into the most enchanting of all seats . . .[50]

The first of these sentences projects sexual fantasy onto the bicycle, comparing it favourably to the bipedal humans of the narrator's past. That comparison then gives way to synthesis and the bicycle acquires its feminine pronoun. This bicycle is, for the narrator, a fantasy woman in the worst possible sense: it is presented here as an idyllically docile lover, a blank surface into whose phenomenal interactions the male ego can project whatever solipsistic desire. And so, as the narrator's pleasure increases through fantastical imposition, the figuration intensifies, passing into the simile, 'like a tame fowl', which objectifies the autoerotic fantasy into a vision of gallinaceous bird life. Here, and finally, we face the metonym of masturbation, which subjoins the apparently inviting 'spread' of the bicycle's saddle, registering a moment in which the autoerotic act begins to produce its own prose and to simultaneously allegorize that production. From the image of the fowl, conjured up in lyric simile, the prose and its narrative together take flight, ascending on an object correlative for the unreconstructed lyrical subject in solitude with the sexualized object of its own imagination: 'She moved beneath me with agile sympathy in a swift, airy stride, finding smooth ways among the stony tracks, swaying and bending skillfully to match my changing attitudes. . . .'[51] This moment of un-alienated lyricism is the aesthetic impress of a short-lived departure from biopower, an entry into solitude that nonetheless takes the capitalist thing for its vehicle and so which must be compromised. It is an unearned moment of aesthetic pleasure that leads the narrator right back to where he started, standing face to face with the policeman. This temporary freedom, which generates for itself a lyricism all too delicate for a book so deeply

[50] Ibid.
[51] Ibid., 380.

aware of its historical situation, cannot hope to last beyond the few pages it should occupy, and so it rings out falsely and for only a short period of time, all the while acknowledging yet denying its imminent arrest: 'I sighed and settled forward on her handlebars, counting with a happy heart the trees which stood remotely on the dark roadside, each telling me that I was further and further from the Sergeant.'[52] O'Brien's novel refuses to triumph over its conditions of production because it knows they are ultimately inescapable. However, in this moment and through the masturbatory trope it discloses the secret of its own aestho-autogamy: that it obtains both within and against the productive matrix of capital.

---

[52] Ibid.

15

Modernist Wheelmen

Mark Byron

The bicycle is the preeminent vehicle of the modernist literary avant-garde. From Alfred Jarry's apotheosis of masculinity, the 10,000 km race in *The Supermale* (1902), to Moran's loss of wheels – literal and figurative – in Samuel Beckett's novel *Molloy* (1951), the bicycle is ritually coupled with male characters and serves as an acute marker of their identities. As a means of self-propelled locomotion, the bicycle is also an expression of existential and ideological agency: neatly expressed in Hugh Kenner's formula for Beckett's cyclist, the Cartesian Centaur.[1] The bicycle is also a mode of protest against and liberation from ever-encroaching automation by way of rail and road: known in earlier times as the velocipede – literally 'fast foot' – this mercurial device provides a means of protest in its locomotory self-reliance. The literal and figurative power of the bicycle as vehicle of the avant-garde reaches its still point – ever turning – in Flann O'Brien's novel *The Third Policeman*, composed in 1940 but first published only in 1967. This compendium of the Varieties of Velocipedal Experience ranges from the instrumental use of the bicycle pump as weapon, the Gnostic mystery of missing lanterns, the ontologically hybrid man-becoming-bicycle, and the mounted cycle as apotheosis of erotic desire charading as a corpuscular cosmology. How do O'Brien's bicycles inflect the rich discourse of modernist wheelmen? How do they enable or prohibit their riders' contemplative faculties? Do they embellish or subsume their riders' identities? What does it mean to push a bike, to take it on a train? How does it compare to walking?

Proliferating wheels

The concept of the bicycle has a long history, from a suggestive sketch in Leonardo's Codex Atlanticus notebook, now widely considered to be a

---

[1] Hugh Kenner, 'The Cartesian Centaur', *Samuel Beckett: A Critical Study* (Berkeley and Los Angeles: University of California Press, 1961), 117–32.

later forgery or addition,[2] to developments in bicycle design in the late-eighteenth century. This history is framed by developments in automotive technology. Although historically the bicycle precedes both the train and the motor car, it comes into being in the age of steam mechanics, and therefore is subject to discourses of machine representation in art and literature of the age.[3] The promise and threat of automated transport is abundantly represented in nineteenth century art and literature, perhaps most luridly captured in the phenomenon of traumatic disorientation Julie Wosk has called 'breaking frame',[4] a profound perceptual rupture incurred by sudden violent technological malfunction. The train, for example, has literary pride of place as the efficient cause of Anna Karenina's suicide, and when captured on film in the Lumière brothers' *Arrival of a Train at La Ciotat*, is said to have produced an uncanny effect of endangerment in the film's first audiences at the Café Grand in Paris in January 1896.[5]

The bicycle might seem a comparatively gentle mechanism, made to the measure of the human body. Yet this humble vehicle is literally revolutionary: the first modern bicycle prototype appeared in Paris in 1791. Although it comprised a wooden bar, two forks, and a carriage wheel at each end, the *célérifère* ('to carry fast') became a popular if uncomfortable vehicle.

After the Revolutionary period this steerless mechanism became known as the *velocipede* ('fast foot'), and caught on in England, Germany and Italy. Such was its popular appeal that in 1811 the General Director of Police in

---

[2] Prof Dr Hans-Erhard Lessing provides a comprehensive refutation of the drawings' Leonardine provenance in 'The Leonardo da Vinci Bicycle Hoax', a paper presented at the 8th International Conference on Cycling History, Glasgow School of Art, in August 1997. The text of this paper is available at http://www.cyclepublishing.com/history/leonardo%20da%20vinci%20bicycle.html.

[3] Two comprehensive accounts of technological innovation from the time of the Industrial Revolution to the mid-twentieth century are David S. Landes, *The Unbound Prometheus: Technological Change and Industrial Development in Western Europe from 1750 to the Present* (Cambridge: Cambridge University Press, 1969); and Francis D. Klingender, *Art and the Industrial Revolution* (1947; New York: Schocken, 1970).

[4] Julie Wosk, *Breaking Frame: Technology and the Visual Arts in the Nineteenth Century* (New Brunswick: Rutgers University Press, 1992).

[5] The abiding myth that the first audience of the film recoiled in terror has long become a verity of mainstream film criticism, but seems unlikely considering the subject matter – an everyday event – was the most common theme in early film. Martin Loiperdinger challenges the credibility of the myth in 'Lumière's *Arrival of the Train*: Cinema's Founding Myth', *The Moving Image* 4, 1 (2004): 89–118. Conversely, a mitigating historical circumstance that rarely rates a mention in histories of early cinema is the catastrophic Montmartre train disaster of 23 October 1895. As Ray Zone notes, only weeks before the screening of the Lumière film 'a runaway locomotive at the Montmartre Station in Paris broke through a second story wall and plummeted down into the street', and was very likely in the public consciousness for months afterwards. See Ray Zone, 'A Note on "Cinema's Founding Myth"', *The Moving Image* 5, 2 (2005): 146–7.

Figure 1 The *célérifère* of Comte de Sivrac, c.1790.

Milan issued a ban on riding in the city at night: 'Prior experience has shown that rushing about on the aforementioned velocipedes presents a danger to pedestrians.'[6] The ordinance lays out a number of compliance orders in response to the more acute dangers presented by the new vehicles:

I. It is forbidden to ride bicycles at night in the streets and piazzas of the city.
II. It will be tolerated, however, to race around the city ramparts or in piazzas far from the city centre.
III. Those who fail to comply with this ordinance will be punished with confiscation of their vehicle.

The German inventor Karl von Drais honed these early designs in 1817 into a machine he called the *Laufmaschine* (running machine). This vehicle, comprising wheels, a steering mechanism and a cross frame, was propelled by foot on the ground. It became known in English as the *draisenne*, and was also referred to as the hobby-horse or dandy horse, an indication of its class status. This design remained remarkably consistent until the introduction of the pedal in the 1860s, and bore implications for the gender of the rider, since

---

[6] Police Ordinance, Milan, 1811, from *Le Biciclette*, ed. Fermo Galbiati and Nino Ciravegna (San Francisco: Chronicle Books, 1994), 111. My translation.

Figure 2 Police Ordinance, Milan, 1811.

'[t]o ride the machine one sat astride the beam, a position which interfered too much with a long skirt to make riding practicable for a respectably dressed woman'.[7] Ernest Michaux exhibited his *Michauline* at the Paris Universal Exhibition of 1867, a model that included a rudimentary braking system. This model was the first mass-produced bicycle and became known as the bone-shaker: a product of its solid wheels and an English inability or

---

[7] Nicholas Oddy, 'Bicycles', in *The Gendered Object*, ed. Pat Kirkham (Manchester and New York: Manchester University Press, 1996), 61.

Figure 3 Henri Toulouse-Lautrec, 'La Chaîne Simpson', 1896, lithograph publicity poster, 87.6 × 124.7 cm, Designmuseum Denmark. Image: http://www.toulouse-lautrec-foundation.org/The-chain-Simpson.html. The cyclist Constant Huret is riding a bicycle with a Simpson chain behind a Gladiator tandem pacer at the Velodrôme de la Seine.

unwillingness to pronounce its French moniker. The chain was added in the 1870s, captured most famously, some years later, in Henri Toulouse-Lautrec's famous advertising poster for the Simpson Chain.

The innovation of the chain led to the production and popularization of more familiar models of bicycle in the following decade, including the penny-farthing or 'ordinary' (its name an indication of its ubiquity at the time). The process of 'frame-closure' from early models to the diamond frame was complete by the 1890s, ushering in the bicycle craze in the middle of that decade. These new mass-produced machines broke down class barriers, but with the introduction of the crossbar, further entrenched a potent physical and symbolic barrier to potential female cyclists: 'The more or less universal adoption of the diamond frame in the 1890s is the key element in the establishment of the gendered bicycle in the post-high-wheel period.'[8]

As the technical evolution of the bicycle frame smoothened the relation between bicycle and rider, another major transformation occurred between bicycle and road: that of the tyre. Work on the pneumatic tyre during the

---

[8] Oddy, 'Bicycles', 63.

nineteenth century aimed to replace the jarring wooden wheels of the earliest models or the iron bands on mid-nineteenth-century bicycles. This work produced a catalogue of proper names which remain at the centre of the rubber tyre trade: in 1839 Charles Goodyear, a chemist, discovered the process of vulcanization by which rubber is made elastic through the application of heat and chemicals; in 1889 a Scottish veterinarian, John Boyd Dunlop, created the inner tube; and in 1891 Edouard Michelin perfected the removable pneumatic tyre and the modern bicycle was born.[9] The slow improvements in road surfaces during the nineteenth century – particularly by Scottish road engineers Thomas Telford and John McAdam (from which the term macadam derives) – combined with the cushioning effects of the pneumatic tyre to produce a viable and durable means of self-propelled transportation.

By the last decade of the nineteenth century there were approximately a million bicycles in Western Europe: half of those were in Britain, a quarter in France, and the rest mainly in Germany, Italy and Belgium. National cycling championships had been held since the 1880s when the national cycling bodies were formed. Most of these races were held on dedicated tracks, although the Paris-Rouen road race, in which women also competed, had been held as early as 1869. The Florence-Pistoia race was first held in the same year (with a pistol as first prize, naturally).[10] But it took until the twentieth century for the greatest of them all: the first Tour de France was held in 1903, over six stages and nearly 2,500 kilometres. It very quickly came to be considered the ultimate test of endurance and strength of the cyclist, as well as the best testing ground and promotional venue for manufacturers.[11] That Jarry's 10,000 km race appeared in *The Supermale*, published only the year before, tells us that in the early years of the century the racing bicycle was seen as the truest test of masculine potency and the most integrated mechanical extension of his body and its powers of propulsion. However it serves well to remember that the Wright Brothers took flight at Kitty Hawk also in 1903, and Karl Benz had patented his first car 20 years earlier. How could the romance of bicycles and the machismo associated with the feats of their riders possibly stand up against motorized transport?

---

[9] For a general history see David V. Herlihy, *Bicycle: The History* (New Haven: Yale University Press, 2004); and David Gordon Wilson, *Bicycling Science*, 3rd edn (Cambridge, MA and London: MIT Press, 2004), especially 8–26.

[10] James L. Witherell, *Bicycle History: A Chronological Cycling History of People, Races, and Technology* (Cherokee Village, AZ: McGann, 2010).

[11] For a general history, see Bill McGann and Carol McGann, *The Story of the Tour de France*, vol. 1: 1903–64 (Indianapolis: Dog Ear Publishing, 2006), especially 4–50.

Locomotion and modernism

The spectrum of modernist aesthetic production is intimately bound up in and enabled by revolutions in transport technologies. Among well-known literary and artistic representations of trains, turbines and steam engines, the bicycle gained attention as a mode of self-expression or even protest at the incursions of automated mass transportation. The cycling stories of Somerset Maugham, Henry Miller, William Saroyan, Mark Twain and Jerome K. Jerome maintain a slightly antiquarian air, self-evident in such literary-cycling anthologies as *The Noiseless Tenor*.[12] Yet modernist identifications with transport technology tend to begin with the Italian Futurist apostrophe to the motor car in the First Manifesto of 1909:

> We declare that the splendor of the world has been enriched by a new beauty: the beauty of speed. A racing automobile with its bonnet adorned with great tubes like serpents with explosive breath . . . a roaring motor car which seems to run on machine-gun fire, is more beautiful than the Victory of Samothrace.[13]

This glorification of speed, and its implied violence, extended into endorsements of war and military hardware: 'It is in Italy that we are issuing this manifesto of ruinous and incendiary violence, by which we today are founding Futurism, because we want to deliver Italy from its gangrene of professors, archaeologists, tourist guides and antiquaries' (180). The irony of this enthusiasm was probably not lost on Marinetti when World War I expended a good number of his Futurist cohort. Further, the iconography of powered flight in that war saw an increased representation of the destructive capabilities of aircraft in second generation Futurist art, in the so-called style of Aeropainting of the 1930s and 1940s.

Yet there was a legitimate place for the bicycle in the mechanic menagerie: Marinetti was enthusiastic about the bicycle's ability to extend human capability, and in his essay 'Destruction of Syntax – Imagination without Strings – Words-in-Freedom', it appears in a long unsorted list of transportation kinds that implicitly shape the subject's worldview:

> Futurism is grounded in the complete renewal of human sensibility brought about by the great discoveries of science. Those people who

---

[12] James E. Starrs, ed. and intro., *The Noiseless Tenor: The Bicycle in Literature* (New York and London: Cornwall Books, 1982).

[13] F. T. Marinetti, 'The First Futurist Manifesto', in *Three Intellectuals in Politics*, ed. James Joll (New York: Random House, 1960), 181.

Figure 4 Tullio Crali, *Incuneandosi nell'abitato* (*In tuffo sulla città*) [*Nose Dive on the City*], 1939, oil on canvas, 130 × 155 cm, Museo di arte moderna e contemporanea di Trento e Rovereto.

> today make use of the telegraph, the telephone, the phonograph, the train, the bicycle, the motorcycle, the automobile, the ocean liner, the dirigible, the aeroplane, the cinema, the great newspaper (synthesis of a day in the world's life) do not realize that these various means of communication, transportation and information have a decisive influence on their psyches.[14]

Note that Marinetti makes no distinction between manual and automated modes of transport and communication in his itinerary. Other Futurists such as Umberto Boccioni saw tremendous opportunity in the bicycle as an object of artistic consideration, most famously in his painting, *Dynamism of a Cyclist* of 1913.

Amongst the rich source material for this kind of virile artistic and literary representation of cycling, the emphasis seems to rest on the nature of its challenge to the rider, as the power source of locomotion, and the embodied

---

[14] F. T. Marinetti, 'Destruction of Syntax – Imagination without Strings – Words-in-Freedom', *Lacerba* (Florence), 15 June 1913; reprinted in Umbro Apollonio, ed., *Futurist Manifestos* (London and New York: Thames and Hudson, 1973), 98–105.

Figure 5 Umberto Boccioni, *Dinamismo di un ciclista* [*Dynamism of a Cyclist*], 1913, oil on canvas, 70 × 95 cm, Gianni Mattioli Collection, Peggy Guggenheim Collection, Venice.

self-awareness this evokes. Faster than walking, slower than machine-driven transport, the bicycle is the optimum in self-extension. Indeed it commutes runaway autochthonic invention as an aesthetic metaphor, unlike the motor car, keeping the author-artist firmly installed in the saddle: 'Perhaps it is no accident that the history of the self-begetting novel coincides with that of the *automobile*. Both are machines designed to generate their own locomotion.'[15]

The iconicity of the bicycle as an expression of physical potency – and thus of artistic expression – is imbricated in the history of technical innovations in bicycle design. The crude machines of the nineteenth century with their solid wheels, awkward seating positions and ungainly means of propulsion were gradually refined to provide the rider with ever greater means of autonomy in the speed and direction of travel. The addition of steering, brakes, rubber pneumatic tyres, chains and gears over the century gave the cyclist autonomy on roadways yet to be populated with motor transport; and, it must be said, on roads of a correspondingly poor quality given that the major modes of transport were horse-drawn carriages. Yet this new autonomy of the cyclist stood in contrast to the loss of agency

---

[15] Steven G. Kellman, 'The Fiction of Self-Begetting', *MLN* 91, 6 (1976): 1243.

and spatial control associated with more obviously industrialized modes of transport such as the steam train. The bicycle frame functioned inversely to the phenomenon of 'breaking frame', and came to be associated with the bucolic and the pastoral. The bicycle 'boom' of 1894–97 was limited largely to the leisured classes, but once bicycle design settled into the modern diamond-frame safety bicycle, it quickly became uniform, widely available and affordable. Only a generation later cycling was so ubiquitous among men and women that one might ride in the city as an unobtrusive and disengaged spectator: the flâneur on wheels,[16] symbolic of modernity just as Baudelaire's ambulatory flâneur was to be in Paris in the mid-nineteenth century. Yet already in *The Supermale*, Jarry begins to question the symbolic autonomy of the cyclist – by way of an exaggerated hyper-masculinity, a proleptic satire on Futurist virility – and the bicycle was transformed, in art, into the testing ground for masculine libido and ontological inquiry.

Hugh Kenner's Cartesian Centaur provides the best known image in this discourse, where the bicycle in Beckett's fiction is always a bicycle lost or remembered: 'like the body it disintegrates, like the body's vigor it retires into the past: *Hoc est enim corpus suum*, an ambulant frame, in Newtownian equilibrium'.[17] The bicycle joins with Molloy's crutches to form an endoskeleton of sorts, compensating for his corporeal shortcomings. The idealism implied in Molloy's arrangement is teased out by Kenner in an extended quotation from Beckett's novel:

> I was no mean cyclist, at that period. This is how I went about it. I fastened my crutches to the cross-bar, one on either side, I propped the foot of my stiff leg (I forget which, now they're both stiff) on the projecting front axle, and I pedalled with the other. It was a chainless bicycle, with a free-wheel, if such a bicycle exists. Dear bicycle, I shall not call you bike, you were green, like so many of your generation, I don't know why...[18]

Chainless bicycles such as the bone-shaker and the penny farthing were prevalent in the 1860s and 1870s, but did not possess cross-bars. The introduction of the safety bicycle (with chain) democratized cycling, at least among males, in the last two decades of the nineteenth century: a socio-economic impulse symbolized in the overwhelming prevalence of

---

[16] This concept was coined in Glen Northcliffe, *The Ride to Modernity: The Bicycle in Canada, 1869-1900* (Toronto: University of Toronto Press, 2001); see especially 243–6.
[17] Kenner, 'The Cartesian Centaur', 117.
[18] Samuel Beckett, *Molloy* (New York: Grove Press, 1965), 15.

black bicycles.[19] Molloy's ancient green number is, historically speaking, a fictitious manifold. Kenner dwells upon the physical rehearsals and proofs of metaphysical scepticism in the cycling male human figure, and detects a series of alignments with the Cartesian Meditations: the veneration of mechanical systems (typical of Descartes' time) over human cognitive and perceptive imprecision; the combination of bicycle and rider emulating the philosophical dualism of mind and body, movement and thought; and the corresponding diminution of ontological integrity in Beckett's characters as they are dispossessed of cyclometric and ambulatory potential: '[t]he Cartesian Centaur was a seventeenth-century dream, the fatal dream of being, knowing, and moving like a god'.[20]

The Third Policeman

Flann O'Brien's novel collates the Varieties of Velocipedal Experience into an apotheosis of the cyclist as tormented male human agent. The one-legged narrator-protagonist gets around on his two-wheeled contraption, and with the aid of his mate John Divney and his trusty bicycle pump, bludgeons another man, Philip Mathers, to death. The violence with which the narrative begins instigates the first circuit of his recurring arrest, detention and escape (by bicycle) from the station peopled by cycling policemen. The Parish in which the action takes place is perhaps a kind of hell,[21] or limbo, in which escape is futile but where things might still take a turn for the worse. The nameless narrator is careful to frame his story of crime and punishment as a kind of *künstlerroman*, or even as a *Radfahrerroman*: a portrait of the artist as a young cyclist. This aesthetic circularity – where the artist grows to the point of being able to write an account of his growth, the product of which is the narrative describing that process – intersects with other circular literary models such as that of Dante's *Inferno*, a quest echoed in the narrator's quixotic desire to produce the definitive 'De Selby Index'. The indefinite circularity with which the novel ends is a parody of the Odyssean

---

[19] See Nicholas Oddy, 'The Flaneur on Wheels?', in *Cycling and Society*, ed. David Horton, Paul Rosen and Peter Cox (Aldershot and Burlington, VT: Ashgate, 2007), 97–112.
[20] Kenner, 'The Cartesian Centaur', 132.
[21] O'Brien wrote to William Saroyan on 14 February 1940 about his newly completed novel, where 'all the queer ghastly things which have been happening to [the killer-narrator] are happening in a sort of hell which he earned for the killing'. Qtd. in Flann O'Brien, *The Third Policeman* (1967; London: Harper Collins, 1993), 207. All subsequent quotations from the novel are from this edition, page references for which will be incorporated parenthetically in the text.

nostos or homecoming, following a picaresque journey on wheel and foot.[22] But this circularity is modulated, where Divney accompanies the narrator back to the police station: is the killer-cyclist being caught by the peleton of Fate, or does this signal the support of his *equipe* on the next lap? Divney disappears on his bicycle for 3 days some time before the narrator's untimely death, and when the appointed time arrives to retrieve the precious cash-box, the pair approaches Mathers' house on foot: 'As my own bicycle was punctured we walked the distance' (20). The ubiquity of bicycles in the narrator's afterlife comprises a form of poetic retribution for the murder, compelling the narrator to seek out a way to graduate from foot to wheel in wandering The Parish.

The strange afterworld of The Parish abides beyond the laws of physics and architecture, and comprises an exclusively male population of policemen, cyclists and bicycle thieves. The two working policemen, Sergeant Pluck and MacCruiskeen, filter their worldviews through the lingo of cycling: on entry into the station Pluck asks the narrator for his 'cog' or surname (*cognome* in Italian). His procedural work begins from a first assumption that any crime is velocipedally related: 'Is it about a bicycle?' (57). He persists with a catalogue of identifying bicycle parts: 'One with overhead valves and a dynamo for light? Or with racing hande-bars?' This strategy falls flat – it is in fact a classic blazon, motivated by a desire for an absent, ideal beloved – and Pluck changes tack, enumerating a brief history of the bicycle's evolution (tricycle, patent tandem, velocipede, penny farthing) in the vain hope of identifying a worthy object for forensic investigation (58). At an impasse, he regales the perplexed narrator with previous years' crime statistics:

> Last year we had sixty-nine cases of no lights and four stolen. This year we have eighty-two cases of no lights, thirteen cases of riding on the footpath and four stolen. . . . Before the year is out there is certain to be a pump stolen, a very depraved and despicable manifestation of criminality and a blot on the county. (62)

The problems of loose handlebars and poor braking systems also occupy Pluck's procedural vision. The Parish swarms with bicycle thieves – 'Never

---

[22] There are strong affinities between *The Third Policeman* and Charles Maturin's novel, *Melmoth the Wanderer*. Both novels are framed by male companionship narratives: in O'Brien's novel, the narrator and Divney remain inseparable concerning their degraded grail-quest for the cash-box, just as Moncada joins forces with the murderer bearing the golden key in Maturin's novel. See Thomas F. Shea, *Flann O'Brien's Exorbitant Novels* (Lewisburg: Bucknell University Press; London and Toronto: Associated University Press, 1992), 119.

in my puff did I hear of any man stealing anything but a bicycle when he was in his sane senses' (63) – confirmed when Michael Gilhaney arrives to report the theft of his two-wheeler which instigates a detailed compilation of the bicycle's profile. The narrator's first conversation with MacCruiskeen follows a similar logic: 'Surely you had a three-speed gear for the hills?'

> "I had no three-speed gear," I responded rather sharply, "and no two-speed gear and it is also true that I had no bicycle and little or no pump and if I had a lamp itself it would not be necessary if I had no bicycle and there would be no bracket to hang it on . . . and I do not believe in the penny-farthing or the scooter, the velocipede or the tandem-tourer." (68–9)

The absurdity of these exchanges proves to be a short-term irritant, but the real problem lies ahead: the narrator has seen the future and it revolves. The narrator accompanies Pluck and Gilhaney in search of the errant cycle, on foot. The discussion turns again to the history of the bicycle, including the relative virtues of rat-traps (bicycle pedals). In a moment of passion Pluck declares, in Wordsworthian augury: 'The high saddle was the father of the low handlebars' (82). Pluck's preternatural ability to sniff out lost wheels sees him miraculously locate a dismembered bicycle buried beneath a remote hedge. Pluck suggestively urges Gilhaney to 'root' around in the nether regions of the bush – 'a lady member of the tribe you might say' (81) – where he finds his pump, lamp and bell. This performance almost adheres to a conventional police procedural, in the cyclometric subgenre, except that Pluck later admits to have stolen, dismembered and buried the bike himself. Other mysteries arise in this vein: the fabled third policeman, Fox, is said by Pluck and MacCruiskeen to be inseparable from his bicycle, and perhaps to have entered an undefined zone of psychic communion, or else simple madness, as a result; and Pluck himself covets his bicycle to the extent that he keeps it locked in the most secure cell in the station.

Following the miraculous discovery of Michael Gilhaney's bicycle, MacCruiskeen explains his Atomic Theory to the narrator. This thesis of the man-becoming-bicycle operates on a corpuscular or atomic principle (very loosely in the Democritean sense): continued riding over rocky terrain will eventually admit to a mingling of the rider's particles with those of the bicycle, producing not a hybrid unity, but a bicycle that is half-human, and a rider half-bicycle. Pluck expands on his theme, intimating how common the problem of atomic interchange is in The Parish, even leading to the execution by hanging of a bicycle for its part in a murder committed by its owner (108). Pluck adheres to the virtues of cycling in moderation, however, as the alternative of walking is deemed unsafe: 'The continual cracking of your feet on the road makes a certain quantity of road come up into you' (93). This conversation profoundly affects the narrator, the full consequences of which are not evident until his escape from the police lock-up towards the end of the narrative. He is left alone as Pluck and MacCruiskeen wage battle with the one-legged army seeking to save the narrator from the gallows (a confederacy borne out of their wooden prosthetic legs), and he notices Pluck's bicycle edging its way out of the unlocked cell. The bicycle becomes a getaway vehicle, but in the process, brings to fruition the earlier intimation of universal intermingling of matter and energy. The narrator becomes erotically united with the bicycle, which is identified as female due to the intermingling of its particles with those of a previous owner:

> Notwithstanding the sturdy cross-bar it seemed ineffably female and fastidious, posing there like a mannequin rather than leaning idly like a loafer against the level floor. I passed my hand with unintended tenderness – sensuously, indeed – across the saddle. (177)

With this encouraging turn, the narrator decides to eff the ineffable and make haste from the station with his new erotic object. This leads him to Policeman Fox's station, hidden in the walls of Philip Mathers' house, where the Sergeant informs him of the fate of the black box: 'I sent it to your house today by express bicycle and you will find it there before you when you travel homewards' (194). Ultimately, after misplacing his new bicycle, the narrator confronts his next cycle of torment with Pluck and MacCruiskeen, but now in John Divney's newly posthumous company.

The rational, reflectively self-conscious rider has no place in the world of the novel: instead the irrational, paranoid, conspiratorial or even erotically inclined cyclist holds sway. Indeed, the romantic entanglement of man and bicycle ('the pleasures of the saddle') so late in the narrative might be seen as the breakthrough moment that makes the act of writing possible in the first place: 'The confirmation of self in sexual excitement and virility is procreative in that it begets its own re-presentation in language.'[23] The figuration of bicycles as docile and female might appear to echo, at first flush, such Renaissance lyrics as Thomas Wyatt's 'They flee from me.' Certainly Pluck's vigilance concerning his two-wheeler is motivated by its gendered transformation into a bicycle-becoming-woman and its meek hind-like approach inspires the narrator's tender caress. Several critics identify a strong current of misogyny in the world of The Parish, where violence sublimates sexual repression

---

[23] Shea, *Flann O'Brien's Exorbitant Novels*, 137.

and male partnerships underwrite a prevalent sexual anxiety. The bicycle, part-human and gendered female, is symbolic of this general sexual economy, and is considered by one prominent critic to function not merely as a post-structuralist hobby horse:

> a metaphor of atomic physics; as a sub-Joycean, Viconian bi-cycle that auto-critically declares its own circular design; as an anthropomorphic allegory of dehumanisation. But to a critic mindful of the Irish comic tradition, and aware of the censorship mentality that existed in 1940s Ireland, the bicycle is also a metonymic discourse of repressed sexuality and Catholic catharsis; an index of social ideology in a new, post-colonial state.[24]

The social history of the bicycle supports this gendered reading of it as a vehicle of a different kind: one of constraint upon female riders, by virtue of design. From the earliest running machines to the diamond frame at the heart of the 1890s craze, bicycles required a straddling manoeuvre not socially acceptable for women of the classes to which cycling was available. The bicycle thus functions as an apt metaphor of social constraint in its very engineering, and this function translates neatly into the social world of The Parish. If the bicycle functions as an erotic aid or substitute for Pluck, MacCruiskeen and the narrator, can it also function as a credible vehicle of cogitation, whether in the Cartesian mode or otherwise?

Locomotion in *The Third Policeman* is punctuated by extended narrative digression, centring on the dubious scholarship concerning the theories of de Selby, and is framed by the epic structure of the *katabasis*, the visit to the underworld. The narrator and Pluck trace out the opening of Dante's Inferno, travelling by foot into the *selva oscura* to the entrance of the underworld. This surreal space is known only to the police, in which all conceivable things can be made and dissolved, but not removed. The endless system of identical hallways and furnaces bears Homeric and Dantescan signatures, and allusions to Hephaestos or Vulcan ring out with the distant but incessant hammering. This is also a subtle reminder of the process by which pneumatic tyres are made: vulcanization. The scholar-cyclist protagonist cannot escape his fate, in which bicycles are always implicated. The underworld zone forestalls logical and forensic thought processes by opening out to a surreal range of possibility, but the active modes of creation are strictly circumscribed to the zone itself. On the other hand, the

---

[24] Keith Hopper, *Flann O'Brien: A Portrait of the Artist as a Young Post-Modernist* (Cork: Cork University Press, 1995), 56–7.

geography of the parish – 'queer country' (80) – provides opportunities for cycling and perambulatory meditation. The narrative provides several extended descriptions of bucolic scenes rising up before the road cyclist or the walker: 'I walked quietly for a good distance on this road, thinking my own thoughts with the front part of my brain and at the same time taking pleasure with the back part in the great and widespread finery of the morning' (40). One might expect to witness the 'flâneur on wheels' at these moments. Baudelaire's preternaturally modern male figure haunting the Parisian streets of the Second Empire was transformed during the cycling fashion of the 1890s into a new mobile observer of social change and memorialist of past charms: 'The cycling flâneur could easily venture into the countryside, where traces of the past, which so interested the original flâneur, still could be found and the bustle of the city avoided.'[25] Do not the policemen in this odd world function in this way, in their pursuit of patently unproductive police work? The flâneur on wheels is distinctive in his detachment from productive work, and 'take[s] a detached intellectualised viewpoint, different from that held by those in the river of life'.[26] The narrator betrays this mode of contemplation at a few singular points in the novel, such as when he divines the industry in nature: 'The world rang in my ear like a great workshop.... The earth was agog with invisible industry' (129). It would seem that the narrator assumes the mantle of the questing pilgrim or the detective, actively observant, while the policemen merely simulate the aspiration to resolve intellectual and practical sphinxes: they are 'all crank and no chain'.

The cycling man of reason is emptied out of his cognitive faculties, and even any residual erotic potency is relegated to the incomplete substitution of female partner and bicycle. In addition to the implied sexual economy of MacCruiskeen's Atomic Theory, several characters allude to other forms of mechanization. At the outset, the narrator swings his murder weapon 'mechanically' (17) and remembers his death in similar terms: 'I noticed several things in a cold mechanical way as if I were sitting there with no worry save to note everything I saw' (25). The dead visage of Mathers observes him through eyes that seem 'not genuine eyes at all but mechanical dummies animated by electricity or the like' (26), and his reaction is correspondingly automated: 'Words spilled out of me as if they were produced by machinery' (27). The subsequent roadside encounter with the one-legged robber Martin Finnucane provides another catalogue of such fare: in his ennui and disillusion he compares the pointlessness of

---

[25] Glen Northcliffe, *The Ride to Modernity*, 244.
[26] Nicholas Oddy, 'The Flaneur on Wheels?', 109.

life with 'bread manufactured with powerful steam machinery' (46), and figures it as a 'queer contraption' (47). The narrator asks if his occupation is that of '[d]riving a steam thrashing-mill' (47), and he responds by saying he is a 'robber with a knife and an arm that's as strong as an article of powerful steam machinery' (48). Elsewhere Sergeant Pluck says of MacCruiskeen: 'He is a comical man . . . you'd think he was on wires and worked with steam' (78). MacCruiskeen's mechanical fetish reaches an apotheosis in the 'little black article like a leprechaun's piano with diminutive keys of white and black and brass pipes and circular revolving cogs like parts of a steam engine or the business end of a thrashing-mill' (71). Upon demonstrating his wares, he declares in the rhetoric befitting a World Exposition: 'All these things are what are called Examples of the Machine Age' (73). The narrator elsewhere describes MacCruiskeen's black box as 'the most complicated mangle I ever saw and to the inside of a steam thrashing-mill it was not inferior in complexity' (110). This habitual analogy to steam mechanisms emphasizes the ideal distinction of cyclometric locomotion: its relative autonomy from fuel (apart from a functional body to propel the bicycle), and the mindful, attentive rider, who must think through every stage of propulsion rather than rely on any form of automation. This trope of the riderly bicycle approaches Kenner's Cartesian centaur, but *The Third Policeman* redirects the rider and his machine from the realm of the rational to that of the affective and the erotic. But bicycles are lost, dismembered or depart of their own volition; the cycling policemen are thwarted in their duties; and the narrator is largely relegated to ambulatory motion, his wooden leg, his body and the road surface interpenetrating each other in a triangulated process. The walking cyclist is ejected from the erotic economy: he manifests the logical cul-de-sac of the once-potent cyclist in a world he cannot understand, a one-wheeler, onanist.

Conclusion

The Third Policeman might be seen as a deeply ambivalent bicycle manifesto: the novel is pessimistic about the bicycle's tool function, seeing it dismembered and transformed into a means of physical violence within an instrumental economy. Yet in the limbo-world of The Parish, the two-wheeler is a vehicle of almost mystical psychic transformation in the 'becoming-bicycle' of Gilhaney, enabling a truly strange enlightenment. The human-bicycle dyad suggests a first step into an enhanced perceptual mediation with the world. It promises to become a sensorial apparatus that thinks and moves its way through its field, but the narrator's failure to achieve a *velontology* is ultimately consistent with the impotence of the cycling police force.

> With the help of Marlowe (and Goethe) *The Third Policeman* becomes a tale of a scholar who sins for de Selby (the self) to attain the book of knowledge (the black box containing "omnium," or omniscience). On this scale of values the female bicycle becomes the equivalent of Marlowe's Helen of Troy (*Dr Faustus*, 1594), who represents a redemptive alternative through human love and desire, an a tantalising vision of life that is lost. . . . Implicit in this Faustian appropriation is the belief that a woman's love could have been an antidote to the brutal self-absorption of the narrator.[27]

The narrator is relegated to his own propulsion, literally and figuratively. The wheel in motion, a childhood fascination since antiquity, captures a ludic impulse that in turn invokes a complementary delight in artistic representation.

Figure 6 Macron, Eromenon, Attic red-figure kylix, c.470 BCE, Vulci, Staatliche Antikensammlungen, Munich.

---

[27] Keith Hopper, *Portrait*, 98.

Figure 7 Peter Brueghel the Elder, detail from *Kinderspiele* (*Children's Games*), 1559–60, oil on panel, 118 × 161 cm, Kunsthistorisches Museum, Vienna.

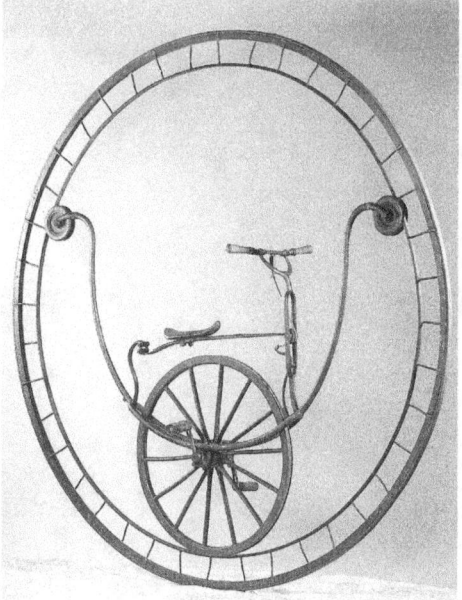

Figure 8 The Rousseau Monocycle, 1869, Museo Fermo Galbiati, Milan, Italy; photograph from *Le Biciclette*, ed. Fermo Galbiati and Nino Ciravegna (San Francisco: Chronicle Books, 1994), 21.

This self-manifesting aesthetic-erotic impulse of the wheel in motion is piquantly captured in the self-sustaining, precarious motion of the one-wheeler: allowing the rider-narrator-solipsist to remain still but to move his world. The narrator of *The Third Policeman* finds his one wheel in the narrative of the *Radfahrerroman*: the portrait of the artist as a young cyclist. It cycles through his first circuit of the afterworld, providing the conditions from which he may begin, at the same point, to tell his story, knowing already how and where it will eventuate. An indefinite rehearsal before an audience of one: a solipsist could not ask for more.

Index

Abbey Theatre   44–5, 97
Adorno, Theodor   136–8, 201
Anderson, Perry   5
Aristotle   16–17
Augustine   11–19, 21, 24–5, 32–3
Austin, J. L.   35–6, 38

Badiou, Alain   149–50, 157–8
Bakhtin, Mikhail   42–3
Ball, Robert   108, 111, 114, 118
Banville, John   130
Barthes, Roland   62
Bataille, Georges   205
Beckett, Samuel   4–5, 58, 74, 97, 107, 114, 116–18, 136, 143, 164, 197–9, 200, 206, 213
Behan, Brendan   93
Bell, The   95, 100, 103
Benjamin, Walter   188
Berkun, Scott   110
Berman, Marshall   142
Betjeman, John   94
Blather   103
Bloom, Harold   56, 68
Booth, Wayne C.   34
Borges, Jorge Luis   75, 124
Byron, George Gordon (Lord)   200

Cantor, Georg   129, 130–1
Capek, Josef and Karol   48
Carroll, Lewis   124
Cassirer, Ernst   116
Catholic Standard   104
Chalmers, David J.   108
Churchill, Suzanne W.   38
Clark, Andy   108
Coffey, Brian   93
Comhthrom Féinne   96, 103
Connolly, Cyril   28–9

Conrad, Joseph   28, 74
Cronin, Anthony   39, 55, 57, 93, 99, 103, 138, 145
Cronin, John   34, 39
Crosby, Donald A.   141

Deane, Seamus   145
Dennett, Daniel C.   116
Derrida, Jacques   57, 62, 80, 86–7
Descartes, René   107, 115–16
Devlin, Denis   93
Donoghue, Denis   22, 138
Dunne J. W.   112, 115–16
Duthuit, Georges   116

Eagleton, Terry   20
Eliot, T. S.   7, 27, 74
Ellmann, Richard   4
Engels, Friedrich   200
Envoy   95, 103

Foucault, Michel   199, 203, 205
Frankfurt, Harry   33–4, 38
Friedman, Susan Stanford   5–6
Friel, Brian   80–1

Gabler, Hans Walter   108
Gauss, Carl Friedrich   131
Gogarty, Oliver St. John   61
Gregory, Lady Augusta   77, 97

Halley, Edmond   111
Heaney, Seamus   97, 105
Heidegger, Martin   137, 147
Higgins, F. R.   104
Homer   227
Hopper, Keith   75, 107, 112, 115
Huxley, Aldous   178
Hyde, Douglas   83

Irish Farmers' Journal 104
Irish Press 104
Irish Statesman 94
Irish Times 94, 97–9, 104

James, Henry 29, 34, 39
Jameson, Fredric 139, 203
Jarry, Alfred 213, 222
Jay, Martin 32
Joyce, James 2, 4–5, 12, 32, 42–3, 50–1, 56–66, 68–9, 72, 93–5, 97, 107–13, 117–18, 136, 138–9, 164–7, 177–8, 181, 184, 186–7, 194, 197–8, 200, 206
Jünger, Ernst 137

Kafka, Franz 74, 136
Kahler, Erich von 108
Kant, Immanuel 116, 199
Kavanagh, Patrick 55, 93–106
Kavanagh, Peter 104
Kavanagh's Weekly 95, 104–5
Keats, John 200
Kemnitz, Charles 112
Kenner, Hugh 4, 31, 207
Kerouac, Jack 106
Kiberd, Declan 36, 75

Lawrence, D. H. 29, 34
Lemass, Seán 106
Lewis, Wyndham 7
Lukács, Georg 136

Mallarmé, Stéphane 28, 43
Marinetti, F. T. 219
Marx, Karl 142, 150–1, 161, 184–5, 194, 200–2, 208–9
McHale, Brian 24
McNamara, Brinsley 84
Miller, Tyrus 4
Mitchell, Margaret 98
Montgomery, Niall 93, 99
Moorhouse, Frank 175–6, 185–94
Muldoon, Paul 97

Murphy, Neil 107
Murry, John Middleton 28

Neyt, Vincent 114
Nietzsche, Friedrich 27–8, 137–8, 147, 156, 159–60, 196
Nixon, Mark 108–9

O'Brien, Edna 107
O'Brien, Flann (works)
   'A Bash in the Tunnel' 59, 63, 165, 172–3
   An Béal Bocht/The Poor Mouth 16, 23, 24, 71–80, 95, 97, 101–3, 135
   At Swim-Two-Birds 1, 15–19, 23, 25, 31, 33–9, 45–53, 58–9, 67–76, 94, 106, 135, 138–9, 165, 167–71
   Cruiskeen Lawn 37–8, 59, 67, 77, 95, 103
   Faustus Kelly 42, 44–5, 47–8, 51, 95
   Rhapsody in Stephen's Green: The Insect Play 42, 46–9
   'Scenes in a Novel' (O'Brien's short story) 19n. 25, 177n. 5
   'The Bog of Allen' 96–7
   The Dalkey Archive 11–12, 20, 24, 31–3, 56–66
   The Hard Life 13, 20
   The Third Policeman 17, 20, 21–3, 31, 34–5, 39, 41, 45, 81, 101, 135–48, 150–61, 164, 172, 177n. 5, 185n. 20
   'The Trade in Dublin' 171–2
   'Thirst' 42, 172
   'Time and Drink in Dublin' 166
O'Casey, Sean 49, 74, 78
O'Connor, Frank 44
Ó Criomhthain, Tomás 71–2, 77
O'Faolain, Sean 44, 95
O'Grady, Standish H. 36
Ó Grianna, Séamus 85
O'Keeffe, Timothy 86

Paulhan, Jean 28
Peirce, C. S. 155, 157
Perloff, Marjorie 30
Pessoa, Fernando 2
Picasso, Pablo 2
Pirrandello, Luigi 2, 45–6.
Pound, Ezra 27, 30
Power, Patrick 83–5
Proust, Marcel, 197–8, 200, 206

Quinn, Antoinette 105

Rancière, Jacques 28, 30, 207
Reeve, Alan 94–5
Reich, Wilhelm 205
Richards, I. A. 30–1, 36
Rousseau, Jean-Jacques 199
Rousseau, Pierre 109
Russell, George (*AE*) 94, 97
Ryan, John 55, 93, 95

Said, Edward 106
Saroyan, William 41–2
Sartre, Jean-Paul 142
Schoenberg, Arthur 2
Searle, John 38

Sedgewick, Eve Kosofsky, 200
Sheridan, Niall 57, 93
Slote, Sam 117
Smith, Adam 201–8
Smyllie, R. M. 93–5
Smyth, Gerry 104
Soyinka, Wole 105
Synge, J. M. 45, 77, 97, 104, 142

Taaffe, Carol 35
Tóibín, Colm 24
Toulouse-Lautrec, Henri 217
Trotter, David, 196

Weber, Max 136, 142
Whitehead, Alfred North 123–4
Wilde, Oscar 1
Williams, William Carlos 28
Wittgenstein, Ludwig 39
Woolf, Virginia 29, 34, 39, 195–6, 209

Yeats, W. B. 1, 4, 77, 93, 97

Žižek, Slavoj 205–6